The Blame Game

The Blame Game

SPIN, BUREAUCRACY, AND SELF-PRESERVATION IN GOVERNMENT

Christopher Hood

PRINCETON UNIVERSITY PRESS

PRINCETON AND OXFORD

Published by Princeton University Press, 41 William Street, Princeton, New Jersey 08540
In the United Kingdom: Princeton University Press, 6 Oxford Street, Woodstock,
Oxfordshire OX20 1TW
press.princeton.edu

Library of Congress Cataloging-in-Publication Data

Hood. Christopher, 1947–
    blame game : spin, bureaucracy, and self-preservation in government / Christopher
Hood.
    p. cm.
  Includes bibliographical references and index.
  ISBN 978-0-691-12995-2 (hardcover : alk. paper) 1. Government accountability.
2. Blame—Political aspects. I. Title.
  JF1351.H67 2011
  320.01—dc22

2010031676

British Library Cataloging-in-Publication Data is available

This book has been composed in Sabon

Printed in the United States of America

10 9 8 7 6 5 4 3 2 1

Contents

Illustrations

Preface

Talk about "blame games" has become pervasive in modern organizations and politics. Type the term or its variants such as "blame culture" and "teflon politics" into a search engine and you will get tens of millions of hits. This book aims to describe, dissect, and explain the blame game, showing how blame avoidance shapes politics and organizational life and what strategies the various players in "blameworld" from top-level leaders to front-line workers, can use to limit or deflect it. But while the tone of most commentary on the "blame game" and "blame culture" is unequivocally disapproving, I argue that blame is not all bad in social and institutional life. A world without blame would have some major shortcomings, however much we might be jaded by adversarial legalism or by the petty point-scoring of political life. So I go beyond an account of how blame games and blame avoidance work by identifying what is "good" and "bad" blame avoidance and by offering some ideas about how to achieve the right balance between the two.

Any book on the subject of blame avoidance in government and public services should of course begin with an excuse. To explain why it took me nearly a decade to write this book since the inaugural lecture I gave on the subject in Oxford 2001, I could plead the usual academic excuse of administrative distraction, and I've certainly had plenty of that in the 2000s. Or, since they say justification is often a better way of avoiding blame than making excuses, I might perhaps try to argue that leaving the argument to ferment and mature was calculated to produce a better book than one that was written more quickly. But it is the reader who has to be the judge of that.

So just what is so fascinating about blame avoidance? Perhaps three things. One is that having become alerted to blame avoidance as a phenomenon, you start to see it everywhere. For instance, where I live the traditional concept of twenty-four-hour policing has been repackaged into something with the warm and cuddly title of "safer neighborhoods" (and who could possibly be against those?). But when you inquire further into what lies behind this unexceptionable slogan, it turns out to mean that the concept of twenty-four-hour policing has been replaced mostly by answering machines that explain that no one's available to take your call just now. So who exactly do we blame when we're trying to alert an official someone to (for example) the rampant drug dealing in our local neighborhoods?

A second source of fascination is that blame avoidance is capable of being discussed at all levels, from abstruse philosophical analysis of the nature of responsibility to everyday conversations on the bus or in the bar that swap battle stories about the frustrations of dealing with big organizations whose systems and structures seem to be carefully designed to make ordinary human communication with them as difficult as possible. Cases in point include those organizations that don't put phone numbers on their websites, that send you emails from "teams" rather than from named individuals, or which allow you to complain about them only on special forms that are guaranteed to put off all but the most pertinacious individuals and whose categories are invariably designed not to fit your own particular grievances.

Third, and more specifically for someone who has spent four decades studying politics and public administration, blame avoidance is a way of linking together three things that normally live in separate academic boxes in these fields, namely the way that public organizations and programs are structured, the way the world of spin and public opinion works, and the politics of the standard operating routines to be found in the world of public services and government. Blame avoidance is a way of bringing the analysis of all these normally separated elements to a single point, and also of linking the behavioral or institutional analysis of how organizations work or individuals behave with ideas about how things ought to be (*deontology*, for the professionals). Is blame avoidance all bad? How can we tell the bad from the good varieties? And can we do anything to encourage the good sorts and discourage the bad?

I have incurred many debts over the long years this book has been in the writing. Institutionally, I am grateful to the ESRC Centre for Analysis of Risk and Regulation at the London School of Economics for moral and intellectual support, for financial help for some of the work that went into the book and for granting me the status of research associate for the whole time that this book was in preparation. I am also indebted for support from the ESRC Programme on Public Services which I directed from 2004 to 2010. I am grateful to the individuals who helped me with researching and honing the material that went into the book, and most particularly Ruth Dixon and Bryony Gill. I owe a lot to the many people who have taught me about the analysis of blame avoidance and shaped my thinking about it, especially my former research students (and now my teachers and collaborators) Raanan Sulitzeanu-Kenan and Will Jennings. I am deeply grateful to Martin Lodge for reading through all the chapters of the book in draft and helping me to improve the argument, and to anonymous reviewers from Princeton University Press who provided the right kind of mix of encouragement and criticism. I am grateful to the various audiences on three continents, in places as far apart as Beijing,

Granada, Florence, and Dayton, who have been subjected to various parts and stages of the argument over the years, for the mixture of encouragement and sharp questioning that helped me to move forward. I'm grateful to Richard Baggaley, formerly of Princeton University Press, for combining persistent progress monitoring with forbearance over delays and very helpful suggestions for improvement while the book was being written; and I'm also indebted to Chuck Myers, Kim Williams, and all the other people at Princeton University Press who helped and encouraged me to get the manuscript into shape. For the many errors that no doubt remain after all this help, I really cannot think of any way to avoid taking the blame myself.

Christopher Hood
Oxford

PART ONE

Blame, Credit, and Trust in Executive Government

CHAPTER ONE

Credit Claiming, Blame Avoidance, and Negativity Bias

> There are ... more winners than losers [from extending free trade]. But it's the losers you see in the streets.
> —Pascal Lamy, Director-General of the World Trade Organization, interviewed after international trade talks in Hong Kong in December 2005[1]

> The small group of journalists who shouted questions at the press secretary every day in the White House Briefing Room had a very different agenda [from that of Bill Clinton's spin doctors]. They were focused, almost fixated, on scandals, on ... malfeasance and misfeasance and plain old embarrassments.... They were interested in conflict ... in behind-the-scenes maneuvering....
> —Howard Kurtz 1998: xix

STRIKING ATTITUDES AND OBSERVED PERFORMANCE: THREE PUZZLES ABOUT MODERN GOVERNANCE

You're riding on a city bus in the middle of a heat wave following a cold snap.[2] To everyone's extreme discomfort, the bus has its heating turned full on. You go to the obvious point of contact—the bus driver—to express your anger at this absurd state of affairs and ask for the heating to be shut off immediately. But you find the bus driver claims not to be to blame and says many of the buses in the city still have their heating on, because only the company mechanics can alter the heat settings on the buses. If you have the time and patience to pursue the matter further, you may find that the mechanics deny all blame as well, and tell you their labor union blames the company for not hiring enough mechanics to service the buses properly. But then you find the bus company managers blame the city's transport licensing authority for setting the fares for riders at a level that doesn't allow the company to hire more than a few mechanics. And the licensing authority says ...

Welcome to "blameworld" and the blame game. Most readers will have been there, in some form. The example given above might seem fairly trivial, though even that scenario might be life-threatening for some people.

But the same pattern can often be found in graver situations—for example, when large numbers of people lose their life savings or pension entitlement as a result of some policy change or company collapse, after years of careful saving for the future. So why do we find such a pattern so commonly repeated, in spite of decades of expert suggestions (Hirschmann 1981: 463) and high-flown rhetoric from reformers promising to make government and public services more customer-focused and better coordinated than before?

Similarly, why do we so often find the handling of risk in public services to be inflexible and unintelligent, often increasing our exposure to some kinds of risk in the name of reducing the incidence of others? Why does so little seem to come out of all those earnest reports, task forces, and government initiatives calling for imaginative, proportionate, results-focused regulation? For instance, how do we account for the sort of logic that causes rural railways to close down by insisting on unaffordable safety upgrades and thereby forces their erstwhile passengers to travel on the roads instead, with much higher risks of death and injury?[3]

Finally, when we get caught up in the aftermath of some unfortunate event that has taken its toll on our peace of mind, our bank balances, or even life and limb, why does responsibility so often prove to be extraordinarily elusive? Public organizations almost everywhere are exposed to successive reform and restructuring exercises purporting to clarify responsibility and improve accountability. So why do official and media inquiries after major failures time and time again find "smoking gun" evidence of who knew or did what when so hard to pin down?

These questions go to the heart of the conduct of modern executive government and public services, and this book argues that the answer to them lies in large part in the way blame avoidance shapes the conduct of officeholders, the architecture of organizations, and their operating routines and policies. It aims to dissect and describe some of the main strategies of blame avoidance, showing how they work and how they play into blame games. But it will also argue that blame avoidance, though often derided, can have positive as well as negative effects sometimes, raising the question of what should count as "good" or "bad" blame avoidance.

A KEY TO THE PUZZLE? THE LOGIC OF BLAMEWORLD

This book argues that there is a link between the types of behavior highlighted at the outset. The common thread is that they are all a product of the logic and politics of blame avoidance triumphing over the "good governance" bromides that pervade—or pollute, as some might say—modern government and public services. The mechanisms by which that sort of triumph occurs are subtle, and they are to be found deep in the way organizations work and their members behave. The triumph is unintended, at least in the sense that it goes against the declared thrust of reform policies for government and public services for at least a generation. The blame-avoidance imperative applies as much, if not more, to the behavior of appointed officials in government as to that of elected politicians. It often extends to private or independent sector providers of public services too.

What we are dealing with here is a type of risk that seems curiously unmentionable in the official corporate lexicon of risk management—namely the risk of blame. And that is curious, because risk in general is anything but unmentionable in today's world.[4] Indeed, over the last decade or so, risk has acquired all the conventional academic trappings of research centers, specialist journals, PhDs, and elaborately titled professorial chairs. In the business world it became central to the world of audit and corporate governance, in the attempt to control the kinds of failures that led to the great financial crash of 2008. In government it became the heart of a set of growing bureaucratic empires that regulate risks at work, environmental risks, food and drug risks, medical risks, financial risks, and many others besides, typically declaring their regulation to be "risk-based" in the sense that it purports to proportion the weight of regulatory action or monitoring to the perceived risks posed by different organizations, rather than treating all organizations equally.[5]

All that risk management activity in contemporary government and business has often been noticed, documented, and commented on.[6] But most of it is officially concerned with risks to society or to corporate organizations. In contrast, this book puts the spotlight on the risk of personal blame faced by public officeholders, including politicians, managers, professionals, and front-line bureaucrats. That is a type of risk and risk management that is rather less commonly identified on the management-seminar circuit. And curiously—or tellingly—it does not have any conventional term-of-art label. We could call it "reputational risk," one of the conventional categories of modern risk analysis, but that term is more often used for corporate brands rather than individual officeholders. We could call it "political risk," but that term is conventionally used in the risk management industry to mean risks to which businesses or investors are exposed by government decisions that are adverse to them, for instance the likelihood of expropriation of property, predatory taxation, or obstructive regulation. So we shall simply call it "blame risk" for the purposes of this book.

Accordingly, this book puts blame risk in government and its associated organizations into the foreground and under the spotlight. By doing that, we can both become more aware of blame-avoidance practices across

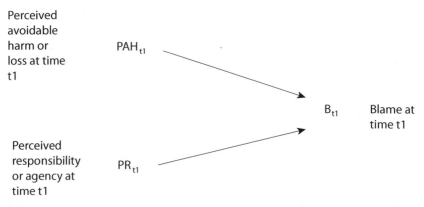

Figure 1.1. Two Key Elements of Blame. Source: Adapted from Sulitzeanu-Kenan and Hood 2005: 2.

the institutional world and start to find answers to some of those puzzles that we began with, about disjunctures between officially stated claims and observed behavior. That is because the management of blame risk— perhaps contrary to intention and usually in an unacknowledged way— so often shapes the organization and operation of modern executive government, producing its own curious logic of administrative architecture and policy operation.

So what exactly are blame and blame risk? Conventionally, blame is taken to mean the act of attributing something considered to be bad or wrong to some person or entity.[7] And it therefore involves at least two components that are depicted in figure 1.1. One, denoted as PAH, is some element of perceived and avoidable harm or loss—something is seen as being worse for some person or group than it could have been if matters had been handled differently. A second, denoted as PR, is some attribution of agency—that harm was avoidable because it was caused by acts of omission or commission by some identifiable individual or organization or possibly some more abstract institution such as "capitalism" or "patriarchy" (Sulitzeanu-Kenan and Hood 2005: 3). Both of those components can vary according to the point in time when avoidable loss and agency are perceived.[8] That aspect of blame may seem less obvious, but to see its relevance you need only think of all those cases where parents say to their children, "This may upset you now, but you'll thank me for it later" (or words to that effect). Attempts to deflect blame often involve working on the time dimension, as well as on the agency and loss dimensions. And, as we shall see later, some forms of blame avoidance are anticipative—they involve efforts to "stop blame before it starts"—whereas others are reactive, and involve operating in a fire-fighting mode after trouble has started.

Individuals can of course blame themselves for avoidable losses and harms (there is a substantial literature on self-blame in psychology), and indeed if you are alone on a desert island, you will have no one—or at least no human being—to blame but yourself. But as soon as there are at least two people on that desert island, blaming becomes a social or political activity, and that is the focus of this book. Blaming in that social sense is something that in principle extends across the whole spectrum of society from high-level potentates to the person in the street. Who you blame for what is a central marker of your culture and attitudes (Douglas 1990). As a social process, blaming must involve at least two sets of actors, namely blame makers (those who do the blaming) and blame takers (those who are on the receiving end). Those two roles come together in "blame games"—a term that came to be heavily used in the 2000s[9]—when multiple players are trying to pin the responsibility on one another for some adverse event, acting as blamers to avoid being blamees. And the consequences of blame can vary from mild social embarrassment to deep shame or extreme legal sanctions involving loss of life or liberty.

Blaming is often distinguished from "naming" and "claiming," following a well-known sociological account of the emergence of legal disputes, developed by William Felstiner and his colleagues (1980) thirty years ago. In that analysis (Felstiner et al. 1980: 635), naming means the identification and recognition of some experience as injurious. Examples include Gulf War syndrome, repetitive strain injury, pension mis-selling, subprime lending. Such naming is a necessary first step for blaming, which is the attribution of responsibility for injurious experience (to departments of defense, employers, and banks in the examples given above). The Felstiner scheme is thus another way of identifying perception of avoidable loss and attribution of agency as central elements in blaming. And in the Felstiner analysis, blaming is in turn a necessary precursor for claiming in the sense of seeking some remedy from the individual or entity held to be responsible. The claiming can range from demands for explanation to monetary compensation, the resignation or dismissal of those who are culpable, or official expressions of sorrow ranging from corporate apologies to more or less drastic acts of contrition by individual officeholders.

Why—or when—should public officeholders care about the risk of blame? On the face of it, that might seem an odd question. After all, most of us as human beings can be expected to care about blame simply because wanting to be well thought of is a normal psychological trait. Beyond that, public officeholders have obvious reasons for concern with management of blame. Elected politicians will care about blame if they think it will reduce their chances of re-election. Managers will care about blame if they think it will reduce their prospects of promotion, bonuses, staying in their current jobs, or moving on to better ones. Professionals will care about blame if they think it will diminish their reputations in ways that could damage their careers or produce expensive lawsuits over malpractice. Front-line bureaucrats will care about blame if they think it will cost them their jobs or their bonuses or their chances of promotion, or bust them back down to the ranks.

Even so, not everyone can be expected to care equally about all types of blame in all circumstances. After all, that psychological need to be well thought of and therefore to avoid blame is not equally distributed in human populations. Some personality types seem to have less concern to avoid blame than others, as in the case of psychopaths who do not exhibit the "usual" sense of moral responsibility (Elliott 1992). At the other end of the scale are those whose lives can be shattered by the smallest damage to their reputations. Our aversion to blame may vary over the course of our lives as well. We will be more motivated to engage in efforts to avoid blame the more likely we think blame will occur and the more serious we think the consequences will be for us if we do come to be blamed.

Variations in concern about blame are not just a matter of individual personality. Social settings and institutional background also seem to play a part. In so-called blame cultures, when every trifling error is watched for and the least step out of line pounced upon, there will be more pressure to avoid blame than in social settings where there is higher tolerance of others' faults and failings, such as therapy groups for those suffering from addiction or intimate gatherings of old friends.

Indeed, there is a whole literature on "high-reliability organization" (for example, Sagan 1993) that makes much of the idea that concentration on blame varies from one kind of organization to another. In politics and government bureaucracy too, concern with blame is likely to vary with circumstances. A politician who has just won a landslide victory or is about to retire from office is likely to be less concerned with blame than one on the eve of an election in a close race. Similarly, a judge or bureaucrat (or professor) whose continuing tenure does not depend on re-election or reappointment can normally afford to be more relaxed about blame than one in different circumstances.

So the importance of blame risk is not a constant but a variable, and that variability may explain the extent to which we can observe behavior of the type highlighted at the outset (that is, defensive lack of integration among organizations, defensively disproportionate regulation, defensively vague accountability trails). If social developments make blame risk more or less salient over time, we might expect the incidence of such behavior to vary accordingly. And we might expect exceptions to such defensive behavior to be found in those cases where individual personality, social setting, and institutional conditions put the least premium on avoiding blame. The next section explores that issue a little further, and we shall be returning to it later in this book.

naming → crediting → claiming

CLAIMING CREDIT VERSUS AVOIDING BLAME: NEGATIVITY BIAS

The opposite of blame is credit, and we can define credit as the act of attributing something considered to be good or positive to a person or entity. Just like blame, credit is also directional, temporal, and based on perceptions of gain, so we can turn Felstiner and colleagues' analysis around and say that "naming" and "claiming" are necessary conditions for gaining credit in exactly the same way that they are for attracting blame. So politicians, organizational leaders, and governments are normally concerned with painting a relentlessly upbeat picture of progress and improvement within their domains of responsibility and with associating any such progress with their own personal sagacity and hard work (rather than sheer luck or benign environmental conditions). Such players can be expected to seek credit for exactly the same reason that they will want to avoid blame—because credit can be expected to increase their chances of re-election, reappointment, promotion, and favorable repute during or even after their lifetimes.

But what if the chance of credit has to be weighed against the risk of blame? After all, that happens all the time in politics, in bureaucracy, and indeed in most areas of our lives. A new scheme that is successful can bring credit to its promoters, but if it flops they are likely to face blame instead. So when politicians and bureaucrats are considering courses of action involving both the chance of credit and the risk of blame, their attitudes to risk come onto center stage. Again, we can assume that risk preferences are likely to vary in the population, with some people more prepared than others to risk blame for a chance of credit. But psychologists have often noticed that risk preferences in aggregate tend to be asymmetric in human decision making.

By that is meant that potential losses are commonly weighted more heavily than equivalent gains, and (as noted in the first epigraph) losers are more likely to notice and act on the basis of their potential or actual losses than gainers are to notice and act on equivalent gains. That is a phenomenon that goes under various names, one of which is "negativity bias." Negativity bias denotes a commonly observed cognitive tendency for more attention to be paid to negative than to positive information and for losses to be valued more highly than gains of an equivalent amount.[10] The causes of negativity bias are debated (notably as between competing "figure-ground" and "loss aversion" explanations), but the existence of the phenomenon is well established and several studies have suggested that losses are commonly weighted at between two and four times more than equivalent gains (see Heath et al. 1999).

Negativity bias has been found in various forms in politics and government. Indeed, it has been said that politics is at its purest when action is prompted more by hatred of enemies than by attachment to friends (Carr 2009). Dissatisfaction is often said to produce proportionately higher levels of activity and changes in allegiance than corresponding levels of satisfaction. For instance, some voting studies have revealed that dissatisfied voters are more likely to turn out to vote than satisfied voters and to switch their vote among parties (see, for instance, Kernell 1977), though the claim that dissatisfied voters are more likely to turn out has been contested by others (see, for instance, Radcliff 1994). We occasionally see groups out in the streets celebrating what they see as just punishment of offenders, but protests against allegedly unjust punishment or imprisonment are far more common. It is often said that political failures tend to be remembered more than successes,[11] and indeed politicians often turn out to get less credit from the voters for their successes than the blame they get for failures.

For example, Olivier Borraz (2007: 226), analyzing the response to rising concerns in France in the 1990s about the traditional practice of using urban sewage sludge for agriculture, uncovered little evidence of any electoral payoffs for the local authorities who handled the issue well, finding only punishments for those who failed dramatically. Oliver James and Peter John (2007) found something similar when they looked at local government election results in England in the early 2000s as against performance data produced by the Audit Commission, the official audit and rating agency for municipal services. They found that incumbent politicians tended to be punished by the voters for exceptionally poor performance on those indicators, but were not correspondingly rewarded for exceptionally good performance.

Negativity bias is also often said to be institutionalized in news media, as is illustrated in the second epigraph to this chapter, quoted from Howard Kurtz's account of President Bill Clinton's once-legendary propaganda machine. Long before that, Spiro Agnew, vice president of the United States under Richard Nixon until forced to resign in 1973 over financial irregularities during his time as governor of Maryland, repeatedly attacked media negativism, famously dubbing the press "nattering nabobs of negativism" on one occasion in 1970 (Morrow 1996). Alastair Campbell, chief spin doctor to Prime Minister Tony Blair, often expressed similar frustrations in his diaries about what he saw as the tendency of the British press to focus on the negatives rather than on the good news stories coming out of government. For example, on one particular day early in the Blair government, Campbell noted in exasperation, "You had Ireland, public sector pay, welfare, serious issues and they went on endlessly about his [Robin Cook's] bloody secretary" (Campbell and Stott 2007: 273).[12]

The media are said to shape negativity bias by amplification of figure-ground effects (in this case, by foregrounding what is perceived to be negative and backgrounding the positive). That process is highlighted by Roger Kasperson's (1992) controversial notion of "social amplification of risk,"[13] and the related idea that media tend to expose society to more information that decreases trust or reduces credit than to information that increases trust and credit (Koren and Klein 1991). Indeed, as in the Alastair Campbell quote given above, politicians and their entourages often rage against what they see as a systematic tendency for media to ignore their successes and focus on their failures.

Negativity bias is often at the heart of bureaucratic behavior too. Some twenty-five years ago, Matthew McCubbins and Thomas Schwartz (1984) famously argued that, far from being helpless amateurs when it came to controlling bureaucracy, as some earlier theorists of bureaucratic power had suggested, the United States Congress could achieve effective control by acting on what they called the principle of "fire alarms" rather than "police patrols"—that is, focusing on things that go wrong rather than those that are working satisfactorily. The argument was that by working in that way legislators could avoid what would otherwise be very high monitoring costs in keeping tabs on large complicated organizations. And such behavior by legislators is readily observable in many other countries too, with much less scrutiny being applied to the successes of executive government than to its alleged failures and foul-ups.

What McCubbins and Schwartz did not point out was the bias that such a system of control introduces into bureaucratic incentives, because it means that success is ignored while failure gets all the attention from the legislature. So it is no wonder that bureaucrats are often found to show biases towards what is loosely called "risk aversion." A German federal bureaucrat I interviewed with a colleague some years ago put the point graphically: "In this kind of bureaucracy, the mechanisms are harsh. For good initiatives one receives some praise ('OK, not bad, but could have been done better') but when it *geht in die Hose* ["goes down the toilet," loosely translated] ... it is a disaster. In politics, a good initiative appears once in the newspaper and if one is extremely successful then our industry has an additional growth rate of 0.2 per cent. Nobody notices it. [But] a politician is remembered for ten years if there is a flop. That is why we are very risk averse here" (Hood and Lodge 2006: 102). Negativity bias in the form of fire-alarm controls by the legislature will tend to produce a mediocrity bias in those they control. Often it seems to pay better to be average than to be excellent.

So negativity bias may help us to go at least some way in understanding the puzzles we started with at the outset—the persistence of muddled and ambiguous relationships between public service organizations, the continuing triumph of rigid rules over intelligent flexibility, and the difficulty of establishing clear accountability when things go wrong, in spite of decades of good governance clichés inveighing against such things. Those forms of behavior start to make perfect sense once they are understood as the product of a persistent logic of defensive behavior to avoid blame in government and public services. Complex partnership and subcontracting arrangements may or may not deliver better public services on the ground than simpler, more easily understandable organizational arrangements. But what they can do is spread the blame when things go wrong. Rigid rules may or may not make for a safer society than the application of common sense. But what they can do is help to protect those applying the rules from blame for using discretion that turns out to be wrong. Crooked and ambiguous accountability trails may not serve democracy or good governance. But they can protect the political and administrative class from blame after failure. In a society whose politics and government exhibited strong negativity bias, isn't that precisely how we would expect politicians and bureaucrats at every level to behave?

Even so, there are several important things we don't know about negativity bias in government. One is why technocrats and even experienced politicians often come to grief because they underestimate the effects of such bias. As our first epigraph recalls, negativity bias is the reef on which international trade talks often falter, even if, as is claimed there, there might be more winners than losers from liberalizing world trade. Margaret Thatcher's remarkable reign as Prime Minister of the United Kingdom came to an abrupt end after she failed to calculate that the losers from the poll tax, a short-lived new form of local taxation she introduced in Britain in 1989, would prove to be far more voluble than those who had benefited from the shift to that system of taxation from the previous one (Butler, Adonis, and Travers 1994). And the long career of Jacques Chirac in French politics never recovered after he failed to calculate that a referendum on a new European constitution in 2005 would act as a catalyst for everyone in France who was discontented with his rule rather than a grateful endorsement of a new grand vision of European unity. How are we to explain why such seasoned and successful politicians sometimes fail to leave negativity bias out of their calculations? Is it a case of "positive illusion"—the sort of unrealistic exaggeration of their ability or strength that humans are sometimes prone to and that is often said to lead to traffic accidents and even the outbreak of wars? (See, for example, Armor et al. 2002; Taylor and Brown 1994.) Or are such cases the exceptions that prove the rule?

Second, negativity bias does not always seem to sweep all before it. There must be some other and countervailing behavioral processes that work to limit such bias, or trust of any kind would seldom or ever exist or survive.[14] Moreover, as we shall see later, governments, public managers, and political leaders put a lot of effort into countering negativity bias. In fact, in their constant search for ways to accentuate the positive, modern governments and public managers put out stirring tales of achievement, facts and figures about their claimed successes, and carefully selected research findings that support their positions and reform programs. Nor is such behavior entirely new: in the late, and by some lamented, Soviet Union, government broadcasts gave an endlessly upbeat picture of life in the workers' state, in their ultimately vain attempt to counter the cynicism and disillusion of the population at large about the conduct of their rulers.

Moreover, government reform programs often include strong aspirations to counter excessive blame aversion in public administration through red-tape-busting activity—for instance, in attempts to reduce the incidence of back-covering checking processes inside government, or to assess the worth of extra regulatory burdens against the risks or mischiefs they are intended to reduce. As noted earlier, a whole new bureaucratic language and practice of risk management has emerged, sharing at least its vocabulary with business practice, to balance desires to avoid blame if things go wrong against cost and other desiderata. (But it is at least an open question as to whether such mechanisms in practice counter or augment blame-avoidance imperatives in government.) Are such activities to be best understood as no more than symbolic activity, like buying one of those New Age crystal pendants said to counter "negativity?"[15] Or can they have positive payoffs?

A final thing we do not know about negativity bias is to what extent it is some sort of constant in human affairs, and to what degree its strength depends on circumstances, as mentioned earlier. Is it a relatively unchanging feature of human behavior that is hard-wired into our cognitive processes as a result of millions of years of evolutionary selection (programming us to focus on threats and dangers to our survival, while taking the positives for granted)? Or is it a product of a particular kind of society or culture? We have little direct survey evidence for changing negativity bias (let alone any developed "negativity bias index"). But some observers, notably Kent Weaver (1986 and 1988), have claimed that political negativity bias increased in several ways in the United States and other developed democracies in the 1970s and 1980s.

Indeed, Frank Furedi has written of the rise of "fear entrepreneurs" in modern societies, arguing that "the politics of fear appears to dominate public life in Western societies" (Furedi 2005: 1), and that the unchecked promotion of fear by politicians, experts, and special interest groups has become a marked feature of the age.[16] In a more institutional vein, Dan Kelemen (2006) has argued that, despite pious aspirations to the "open method of coordination," the European Unions's institutional structure has strong built-in incentives for the growth of adversarial legalism. And John Dryzek (1996) has commented in a similar vein on the development of the "risk industry" in a number of developed countries. Such ideas suggest that negativity bias can be encouraged and reinforced by institutional, technological, and social factors. If actual or potential loss tends to attract more political, legal and legislative activity than equivalent gains (for instance, if victims are easier to mobilize than beneficiaries, or compensation claims more readily attuned to legal and policy entrepreneurship than feelings of contentment or gratitude), the more focus there will tend to be on potential instances of failure, malfeasance, and avoidable risk.

Similarly, the more journalists, lobbyists, scientific experts, compensation lawyers, elected politicians, and their sidekicks there are (and the proportionate growth of all these actors is indeed a marked feature of modern developed societies), the greater will be the demand to discover and act upon such instances. If that is the case—and we will be exploring such issues further in later chapters—we might expect to find increasing investment by governments and bureaucrats in blame-avoidance activity, and indeed a tendency toward growth, rather than any decrease, in the sort of behavior we noted at the outset.

Blame Avoidance as Craft and Science

So if negativity bias produces a strong drive to avoid blame in public services and government, even sometimes at the cost of claiming credit, what strategies are available to politicians and bureaucrats in their quest for a blameless existence, and how well do they work? We might expect there to be a large and well developed literature on this subject, and academies running master classes to help would-be practitioners from politics and government develop that perfect Teflon strategy for preventing blame from sticking to them.

But actually blame avoidance has a curiously low profile as a field of study. It is largely a craft activity, self-taught or picked up in an informal way as politicians, bureaucrats, and spin doctors learn by doing to practice their art. That means that most of its "professors" do not have conventional academic titles or university chairs. Not only is the craft separated from the science, but the science itself tends to lack a clear central node.

The academic study of blame avoidance consists of a diffuse body of writing and analysis that is scattered across numerous disciplines including psychology, political science, philosophy, sociology, and institutional economics, and indeed tends to live at the edges of each of those disciplines. Some of it is new and some of it is old, because scholars were analyzing the phenomenon *avant la lettre*, long before the term "blame avoidance" came into currency. For instance, as we shall see later, Niccolo Machiavelli anticipated modern analysis of delegation as a strategy of blame avoidance by some four centuries, and Jeremy Bentham was discussing negativity bias in the early nineteenth century.

However, the modern development of this approach seems to have started in the United States in the 1980s, with the work of a leading institutional scholar, Kent Weaver, to whom we have already referred. Weaver drew heavily on the idea of negativity bias, and he argued that elected politicians in the United States often tended to prefer avoiding blame over claiming credit. The 1980s and early 1990s also saw complementary developments in social psychology and "rational choice theory" about institutions and politics, with the classic work of Daniel Kahneman and Amos Tversky (1979) on risk asymmetry, the analysis of the politics of delegation by leading scholars like Morris Fiorina (1982 and 1986) and Murray Horn (1995), and work at the borderline of political science and social psychology, notably Kathleen McGraw's (1990) experimental work on excuses and justifications by politicians facing blame.

Historians always want to look at ideas in their context, and readers may well ask what precisely was it in the social and political background that prompted such intellectual developments in the United States at that time? Intriguing as it is, that is a question that has barely been asked, let alone answered. Was it something to do with the way American politics developed after the debacle of the Vietnam war? Was it something to do with "partisan dealignment" (the term conventionally used to mean a reduction in the fixity of attachments by voters to political parties) that started to take place in electoral politics in the 1960s? Was it something to do with the growth of federal government activity associated with developments such as the War on Poverty of the 1960s? Could it have been a mixture of all three, or maybe even none of the above? We don't really know. But in the twenty-odd years since Kent Weaver's article and book appeared, political scientists have worked on the blame-avoidance perspective in at least three ways.

First, there have been numerous investigations of the ways that officeholders in democratic political systems can limit their career risks of being punished by voters for the pursuit of unpopular policies that may expose some of their voters to more risk (particularly when they are making cutbacks in welfare entitlements such as state retirement pension benefits while often at the very same time increasing the welfare benefits going to the political class). How can we explain how governments can do such things to their voters and still manage to avoid electoral wipeouts? The answer, according to such studies, takes us into recondite questions of constitutional and institutional architecture, policy program structuring and political tactics in party competition, and framing and packaging policy.[17]

Second, a new generation of scholars has tried to take the study of blame avoidance beyond circumstantial evidence and telling anecdotes. Some have followed the experimental approach pioneered in this field by Kathleen McGraw (1990), as with Raanan Sulitzeanu-Kenan's (2006) exploration of the effect of public inquiries on blame attribution for hypothetical policy failures. Some scholars have also tried to track policy actions and public opinion systematically over time (Jennings 2004 and 2009; Sulitzeanu-Kenan 2007; Hood et al. 2009). And third, the blame-avoidance perspective has been applied specifically to the management of health and financial risks, for instance in the work of Julia Black (2005) on risk-based approaches to financial regulation taken by the British Financial Services Authority in the early 2000s. Other scholars working on the regulation of health and social risks (such as White 2009; Hood, Rothstein, and Baldwin 2001) have developed a similar analysis, in showing how the management of such risks links to the career risks of politicians and public servants at various levels.

Indeed, the blame-avoidance perspective cuts across three different strands of political science that are normally separated—namely the analysis of institutional architectonics (why institutions are designed the way that they are), the analysis of policy processes (how policies play out at all stages from their emergence onto the decision agenda down to the way they operate on the ground), and the analysis of the working of electoral processes and public opinion. In fact, all of those different analytic strands are needed to explore the questions we posed at the outset, about why organizations often don't connect in policy delivery, why rigidity often trumps flexibility and proportionality in organizational functioning, and why opacity tends to trump clarity in accountability after policy fiascos. So we will be drawing on each of those three strands in the rest of the book.

THREE STRATEGIES FOR BLAME AVOIDANCE

In the traditional study of rhetoric, the art of persuasion, much effort went into categorizing and classifying different forms of argument (or substitutes for argument).[18] As yet we have no corresponding definitive categorization of blame-avoidance strategies to show for the twenty years or so since the term began to come into currency in political science and other fields. But in that scattered literature, we can identify three main strategies for deflecting or avoiding blame (see Hood 2002; Sulitzeanu-Kenan and Hood 2005). They are here termed presentational strategies, agency strategies, and policy strategies. The basics of each of those three strategies are summarized in table 1.1 and will be explored more fully as the book goes on.

Presentational strategies deal mainly with the loss or harm perception dimension of blame, but may also work on the time element to have an effect. *Agency strategies* deal mainly with the perceived agency dimension of blame that was discussed above (that is, the issue of who or what can be held responsible for what someone sees as avoidable harm). But such strategies can also approach the blame-avoidance problem by focusing on the time element—for instance, by revolving-door systems for moving officeholders on, so that by the time blame comes home to roost, someone else is in the hot seat. *Policy strategies* also deal mainly with the agency dimension and the time element. But they work through different means, namely through the overall architecture of policy and the standard operating routines that organizations follow rather than with distribution of responsibility in an organizational structure.

Thus, as table 1.1 suggests, "presentational strategies" involve various ways of trying to avoid blame by spin, stage management, and argument. The presentational strategist aims to work on the loss or harm perception dimension of blame, for example by accentuating the positive to counter negativity bias, and focuses primarily on what information to offer, when and how. Presentational strategists aim to find ways of showing that what might be perceived as a blameworthy problem is in fact a blessing in disguise, for instance as short-term pain that will produce long-term gain. They may also search for plausible excuses to mitigate blame on the part of particular officeholders, at the point where loss perception and agency meet. They may actively create diversions or at least contrive to time unpopular announcements at times of minimum public attention, with measures such as increases in politicians' pay sneaked out on public holidays or at a time when media attention is focused on some other big event.

The analysis of presentational strategies takes us into those parts of political science and related fields that are concerned with the framing of arguments, the rhetorical dimension of politics and management, the dynamics of public attitudes and opinion, and the links between media and politics. The former British prime minister Harold (later Lord) Wilson is claimed to have said that "most of politics is presentation, and

TABLE 1.1

Three Types of Blame-Avoidance Strategy

	Aspect of blame dealt with	Works on	Example	Assume
Presentational strategies (Slogan: "*Spin your way out of trouble*")	Loss or harm perception and time	Arguments for limiting blame (excuses) or turning blame into credit (justifications) and other methods of shaping public impressions	Shaping of public perceptions through news management	Presentational activity will limit or deflect rather than exacerbate or attract blame
Agency strategies (Slogan: "*Find a scapegoat*")	Agency perception and time	Distribution of formal responsibility, competency, or jurisdiction among institutions and officeholders in space or time	Formal delegation of potentially blameworthy tasks to "lightning rods"	Formal allocation of organizational responsibility is sufficiently credible and salient to last through blame firestorms
Policy strategies (Slogan: "*Don't make contestable judgments that create losers*")	Agency perception and time	Selection of policies or operating routines to minimize risk of institutional or individual liability or blame	Protocolization and automaticity to remove or minimize the exercise of individual discretion by officeholders	There is a low- or no-blame option (e.g., in choosing between errors of commission and errors of omission or between opting for automaticity and opting for discretion)

Source: Developed from Hood (2002).

what isn't is timing" (Jones 1993: 73), and presentational strategies have attracted much attention in the current age of "spinocracy." The idea of a "spinocracy"—rule by spin doctors—implies the rise to power of a so-called media class, in the form of armies of flak-catchers and public relations professionals or bureaucrats in central and influential positions in all forms of government and public organizations because of their supposed expertise in shaping media debate and public perceptions (see Kurtz 1998; Jones 1996 and 1999; Oborne 1999). And, whether or not spinocracy is as new as some of that breathless commentary suggests, it is true that after a crisis has struck, presentation is typically the main strategy for blame avoidance available to beleaguered officeholders.

By contrast, agency strategies involve various ways of trying to avoid blame by the way lines of formal responsibility are drawn in government and public services. The agency strategist aims to work on the responsibility perception dimension of blame and focuses primarily on government's organogram and on who occupies what position within it at what time. One important strain in agency strategy involves efforts by officeholders to delegate activities that will attract blame while retaining in their own hands the activities that will earn credit. Other ways to diffuse blame include partnership working, multi-agency arrangements, or institutional machinery so complex that blame can be shuffled about or made to disappear. As we shall see, organizations often engage in processes of defensive reorganization and revolving-door movement of officeholders, so that by the time blame comes home to roost, the organizational structure that produced the perceived harm has long been superseded and the relevant individuals have all moved out or on, leaving frustrated media and campaigners with no heads available to stick on spikes.

The analysis of agency strategies takes us into the traditional study of public administration—that part of political science that is concerned with all the details of how executive government is organized, including its use of private and independent organizations in partnership or delegation arrangements for public service provision. And as we shall see later, the blame-avoidance perspective may offer us one way of making sense of the much-remarked development of semi-autonomous public bodies, multi-level governance, and partnership arrangements in modern (and not so modern) government. It may also help to explain why elected politicians and senior bureaucrats often seem to spend a remarkable amount of their time on the fine print of organizational design while often professing that all they care about is "results."[19]

Policy strategies, also noted in table 1.1, are ways of trying to avoid blame by the processes that are followed in decision-making or by the substance of what officeholders do, rather than concentrating on the presentation of actions or outcomes, or on who is placed in the front line of responsibility for policy and operations. Policy strategists aim to work on the agency dimension and the time element by choosing policies or procedures that expose themselves to the least possible risk of blame. As we shall see later, there are various possible ways they can choose to do that. When it comes to more or less inevitably unpopular policies such as raising taxes or paying salaries and allowances to politicians, they may choose to rely as far as possible on following whatever they have inherited, so that blame attaches as much to their predecessors in office as to themselves. In addition, they may seek to replace human judgment and the blame it can attract by following automatic formulae.

Commonly observable examples of the latter approach include formula-driven rather than discretionary budget allocations, rigid protocols rather than independent professional judgment in casework decisions, checklist or tick-box approaches rather than qualitative assessment (such as computer-marked multiple-choice tests rather than essays judged in the round by teachers), computer-based decision algorithms rather than direct human contact. Or policy strategies may simply choose to abandon activities that may attract blame (such as the giving of advice or provision of public recreational facilities) rather than relying on being able to spin their way out of trouble or on shifting the responsibility around.

Policy strategies are not institutionalized in the same way as agency strategies or presentational strategies, so the analysis of policy strategies has to be conducted in a rather different way, as we shall see later in this book. We have to look at selective cases rather than at general indicators of development. But the greater the real or perceived negativity bias in the population at large or the particular culture in question, the more policy is likely to be dominated by such defensive approaches all the way down the food chain of executive government and public services. And policy strategies may be the blame-avoidance strategy of choice when agency strategies are not available—for example, by those to whom blameworthy activity comes to be delegated and who cannot delegate it further.

These three types of blame-avoidance strategy, which are summarized in table 1.1 and all of which are recognizable in the literature on public policy, are not claimed to exhaust all the possible approaches to avoiding or limiting blame. Nor are they claimed to be mutually exclusive or jointly exhaustive. They merely represent the most commonly discussed elements in the scattered literature on the topic. We can perhaps think of them as elements of a Venn diagram, a common representation of three separate circles that overlap at the margins, and they are presented as such in figure 1.2. One of the obvious areas of overlap consists of those cases where policy or agency strategies are so plastic (that is, easily changed, ambiguous, lacking clear exposition) that they are hardly distinguishable from presentational strategies. Cases of that kind include those instances

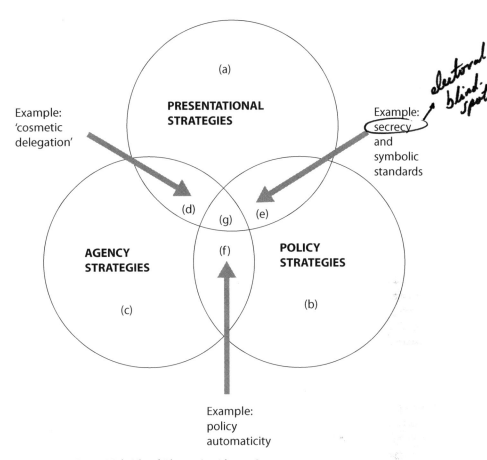

Figure 1.2. Some Hybrids of Blame-Avoidance Strategy.

where the arrangement of responsibilities among organizations or office-holders are so soft that they can be spun at will or where policies and procedures are capable of being interpreted in widely different ways, such that they too are not distinguishable from presentational strategies.

Moreover, as table 1.1 indicates, each of those three approaches to blame avoidance tends to have built-in limits. Agency strategies will reach their limits when formally declared lines of responsibility turn out not to be credible with the relevant public—for example, when voters still blame presidents or ministers even when activities are officially said to be delegated to or shared with other organizations. Presentational strategies, as we shall see later, reach their limits when spin doctors and their devious arts start to serve as blame magnets rather than blame deflectors. And policy strategies reach their limits when there turns out to be no blame-free position or procedure available, as at the point where errors of commission attract much the same amount of blame as errors of omission. But to say that any strategy has its limits is not to say that it cannot be used effectively within some range or in a suitable social context, and each of these types of strategy merits attention in the analysis of blame avoidance.

DEVELOPING THE ANALYSIS

Now that we have sketched out the blame-avoidance perspective and the kinds of behavior it may be able to explain in government and public service organizations, the chapters that follow aim to develop the analysis.

The next chapter aims to explore four different "worlds" of blame avoidance, distinguishing the world occupied by those in the highest offices (the top bananas), those who are in the front line of organizations or public services, and the meat in the organizational sandwich—everyone in the middle between the top officeholders and those in the front line. And a fourth world comprises those who are neither officeholders nor service providers, who can find themselves both on the giving and receiving end of blame. The blame game—the politics of blame avoidance—can be understood as a process of interaction among the players in these different worlds, as they combine or conflict and seek to pass the blame onto those in the other worlds.

Following that account of different blame-avoidance worlds, the next part of the book delves into the three blame-avoidance strategies sketched out above. We devote a chapter to each of them, exploring some of the variations around each theme and exploring some of the ways that each of these approaches have developed over time. We can think of this part of the book as an exercise in "naming the parts" of blame-avoidance approaches, as military recruits have traditionally been trained to do with their weapons (see Finer 1970: x) and medical students with human bones—analysis in the original sense of breaking something down into its various components. Of course this naming of parts is not exactly like identifying the bones of the foot or the parts of a gun, but it nevertheless consists of identifying three broad strategies of blame avoidance and then sketching out some of the different approaches that can be found within each broad strategy.

Thus in chapter 3, we explore presentational strategies, distinguishing those approaches that concentrate on winning arguments from those that concentrate on changing the subject, and differentiating those that involve invisibility or inaction ("taking the Fifth Amendment"[20]) from those that involve preemptive apologies designed to deflect blame or head off major accountability. In chapter 4, we turn to agency strategies and go into practices of hard and soft delegation, various types of responsibility-sharing through partnerships, and officeholder rotation. In chapter 5, we explore policy or operational strategies, looking at forms of protocolization (playing it by the book), varieties of group decision-making (staying with the herd), service avoidance (avoiding blame by not providing service in risky cases, as in the case of doctors not taking on high-risk patients), and ways of passing blame onto individuals, for instance by all those small-print disclaimers that put all the responsibility onto the individual recipient of service rather than on the service provider.

Then, following this analysis of the anatomy and development of blame-avoidance strategies, the next part of the book turns to the analysis of how those strategies can be mixed and matched and what institutional developments can be observed over time. Chapter 6 explores the dynamics, looking for clues as to whether the mix of the various approaches discussed in the previous three chapters is changing over time or that the amount of time and money invested in each of them is altering. For example, behind the high-flown rhetoric of liberal democracy, is government today drifting into a style of officeholding and organizational behavior that emphasizes neither steering nor rowing,[21] but rather blaming everyone else? Chapter 7 then turns to the mixing-and-matching issue, asking whether any combination of strategies can be successful or whether there are some strategies and variants that mix better than others, and whether there are limits on the way different blame-avoidance strategies can be sequenced when individuals or organizations are under blame pressure.

Finally, in chapters 8 and 9, the book returns to the themes we began with in this chapter and explores what the effects of blame-avoidance strategies are on modern executive government, what unintended effects they may produce on public policy, and to what extent they are to be welcomed or deplored as a shaper of government institutions and behavior. How effective are blame-avoidance strategies in keeping blame at bay, and whether or not they work, does the pursuit of such strategies improve or undermine the quality of governance in the sense of rigorous policy debate, sharp accountability, and transparent organization and policy process? And to the extent that the pursuit of blame avoidance can be problematic—as the opening examples in this chapter suggest—are there remedies available to limit the more negative aspects of blame avoidance dominating the behavior of executive government?

CHAPTER TWO

Players in the Blame Game: Inside the World of Blame Avoidance

> The main features [of the speech] were ... that he'd been under a lot of pressure but he'd been very brave, that he had done nothing wrong, that it was all the fault of the Serjeant-at-Arms, that he was the real victim, that he hadn't been told anything ... and that it wouldn't happen again because he was going to be in charge. He was going to form a committee....
> —Carr 2008: 6

INTRODUCTION: FOUR WORLDS OF BLAME AVOIDANCE

In the previous chapter, we looked at the basic idea of blame avoidance as a political and bureaucratic imperative, suggesting that blame avoidance can help us make sense of what otherwise seem to be baffling features of the way organizations and officeholders behave, contrary to the prevailing bromides about good governance and managerial reform. We explored the linked idea of negativity bias and identified three broad strategies that are available to would-be blame avoiders and are discussed in the scattered literature on this topic. In this chapter, we go inside blame-world, exploring blame avoidance from the perspectives of four types of players. Three of these types comprise different actors within government or public service delivery organizations, and the fourth comprises various actors outside such structures. Each of these types of player can either be blame takers (those who are liable to be blamed) or blame makers (those who dish out the blame), as explained in the previous chapter.

Our first world is that of the generals—the people with the grandest titles, who are in top leadership positions, and whose normal habitat is the boardroom or the chief executive's office suite. In modern media-saturated societies, some of these people have celebrity status, but even those that don't are destined to find themselves thrust into the limelight when things go wrong on their watch and a blame crisis occurs.

A second world is that of the infantry, the street-level bureaucrats or case-handling professionals. These are the people who are at the front line of their organizations at the point where they meet their publics, and such people will find themselves at the sharp end in a different sense when failures occur. Most of the time they will be out of the limelight, except for those occasions when a dramatic operational failure or other out-of-the-ordinary (usually negative) event puts the attention of the entire media and the political class onto that particular call center operator, train driver, surgeon, or police community support officer who was at the center of whatever it was.

A third world is more heterogeneous, comprising all those who are to be found somewhere between the generals and the infantry in government or public service organization. Between those two ends of the institutional pecking order we will often find various levels of middle managers, regulators, resource allocators, common service providers, consultants and advisers, spreaders of best practice, bean counters, personnel and safety people, and all the myriad of other intermediaries between the people at the top and the front-line deliverers. These individuals will often be less visible to the public at large than the top-level bosses who may feature in the news media or the front-line professionals or workers they meet in the street or at the service counter. But when adverse events occur, these people too may well find themselves in the line of fire, with the other actors seeking to lay the blame at their doors.

A fourth and final world is still more heterogeneous, since it comprises all the different individuals with whom governments and public service providers deal—their clients, customers, patients, prisoners, students, suppliers, and those who scrutinize or report on them. Some of those people are social isolates, but others are more actively engaged in blaming government or each other, whether as individual blame entrepreneurs, group-based egalitarians, or those belonging to well-defined social hierarchies. From one perspective this heterogeneous world can be seen as constituting those who deal out the blame to officeholders and public service institutions via their impact on public and media opinion and the way they cast their votes. But as we shall see, these "civil society" players can sometimes find themselves on the receiving end as well, when government officeholders and institutions try to turn the tables on them and blame them for what might otherwise be seen as the failures of government organizations on issues such as crime control or obesity.

TOP BANANA WORLD: THE SUMMIT OF BLAME AVOIDANCE

Perhaps the most obvious world of blame and blame avoidance, and the one to which many political scientists understandably tend to pay the most attention, is that of the top officeholders—such as presidents, prime ministers, cabinet ministers, central bank governors, chief executives, and other top bananas of that sort. Such potentates tend to be frequently in the media spotlight in most societies today and are often selected—at least in an evolutionary sense—on the basis of their ability to turn blame avoidance into an art form. Indeed, such individuals tend to be constantly searching for ways to draw credit upwards to themselves (by means such as making good-news announcements in person and appearing in flattering photo-ops with winning sport teams, gallant firefighters, cute children, or other credit-enhancing groups), while pushing blame downwards or sometimes outwards to others. Their world is rich in biographies, autobiographies, anecdotes, and even blow-by-blow accounts of how particular threats and crises have been handled by those at the top.

A graphic example of such material, referred to in the last chapter, is provided by the diaries of Tony Blair's former spin doctor Alastair Campbell (2007), which chronicle a long succession of actual or potential negative news stories that the Blair team frantically worked to forestall, close down, or respond to. It shows how far the people at the top of that government were driven by the imperatives of 11 a.m. press conferences, constantly preoccupied with working out worst-case media blame scenarios and planning lines of defense. It portrays a world of extreme time pressure—with a few hours being a long time to think anything through—and involving a draining ride on an emotional roller coaster that meant moment-by-moment switches from euphoria to anger and despair.

As a condition of survival, those top-level individuals have to find a way to cope psychologically with such an existence—for instance, by developing a special language, self-image, or mind-set, or by forms of superstition.[1] Nowadays they will tend to be well resourced to pursue all the blame avoidance strategies (agency, presentational, and policy) that we sketched out in the previous chapter. Normally they can command some specialized presentational resources and expertise, in the form of spin doctors, press officers, media coaches, and the like. Those specialists are there to help the top bananas monitor what is being said about them, keep track of poll or survey data, and train their charges to be media-savvy enough to present themselves and their policies in the most favorable possible light, to keep blame risk at bay, and to come out of every scrape smelling of roses.

The expertise and technology that can go into such operations is often impressive, from the effort put into scheduling and clearing press releases and public announcements across departments or other organizations, to the technological apparatus that accompanies top people's attempts to control the story. For example, when he was France's Minister of the Interior in the mid-2000s, Nicolas Sarkozy (elected President of France in 2007) maintained his own personal TV camera crew to capture the positive aspects of all his ministerial activities, such as visiting police stations and comforting crime victims. That put him in a position to offer selected parts of that film footage free to France's cash-strapped TV stations desperate to fill airtime.

Taking that approach to its logical conclusion, in Larry Gelbert's satirical 2006 play *Abrogate*, a fictional American President is followed around by an imaginary "photo-op unit," complete with wigs and costumes, ready to dress up as firefighters, disaster victims, and the like, as the political need of the moment demands. And that is only a slight exaggeration of the effort put into favorable self-presentation by some top officeholders.[2] More mundanely, heads of organizations and corporations often invest substantial resources in websites and house publications that carry only positive news about corporate activity, and numerous local authorities in Britain carried that approach a stage further in the 2000s by starting their own free newspapers which were not instantly reconizable as propaganda but which carried only positive news about the council and its leaders.

Not only do they have more resources available to them for controlling the story than those of us who are lower down the food chain, but top officeholders also tend to have more power to structure their organizations. Whereas most of us have to take the organizational structures in which we find ourselves as given, those at the top often have considerable scope to shape organization charts and thus determine who is to be in the front line of blame when things go wrong. For example, when 110,000 tons of rotting garbage had piled up in the streets of Naples in 2008 because there were no more landfill sites available (reflecting a long history of political ineffectiveness, endemic corruption, and control of waste disposal in the area by organized crime), Italy's then prime minister Romano Prodi dealt with the blame by appointing a former police chief, Gianni de Gennaro, as a new "trash czar" and handing that individual the poisoned chalice of fixing the problem within four months.[3]

Of course high officeholders may be limited in such blame-deflecting activity by constitutional or other rules they can't change, or at least not easily. Moreover, as we will see later, their efforts to shift blame by institutional tinkering may be limited by public attitudes that may not pay much attention to the finely crafted details of official lines of reporting when the people at the top try to delegate responsibility for problems like streets filled with mountains of stinking garbage. But within those limits, top-level individuals have numerous ways of shaping the executive structure around and below them in a way that their underlings cannot do, creating blame-sharing advisory groups for this and blame-attracting czars or trouble-shooters for that, to try to keep themselves out of the front line.

Those top bananas usually have a leading role in determining policy and procedures in their institutions as well, at least at the topmost level.

It is true that for an organization of any size much of the small print of detailed operations will inevitably tend to be decided further down the line. That can catch out the top-level people or work against what they are trying to achieve, particularly when it reflects efforts by lower-level people to protect themselves against efforts by the topmost officeholders to pass blame to them. But at least the top bananas can decide what broad projects to back and what services to provide or withdraw, and they will often have a decisive influence on the broad transparency or open-government rules that shape the conditions under which they are made accountable—something that those of us in less elevated positions can rarely do.

But as has already been noted, the downside of all these resources in their possession is that these eminences are also heavily exposed when things go wrong on their watch. Of course they can—and usually do—try to put the blame for any adverse events on their predecessors, on their subordinates, on real or imaginary enemies within and outside their institutions, and on anything else their often fertile imaginations and persuasive tongues can conjure up. But the blame avoidance frontier they have to defend is by definition a long one, given the scale of the organizations and the range of activities over which many of them preside. So in a world of continuous news media coverage, rather than the more measured daily rhythms of a generation ago, they are constantly exposed to the risk of an unexpected blame event coming from left field.

Moreover, for all celebrities—political and managerial as well as sporting or artistic—the downside of using the media as a platform for turning themselves into household names is that the same media that built them up are also likely to find news value in turning the finger of blame on them at some point down the line. [4] And in spite of their carefully cultivated images as supermen or superwomen above the petty concerns or weaknesses that beset us lesser mortals, these top-level individuals are also human beings who are likely to have at least their fair share of human frailty.[5] Like the rest of us, they have the potential to err in matters of personal conduct and judgment that they cannot plausibly delegate to others. And even for those vanishingly rare individuals who do manage to achieve something approaching perfection in such matters, there is no guarantee that their close friends and family will do so. Who among us does not have some embarrassing relatives or ill-judged friendships formed at some point in our lives?

But unlike the rest of us, top officeholders—especially but not only those who are elected rather than appointed—operate in a world that is likely to take a close interest in the smallest details of their love lives, their possibly dubious cronies or associates, their personal financial dealings, habits and lifestyles, family quarrels, the questionable political or religious affiliations they might have had in their early lives. And, particularly in an egalitarian culture, that outside world will be constantly alert for signs of hypocrisy in the form of gaps between the sanctimonious public pronouncements of those top bananas about proper standards of conduct and what they actually do themselves—for instance over such matters as family values, honesty over claims on the public purse, self-restraint over pay and pension deals, green lifestyles or carbon footprints, acceptance of gifts or hospitality from other individuals or organizations, second homes, or special advantages to their children in matters such as employment or private tuition or education.

In some times and places, top officeholders are able to maintain a wall of privacy around themselves on such matters. That often happens in authoritarian states, as with the seclusion in which the first Chinese Communist emperor Mao Ze Dong was able to pursue his "incessant" casual love affairs[6] while successfully presenting an image of puritan simplicity to the outside world. But even in what are ordinarily considered to be democracies, top leaders are not equally exposed to media scrutiny about what they do in their private lives. For instance, the French and German press has traditionally taken much less interest in the sexual peccadilloes of their respective political classes than the British tabloids. Some of that may be due to institutional factors, such as France's stringent privacy laws, but broader cultural attitudes can also play a part. For example, the late François Mitterand (who ruled France as president from 1981 to 1995) was able to maintain his mistress and natural daughter as well as his official family in government accommodation during his presidency without incurring any media comment or public opprobrium, something that would have been unthinkable in Britain or the United States at the same time. Commenting on the contrast between the blame heaped on President Bill Clinton for his well-known affair with the then White House intern Monica Lewinsky and François Mitterand's near-total avoidance of such treatment in spite of his at least equally lurid love life, one of Mitterand's biographers, Ronald Tiersky (2003: 333-34) says:

> The French people forgave Mitterand these "sins" [that is, his "second family" with Anne Pingeot, his long-term affair with the Swedish journalist Cristina Forsne for much of the fourteen years of his presidency, and his numerous other girlfriends[7]], perhaps, foreigners will say, because they are sophisticated and amoral, perhaps because their Catholic traditions teach that sins can be forgiven, or perhaps because it was not their business.... In contrast to the weight put on the necks of recent American presidents by public prudishness and prurience, abetted by the American media, François Mitterand did not have to moralize or discuss his private life (let alone his sexual

life) to do his job. If Mitterand was reproached by some of the French people for his morality, at least as many respected a double life discreetly done.

But even where high officeholders' private lives can be kept out of the blame game in such ways, the cost of maintaining the desired blame-free façade is not likely to be trivial. Living behind high walls, carefully concealing inconvenient details about youthful indiscretions, and keeping potentially embarrassing deals and transactions out of the public gaze can take a lot of time and effort. And when blame does start to emerge on those matters of personal conduct and judgment—as it eventually did even for the wily Mitterand in the matter of his early right-wing political associations and his work in 1942–3 for collaborationalist Vichy France[8]—top officeholders are particularly exposed, since those are precisely the kind of lapses that cannot easily be blamed on others.

FRONT-LINE WORLD: THE VIEW FROM THE STREET

In sharp contrast to the elevated but often frenetic blame avoidance world of the executive suite is that of the people at the front line of service delivery or government decision-making. These people are those who deal more or less directly with the public, such as bus or train drivers, social workers, emergency service crews, health-care professionals such as nurses and doctors, teachers, police marksmen or beat officers, counter or call-center staff in public offices, and everyone else who operates at the point where the individual meets government or public services. Most of the time, no one from the media or political world takes much interest in such individuals, unless they win the lottery, are discovered to be serial killers, or are unusual in other ways. But they are liable to find themselves suddenly blinking in the glare of the blame spotlight when they are involved in something that goes wrong (trains crash, children die in care or during school activities, patients die on the operating table, police shoot the wrong person).

To the extent that blame avoidance shapes the ways these front-line individuals behave, they will aim to claim victimhood. That is, they will try to ensure that when something goes wrong, the blame can be shifted back to the people further up the line—those who are responsible for whatever can be portrayed as the ill-judged orders, inherently flawed policies, unworkable operating systems, bullying management cultures, poor communications, badly designed organizational structures, inadequate resource allocations, or any of the many other possible sources of pressure on front-line staff that could be said to have caused the problem concerned.

For example, when train crash tragedies occur after drivers have passed stop signals (signals passed at danger, in British parlance), the top bananas and the people at the middle levels will naturally want to place the blame firmly at the door of the individual driver who ignored the signal. But the train drivers will often want to tell another story that at least mitigates blame for any individual carelessness on their part. They may aim to point out the accident was waiting to happen, given the operating conditions in which they work, such as fatigue caused by compulsory overtime (which itself might reflect constant crew shortages caused by companies' reluctance to train more drivers) and other safety hazards such as signals sited in such a way that makes them hard to read. Much the same tension between blame focused on the performance of front-line individuals and system blame can be found in the world of health care,[9] and that tension can turn into an ideological divide between the front line and higher management.

Indeed, there is an obvious general blame avoidance logic to front-line individuals in potentially blameworthy operating conditions seeking to portray themselves as merely the 'poor bloody infantry' (in military phraseology). To fit that image, they need to be seen as the gallant combat troops who are victims of a system over which they have little control as a result of being over-stretched, under-trained, and asked to perform impossible feats by inept or uncaring commanders well behind the front line.

Like the top-level people, these frontline individuals also have to cope culturally and psychologically with the ever-present risk of blame. In police services, some of that coping has traditionally been ascribed to the working of the so-called canteen culture (Waddington 1999)—that is, the social mechanisms by which police band together against the outside world to establish and maintain their own informal codes of conduct, sometimes in the face of the official ethics code or the law on the statute book.[10] Similar mechanisms are typically found in other uniformed and civilian organizations whose errors can be fatal or at least very damaging to those with whom they deal (see for example Menzies 1960 for a study of how student nurses in a London hospital handled anxiety). While the frontline troops are likely to be more experienced than those in top leadership positions in dealing with blame at the street level, they will tend to have fewer resources for handling higher-level media blame events. And unlike the top bananas, for whom dealing with such events is likely to be a regular occupational hazard—if not indeed their occupation—frontline people are unlikely to have to deal with such events on a regular basis and may have to learn from scratch the arts the top bananas have honed and practiced over their careers.

But that does not mean front-line players have no resources for trying to deflect blame away from themselves in their dealings with clients or customers. In some cases they may be able to influence their organization's operating practices, turning them into policy strategies (as we termed them in the last chapter) for avoiding blame. For instance, in recent years it has become common in Britain (and to a lesser extent in some other countries) for organizations such as banks, local government offices, hospitals, rail ticket offices, and airport security areas to prominently display large notices containing words to the effect that "our staff are here to help you. It is important that they are never made to feel threatened. We will not tolerate aggression or verbal abuse toward our staff."[11] And of course some of those front-line players will find ways of interpreting such apparently unexceptionable operating policies in such a way as to take any persistent questioning, unwillingness to accept obvious lies, or any complaint about rude or unhelpful treatment as verbal abuse and thus turn the blame onto clients or customers. Indeed, when serious failures occur, and irate and distressed people swarm around service counters and besiege internet sites and call centers with demands for information and remedies, the front-line staff facing all that suffering or complaining humanity will almost as a condition of survival have to pass the blame for the inconvenience or poor service onto their superiors or the systems within which they have to work. That too can be developed into an art form.

Unlike the top bananas, the frontline troops follow a route to blame avoidance that tends to be through collective organization rather than personal staff at their disposal, to protect themselves from blame and shape policies and organization. Such collective organizational resources include labor unions, professional associations and spontaneous organizations of various kinds, including the canteen culture referred to earlier. And those collective resources are more likely to be directed toward blame-avoiding policy strategies than to agency strategies, because frontline troops will usually not be in a position to delegate their powers or to negotiate partnership arrangements and the like on their own initiative.

Policy strategies can be pursued at the individual level too. A generation ago, in a classic account of street-level bureaucracy, Michael Lipsky (1980) stressed the extent to which public employees such as police or teachers who interacted directly with the public at large had *de facto* power to determine policy through their powers of discretion and relative autonomy. Lipsky (1980: xii) wrote that "the decisions of street-level bureaucrats, the routines they establish, and the devices they invent to cope with uncertainties and work pressures effectively *become* the public policies they carry out" (see also Hupe and Hill 2007: 280).

Seen from a blame-avoidance perspective, that policy autonomy stressed by Lipsky and others carries accompanying blame risks, because it makes frontline individuals potentially vulnerable to blame when their exercise of that individual discretion results in an avoidable failure. For instance, if a child suffers death or injury when a social worker fails to recognize abuse or otherwise fails to act on information available, if civilians or hostages die when police or peace-keeping soldiers use force in a way that in hindsight appears unnecessary or disproportionate, if patients die as a result of being given the wrong medication or of surgery that goes wrong, the frontline policy discretion Lipsky and others highlight will be a short route to taking all the blame. It gives the top bananas or the middle-level players a clear opportunity to shift the blame by claiming they had no knowledge of what was happening further down the line or weren't responsible for those ill-judged discretionary decisions at the operating level.

So if negativity bias and blame avoidance considerations dominate the behavior of street-level bureaucrats, they will, perhaps paradoxically, use the de facto policy autonomy noted by Lipsky and others to limit their blame risk. And that logic will often lead such individuals to interact or collaborate with higher levels of the organization to share or shift the blame, or even delegating responsibility upwards, as in Menzies' (1960) study of student nurses. Three of the commonest ways of doing that (which we will come back to in part 2) are to lock in higher-level people to decisions, to follow the bureaucratic "jobsworth" strategy of sticking rigidly to rules and protocols whatever the circumstances, and to use the safety-in-numbers strategy of working as a group.

Locking in means associating superordinates with decisions so they cannot later claim they didn't know or didn't agree with what was being done. A familiar application, costing little in time and effort in today's digital age, is for front-line staff to copy their seniors into all e-mails that could lead up to potentially blameworthy decisions. Indeed, over the last few years the exposure of "killer e-mails" has become a key element in who-knew-what-when blame games between higher and lower officehold-ers.[12] The jobsworth strategy means following rules to avoid blame—for example, when health-care professionals follow standard protocols which offer them a following-best-practice defense when their decisions turn out to be wrong in individual cases. (That is part of a more general approach to defensive medicine, which we shall discuss in later chapters.) The herding approach, also to be discussed later (in chapter 5), means that potentially challengeable decisions or judgements are made by a group rather than an individual, such that no one person can later be blamed for errors of judgement.

All of those blame-shifting and -sharing tactics are widely observable at the front line of public services today, and modern information and communications technologies have produced many new applications. As we have just noted, e-mail can drastically cut the cost of bureaucratic back-covering. Information technology can provide endless new variants of the "it's the computer" excuse for failures to deal with individual cases

→ principal-agent problem

effectively. And indeed modern IT systems often make it hard for front-line staff or professionals to override the software, obliging them to use preset online decision trees or risk-assessment algorithms in dealing with cases and clients (something that hardly existed when Lipsky wrote his classic account of street-level bureaucracy three decades ago and has become widespread in areas such as probation and social work). A case in point is the sort of IT software that prevents staff in job placement agencies from claiming to have placed a job-seeker in work unless that individual is entered in the system as having come off welfare benefits at the same time. Such systems are designed to limit the scope for job placement agency staff to fiddle the numbers (see Heinrich 2002) by curtailing their discretion, but they can also be used by frontline staff for blame avoidance. ("Don't blame me, blame the software and the protocols built into it.")

Of course neither such technology nor more low-tech devices can ever completely remove those front-line individuals' discretion and autonomy and some claim that the reduction of discretion in domains such as social work has been exaggerated (Evans and Harris 2004). For instance, the disposition of front-line troops' time among all the various cases they could be treating at any given moment can rarely be fully protocolized, even with medical triage routines and their equivalents in other domains. Nor can bosses be brought into every time-disposition issue. The technology fix is not always applicable either, for instance in crisis conditions when computers fail for one reason or another or where the technology is otherwise inapplicable.

Even then, the multiple accountabilities that have often been identified in analyses of the work of front-line bureaucrats may sometimes help to deflect or limit blame for the way such people use their discretion. For instance, if police officers make unfortunate decisions such as wrongful arrest or failure to act, they may be able to limit blame by playing on some of their other accountabilities, such as the expectations of the local community, demands from the media, or even health and safety obligations. Indeed, the latter was used by two police community support officers in Lancashire, England in 2007 when they faced a storm of criticism for failing to jump into a pond to save the life of a drowning ten-year-old boy who was trying to help his eight-year-old stepsister. In the aftermath of this tragedy, it emerged that health and safety provisions were being interpreted in other cases to limit the attempts by emergency services to save drowning people.[13]

It might at first seem that front-line troops are just cannon fodder in the blame game. But they too have significant cards to play as blame makers and strategic choices to make over blame avoidance. Indeed, the troops' counter-strategies can sometimes undermine the blame avoidance strategies adopted by the generals back at base, for example when employees who have been fired in a blame crisis counterattack with damaging revelations about their former bosses.

The Meat in the Sandwich: The Middle against Both Ends

In between top banana world and that of the troops at the front line are all the people in the middle—usually less visible, though such players can emerge into the limelight on occasion, for instance to denounce their bosses after they have been made to take the rap for some error. Of course that middle level breaks down into a myriad of different worlds, since there is often a complex array of players crowding into the space between the front line and the topmost command. They include private-sector contractors along with public bureaucracies, common service providers along with middle levels in a chain of command, numerous forms of regulators, auditors, or inspectors, those who allocate money to fund operations at various stages along the line, and those who control various aspects of overall policy, such as greenness, efficiency, equality and diversity, and all the other competing desiderata that jostle for attention in the policy arena and become reflected in special units at various levels in an institutional system.

From the perspective of the generals and the frontline troops, the middle might seem to be the safest place to be when blame over operational failures starts to rear its head. But those in the middle can find themselves on the receiving end of blame directed to them both from top- and bottom-level players. Indeed, in institutional politics, top-level leaders commonly try to form alliances with the frontline people against what they perceive or portray as the obstructionism of the "frozen middle" of the executive structure (a term used by General Motors chief executive Roger Smith in GM's onslaught on middle management in the 1980s [Smith 1994: 251] but often found in the politics of public services as well). And the frontline people equally can try to appeal over the heads of their immediate superiors to those at the very top.

Indeed, when things go wrong in government and public services, the question can often be raised as to whether the front-line operators and the topmost commanders were both let down by bungling or in-fighting in the middle. A common example is the question of who is to blame for the mishandling of materiel supplies for military operations, when there is avoidable loss of young soldiers' lives as a result of delays in procuring or issuing protective equipment. And the middle levels can often figure large in the sort of blame that relates to muddled instructions, inconsistent or even contradictory demands, failure to inform the top-level leaders accurately or to understand the conditions on the ground. In any complex institutional structure, blame in that form is rarely far to seek.

In such an environment, the various players in the middle (like their counterparts at the top and the bottom) will need to find ways of directing blame away from themselves. And while the middle levels can find themselves on the receiving end of blame from both the top and the bottom, the opposite side of that coin is that they have more directions in which they can try to shift blame than do the other players. After all, the top-level players mainly have to move blame downwards and the bottom-level players mainly have to move it upwards. But the middle-level players can try to move it both upwards and downwards, and frequently sideways as well, given the multiplicity of players typically found between the generals and the front line.

Like the other players, the people in the middle have a distinctive set of resources or cards they can play in the blame game. Crucially, they are often the people who control the small print of policy and procedure in organizations, in the commonly noted process by which instructions or policy guidelines coming from the top are translated into standard operating routines (see, for instance, Dunsire 1978: 6–7; Page and Jenkins 2005). If the devil is always in the details in matters bureaucratic, it tends to be the middle-level people who control the details, and that can put them in a position to use their small-print power to put the onus of responsibility onto the other players.

So, like the front-line players, the people in the middle can play the blame game by acting as blame makers and trying to deflect blame upwards to those at the top. One of the ways to do that is to lock in those top-level players to every policy or case decision that could possibly be controversial if it goes wrong, as by clogging their inboxes with more copied e-mails than the top people will ever have time to read or digest. Edward Page and Bill Jenkins (2005), in a pioneering book on British middle-level bureaucrats, stress the extent to which such players follow the path of invited authority, that is, not operating autonomously but seeking out their superiors for approval of every stage of their work, particularly for anything that might be sensitive or "political."[14] Of course such efforts may not always be welcomed by the top-level players, because as we have already seen the top bananas will normally want to detach themselves from middle-level operations so that they can later claim they were not told about anything that comes to be seen as blameworthy.

Further, like the top-level players, the people in the middle can also play the blame game by trying to deflect blame downwards to those in the front line. That means using their detailed policy-shaping resources to ensure that operational failures can be shifted back to mistakes made by those at the front line, to be classed as operator error or individual carelessness and dealt with by disciplinary action against those operators, rather than treated as system failures that could be laid at their door. That can be done by making sure the procedural rules put the onus of making tricky decisions about handling risk and emergencies onto the lower-level operators, such that those front-line operatives are liable to be blamed whatever they do.

For instance, one of the many hazards of operating civil aircraft today, highlighted in Imogen Edwards-Jones' (2006) dark novel *Air Babylon,* is that of handling a death en route. Pilots are liable to be blamed if they fail to follow a rule that says they must land at the nearest airport if a passenger dies during a flight—an event that is far from unknown, particularly as more elderly people have been embarking on long once-in-a-lifetime journeys in the recent era of cut-price air travel. But the aircrew will certainly find themselves under heavy criticism from their passengers and colleagues for all the long flight delays and inconvenience that will result from meticulously observing the first rule. In consequence they may be driven into workarounds such as trying to put the dead body out of sight and inventing the convenient fiction that a person who dies on a flight passed away just as the plane was landing at its final destination.

Middle-level people can also pass blame sideways, and the complexity of the middle-level structures of public services and executive government often provides plenty of scope for sidestepping blame in this way. For example, they may be able to blame others for delays or information lapses, or to use regulatory approval requirements, funding limits, or the incompetence or lack of cooperation of partner organizations as an alibi.

Even within a single service domain, the organizations behind the front line are typically split up into at least three parts, namely the chain-of-command intermediaries, the common service providers (for instance, those who provide training or financial services or IT), and the regulators or inspectors, themselves often multiple and overlapping. For example, during the early years of Tony Blair's Labour government, there were two regulatory bodies for Britain's chronically breakdown-prone rail system, with the (convenient, though possibly unintended) effect that those bodies blamed one another for the many rail failures that occurred during that period (see Hood 2002).

Indeed, complex overlaps at intermediate levels often go much further than those in what John Bryson and Barbara Crosby (1992: 6) call a "no-one-in-charge world," comprising a range of organizations of different statuses (public bureaucracies, private firms, third-sector bodies, and all the various hybrids of those types). And where a problem or case crosses several public service domains (such as the handling of ex-offenders or problem children), those complexities—and consequent opportunities for blame-shifting—are compounded even further.

On top of that, those no-one in charge multi-organizational structures will often be in a process of reorganization as the institutional furniture

is moved around and organizational names are changed to confuse enemies and give an impression of progress and dynamism. Those processes
of transition—which often seem to be perpetual, like the never-ending
road works to be found in many countries today—involve organizations,
frequently under new management, moving from systems or structures
that have been admitted to be flawed to a new regime claimed to offer
better prospects for the future. And they offer further scope for attempts
to shuffle off blame for whatever temporary difficulties arise from those
transitions, or for making it disappear into the cracks of the bedding-in
process of new organizational structures.

The bureaucratic control strategies practiced by top-level leaders can
sometimes unintendedly help the middle-level players pass blame among
themselves. President Franklin Roosevelt was well known for his tendency
to dislike tidy structures in the federal government, instead preferring
multiple overlapping units which increased his chances of playing various
bureaucrats off against one another in their battles for turf and resources
(see Neustadt 1960). And Roosevelt was far from the only top-level leader
to follow such a divide-and-rule control strategy over the bureaucratic
world. But in pursuing such a strategy such leaders also create the conditions for those multiple and overlapping units in the middle to blame each
other for whatever goes wrong.

The middle of the heap in the organizational world lacks both the celebrity stardust of the highest levels and the credibility and respect that
can go with being in the heat of the action rather than behind the lines,
and it traditionally gets less research attention than the first two worlds.
But it too is a world that contains both strong motivations to try to avoid
blame and numerous opportunities for doing so.

Everyone Else

Finally, we need to consider all those who are to be found outside the formal delivery structures and organizational apparatus inhabited by those
top, middle, and front-line officeholders discussed above. This world is
that of the public and civil society organizations that government and
public services deal with—as clients, customers, applicants, inquirers,
detainees, patients, students, and all the many other guises in which the
individual meets organizations providing public services (see Hood and
Margetts 2007).

In one sense, we can think of this world as comprising blame makers
rather than blame takers. After all, in the first chapter we began with the
standard notion of politicians and other officeholders trying to claim
credit and avoid blame from voters and the public at large. But those who

are outside those officeholders' worlds can also find themselves on the receiving end of blame as well as dishing it out. That can happen in at least four ways.

First, governments and public officeholders often try to put the blame for social ills or other kinds of failure onto enemies within the society or organization, or onto international or outside forces, rather than attributing those ills to their own failings. The idea of sinister forces of subversion, sabotage, and immorality is often invoked by governments and other officeholders when things go wrong, and it manifests itself at various levels from low-level sparring between politicians and the media over allegedly biased reporting to outright racist and other forms of stigmatization found in fascist or other regimes based on the politics of paranoia.

An extreme example is the blame game that took place over the hyperinflation and chronic food and fuel shortages, in President Robert Mugabe's Zimbabwe in the 2000s. By 2005, the economy had contracted in real terms for five successive years, Zimbabwe's average income had returned to its 1953 level, inflation was in three figures, half of the country faced serious food shortages, and about a quarter of its population had fled abroad. But Mugabe and his lieutenants tried to put the blame for these problems onto international forces (including what they claimed to be an international gay conspiracy and a drought induced by American control of Zimbabwe's weather) rather than their own economic mismanagement and predatory rule (Clemens and Moss 2005).

Further, as was noted in the previous chapter, governments and officeholders under pressure often try to put the blame onto news media for what they claim to be irresponsibly one-sided reporting, for creating panics by spreading scare stories or unfounded rumors, or for promoting cynicism and undermining public trust in institutions. For instance, Craig Crawford's (2005) *Attack the Messenger* describes how a succession of US presidents have contrived to present themselves as victims of pervasive media bias. Harold Wilson, the British Labour prime minister of the 1960s and 1970s, similarly blamed the media for what he said was "trivialization of politics," but skeptics thought that was political code for media unwillingness to accept obvious untruths in answers to probing questions (see Levin 1971: 341).

A third way that governments and officeholders can try to put the blame onto the world outside is by blaming the apparent victim—for example, when victims of crime are said to have brought their own fate onto themselves by flaunting their wealth, dressing inappropriately, choosing to go into unsafe areas, and the like. How far victims should take the blame for what happens to them is a long-standing issue in law, as in the debate about how much those who are subject to rape can be blamed for "provocation" and in the debates over strict liability in consumer rights law, concerning how far those who harm themselves or their property in using products or services without due care can be held liable for what happens to them. Exactly the same issue arises in politics and government more generally.

A case in point is the much discussed rise of obesity in many countries over recent years, highlighted by a series of alarmist reports and health warnings. We might blame such developments on the activity of governments and employers that produce "obesogenic environments"[15] by chaining more and more of us to a sedentary screen-based existence in every part of our lives (from work to shopping to dealings with government itself). We might blame those who make the planning decisions that can make it harder to shop or commute by walking or cycling. We might blame those responsible for the decisions that make access to basic exercise facilities like swimming pools costly and difficult. But rather than laying the blame for obesity on such corporate and government activity, health ministers often choose to lecture the population about the need to eat less and exercise more, as if it was just an epidemic of personal idleness and greed that was causing the problem.[16]

Similarly, governments and officeholders can seek to deflect blame onto other actors in the world outside by means of what the criminologist David Garland (2001) terms "responsibilization." By responsibilization, Garland means putting the blame for the social problems government is unable to solve onto other actors in the society—for example when police seek to excuse their inability to control crime or terrorism by denouncing inadequate parenting or the breakdown of civil society. For Garland, responsibilization in the sense of attempts by elected politicians to download responsibility to others for crime and security problems is a central feature of modern criminal justice politics in the United States and Britain—for instance, in making communities responsible for crime control and blaming parents for the behavior of their children.

A variant of that responsibilization approach to shifting the blame is putting 'ordinary people' (or those who can be represented as such) onto advisory committees or focus groups, or as lay members among professionals on governing bodies, to help spread the blame when criticism of the actions of such bodies starts to emerge. That can be thought of as a milder equivalent of the "human shield" tactic used by hostage-takers or rogue political regimes to protect themselves. Celebrity endorsements or initiatives—which so commonly feature in sport and art projects, as well as anti-poverty, climate change, and urban development measures—can have similar blame-deadening or -spreading qualities, because they enable celebrities to gain public attention while simultaneously allowing public officeholders to share or deflect the blame.

Some readers will of course think that for politicians or bureaucrats to blame the public at large or particular social institutions for problems such as crime, obesity and waste means getting to the heart of the relevant social processes, if they think change in individual (as opposed to governmental) behavior is the key to tackling such problems effectively. Readers may also think that involving ordinary people in organizational, professional, or governmental processes is a key to good governance. We shall postpone that discussion to the final chapter, where we consider what is to count as good or bad blame avoidance.

These are just a few examples of how governments and officeholders can try to pin the blame for social problems onto players in the fourth world, that of civil society. And of course these players, targeted as blame takers, can just as well be blame makers when it comes to blame games. The poet and playwright Berthold Brecht deftly satirized the blaming-the-public strategy in his famous 1953 poem "Die Lösung" calling for the East German government to dismiss its public and get a new one.[17] And indeed the advantage to those in the first three worlds of blaming the fourth is that it turns the blame-avoiding interactions between top, middle, and lower officeholders from a zero-sum game (the more liability to blame one of these levels assumes, the less is assumed by the others) into a cooperative game in which all can gain by jointly blaming the victim.

Conclusion

Table 2.1 summarizes the earlier discussion of the directions and resources for shifting blame available to the players in the four different worlds of blame avoidance sketched out in this chapter. It suggests that for the first world, blame can be shifted downwards, sideways, or outwards; in the second world, upwards, sideways, or outwards; in the third world, upwards, downwards, sideways and outwards; and in the fourth world, sideways and outwards (where outwards in this world involves pinning blame onto governments or public organizations).

Blame games can be understood as the interactions among the various players in each of these four worlds. Those interactions among the four worlds involve a mixture of conflict and collusion, with some actors engaged in zero-sum battles to lay the blame on one another, and some actors forming more or less explicit alliances against others.

Examples of conflict that have already been mentioned include battles between media and politicians over issues such as lack of public trust in government or between top-level officeholders and those further down the hierarchy as to who knew what and when about blameworthy decisions

TABLE 2.1
Blameworld: Four Sets of Players and Their Strategies

World	Main Available Directions of Blame Avoidance				Main Available Resources for Blame Avoidance		
	U	D	S	O	Presentational	Agency	Policy
Top		✓	✓	✓	Will typically have substantial resources at their individual disposal for pursuing all three types of strategy		
Front-line	✓		✓	✓	Mainly through collective action	Mainly through creative handling of multiple accountabilities to deflect blame	Mainly in interpretation of policy and operations—e.g., in "no abuse of staff" rules to blame clients or customers
Middle level	✓	✓	✓	✓	Unlikely to have presentational resources at their individual disposal	May control or at least influence demarcation in detailed agency relationships	"Small-print" control of detail of enacted policy and procedure
Civil society			✓	✓	Highly variable, given the variety of actors in this world, from major corporate players to social isolates.		

Key to directions of blame avoidance:
U = upwards (e.g., blaming higher management)
D = downwards
S = sideways or inwards (e.g., blaming other agencies)
O = outwards (e.g., blaming media, enemies, saboteurs)

or operations. But we have also seen that although there is always likely to be an underlying "zero-sum-ness" about blame in social systems, there can also be alliances between the players in the different blame-avoidance worlds sketched out here, as when the first three sets of players work together to put the blame on the fourth world, or when top- and middle-level players join together to blame front-line staff for operator errors in disasters. Sometimes those alliances cross over into the fourth world as well—for instance, when top-level officeholders try to bring the public in to put the blame on frontline staff for poor public services.

How those interactions play out among the four worlds discussed here will be shaped both by institutional architecture and by culture in the sense of prevailing attitudes and beliefs. For instance, if all else is equal, we might expect blame conflicts between the top and bottom levels of institutional structures to be more severe in the sorts of structures where people parachute straight up to top levels from outside, as compared with closed-career public service structures (that is, when career progression involves everyone starting at the bottom and working up, rather than lateral entry to higher levels, as commonly applies in police and military organizations). Similarly, systems of divided government and complex multi-level government structures may offer more opportunities for blame-shifting in the sideways and up-and-down directions than simpler structures.

And more generally, the attitudes and beliefs shared within a society or organization can be expected to shape the way blame plays out among the four worlds discussed here. To anticipate a point to be developed later in the book, in some times and places there will be a general propensity to blame the people at the top for everything that can be seen to be wrong, from climate change to obesity and car crashes, and such a cultural environment is unfriendly to blame avoidance efforts by top bananas. But in other times and places, blame or exoneration will be more likely to rest on sometimes complex niceties as to who followed or flouted the relevant official rules or established procedures, and that is an environment which may be less favorable to the denizens of the second and third worlds that we considered above. In yet other social settings, blame will tend to be assigned to those who are considered to be personally inept or maladroit (for example, investors who lose their shirts when the respected financial institutions they have invested their pension funds in collapse)—people who might be considered victims from other cultural standpoints. And in other conditions, blame outcomes will be capricious and hard to predict, not necessarily following any clear social logic. The late Mary Douglas (1990: 15), a well-known anthropologist whose cultural theory identifies four distinct and fundamental worldviews, declared: "In an individualistic culture, the weak are going to carry the blame for what happens to them; in a hierarchy, the deviants; in a sect, aliens and also faction leaders." (We shall be returning to this issue in chapter 7.)

In the next three chapters of this book, we turn to the three main blame avoidance strategies we have already identified—that is, presentational, agency, and policy strategies. We explore some of the variant forms of each of those strategies and consider their scope and limits, before returning to our broader analytic questions about blame avoidance in politics and bureaucracy.

PART TWO

Avoiding Blame: Three Basic Strategies

Presentational Strategies: Winning the Argument, Drawing a Line, Changing the Subject, and Keeping a Low Profile

> The best way to deal with nuclear waste is to hire a PR company
> —*Private Eye* 1144, October 28–November 10, 2005: 26

> Only the future is certain. The past is always changing.
> —Precept number 15 of "pompomism," meaning poodle-like political characteristics, in Paul Flynn's (1999: 24) account of New Labour rule in Wales in the late 1990s.

PRESENTATION, PRESENTATION, PRESENTATION ...

The presentational approach to blame avoidance was briefly sketched out in the first chapter. It denotes attempts to affect the harm perception or agency dimensions of blame by spin, timing, stage management, and various forms of persuasion. The great philosopher Friedrich Nietzsche once wrote (albeit in unpublished notes) that "there are no facts, only interpretations."[1] That statement is an expression of what is known as perspectivism and is itself (of course) philosophically contestable. But presentational strategies for warding off blame certainly operate on an assumption that is close to Nietzsche's famous dictum, and the spin doctor's art is to concentrate on the interpretation or framing of what might otherwise be embarrassing "facts."

The practice of "impression management" (Schlenker 1980) is hardly a new discovery, and framing analysis has long been a central theme of psychology and social science (see, for instance, Goffman 1986; Tversky and Kahneman 1981). But, as the cynical *Private Eye* quote in the first epigraph perhaps reflects, presentational strategies for avoiding blame attract a lot of attention in what is often portrayed as an age of spinocracy. As we noted in chapter 1, much has been written in recent years about spin and presentation as a way of avoiding blame and claiming credit.[2] Numerous commentators (as well as novelists, playwrights, and satirists) have been fascinated by the apparent rise of a so-called media class, comprising powerful public relations professionals or czars who

have come to occupy central and influential positions in government and
public organizations because of their supposed expertise in spin doctoring media debate (see Kurtz 1998; Jones 1996 and 1999; Oborne 1999).
The term spin doctor is itself of fairly recent coinage,[3] though the activity
certainly existed before the phrase came into existence.

Indeed, senior officeholders in modern government, as well as celebrities and leaders of private corporations, often devote a very large part of
their time to presentational activity. Howard Kurtz (1998: xxiv), in his
account of President Bill Clinton's propaganda machine, writes: "The ...
reality of White House life was that the top players spent perhaps half their
time either talking to the press, plotting press strategy, or reviewing how
their latest efforts had played in the press." In some cases, such individuals spend an even larger proportion of their time on such presentational
matters. One senior minister in Tony Blair's New Labour government is
said to have spent most of his day dealing with the news media, and the
rest of his time dealing with concerns coming from the prime minister's
office—which were in turn mostly about the handling of the media.[4]

Further, the more such players see themselves as victims of negativity
bias, the human tendency to put more emphasis on negative than on positive information that we discussed in the first chapter, the more effort
they are likely to put into trying to correct such bias to keep blame at bay.
Many of those at the top of the tree in politics and other walks of life,
perceiving their merits and achievements to be constantly under assault
from an army of malicious and envious critics, would probably heartily
agree with Sir Walter Scott's observation that "detraction ... always pur-
sues merit with strides proportioned to its advancement."[5] Given that
perception, it is not surprising that such individuals invest a lot of time,
effort, and money in presentational strategies designed to accentuate the
positive.

Indeed, if negativity bias can be as important a force in politics as was
suggested in the first chapter, there is an obvious logic in organizations
and officeholders seeking to counter it with as much positivity bias as
they can summon up, to match what they are likely to see as the unrepre-
sentatively downbeat interpretation of their activities and achievements
coming from special-interest malcontents and bitter ex-colleagues. Some
regimes apply that positivity bias in extreme and unsubtle (in fact often
ludicrous) ways, as in the case of the relentlessly upbeat pictures of life in
the workers' state and constant rewriting of history in the official propaganda of the former Soviet Union. But as the second epigraph reminds
us, the spin machines of modern democratic governments are also in the
blame avoidance business.

Indeed, a few years ago the journalist Christopher Fildes (2005) even
coined the tongue-in-cheek term "hedonomics" to denote what he claimed

to be "a newly identified branch of economics" that sought to put a positive spin on the formerly "dismal science." The examples he gave included finance ministers dismissing persistently high inflation as a blip, talking about 'green shoots of recovery' during the deepest of recessions, or more subtly, massaging official statistics to accentuate the positive, for instance by leaving taxes out of official inflation indexes.[6]

This chapter aims to delve into the slippery world of presentational approaches to blame avoidance, and most of it is a sort of stamp collection, itemizing some of the different forms that presentational strategy can take, arranged around variations of four main types. But we conclude with some discussion about the conditions in which presentational strategies have the desired effect in limiting or avoiding blame, and when they have diminishing or even negative returns. What is the scope and what are the limits of the presentational approach?

TYPES OF PRESENTATIONAL STRATEGIES

Presentational strategies can come in different forms. Although rhetoric, the study of argument and persuasion,[7] is the oldest subject of the humanities, there is no definitive catalogue. And indeed such a classification is always likely to be elusive, as culture changes and human inventiveness develops. But to give an idea of some of the variety without making any claim to comprehensiveness, table 3.1 sketches out four broad types of presentational strategy in the blame game that we explore further below.

TABLE 3.1
Some Varieties of Presentational Strategy

Keeping a Low Profile	Winning the argument
Motto: "Keep your head down until it blows over"	**Motto**: "Fight your corner to win over your audience"
Example: Being unavailable for comment	**Example**: Offering persuasive excuses and justifications
Changing the subject	**Drawing a line**
Motto: "Divert the attention of your critics or the public"	**Motto**: "Disarm your critics before they turn nasty"
Example: Finding good times to bury bad news	**Example**: The tactics of "sorry democracy"

They are labeled winning the argument, drawing a line, changing the subject, and keeping a low profile.

Winning the Argument

The most obvious form of presentational strategy is to try to win any argument over culpability in its own terms. That means showing that what organizations or officeholders are being accused of by their detractors is untrue—or if it is true, justifiable in some way. So what we can call winning-the-argument variants consist of some sort of reasoned account offered by the potential blame taker to the potential blame maker, to avoid or limit blame.

In the opening chapter we argued that blame includes elements of avoidable harm, agency, and time. So to win arguments about blame we need to do one of two things. One is to show there is no problem (avoidable harm), so that the question of blame does not arise. The other is to show, if there is such a problem, that blame either lies elsewhere (agency) or can be shuffled off in some other way. Out of these, problem denial is perhaps the most secure basis for blame avoidance, since if there is no perception of avoidable loss or harm, the issue of blame cannot arise (see Schütz 1996: 122). So it is not surprising that organizations and officeholders often play this argumentative card early when criticism starts.

There is more than one variant of problem denial. The purest form—the "crisis, what crisis?" gambit, as it is sometimes known—is that of total problem denial. That is a high-reward but high-risk approach: if it succeeds, it removes all questions of blame, but runs the risk of extra embarrassment and loss of credibility if the problem later turns out to be undeniably real. A more qualified variant (perhaps slightly less risky because easier to row back from) takes the form of admitting that there is some minor problem, but denying that it is serious or significant or out of control in any way. And a third type, often a variant of the first or the second, consists of some sort of problem denial accompanied by a counter-attack.

Such counter-attacks can take the form of portraying any critics of the officeholder or organization concerned as politically motivated troublemakers. Besides such smear tactics, attacks can consist of asserting that the onus of proof rests with the critics rather than with those who are being blamed. They can include dismissals of moles, whistle-blowers, and leakers within an organization, or making threats of various sanctions against those suggesting there might be a case to answer. As we saw in the last chapter, officeholders and organizations can try to pin the blame on the media in general or on named journalists in particular for distortion or fabrication. To quote again from Howard Kurtz's (1998: 302) account of President Bill Clinton's propaganda machine: "[Among] the techniques that had worked so well for so long... [were] blaming the press, denouncing their accusers, assailing right wing enemies....'

Problem denial sometimes requires hair-splitting precision in the words to be used, reflecting a careful choice of which facts to put into the denial and which to leave out. Perhaps the most famous example of that tactic in recent history comes from Bill Clinton's handling of the scandal over his affair with the then White House intern Monica Lewinsky, leading to impeachment proceedings in 1998. Craig Smith points out that the famous presidential denial, issued on January 26, 1998 ("I did not have sexual relations with that woman, Miss Lewinsky.... These allegations are false') rested on a particular legal interpretation of 'sexual relations' as meaning one person's contact with another for that other person's pleasure (Smith 2003: 175). That is a striking example of a form of argument—choosing which facts and premises to put into an argument and which to leave out—that Aristotle (1984: 2236) termed "enthymeme" in his account of the art of rhetoric. Enthymeme is often central to presentational strategies for trying to ward off blame.

Closely related to such tactics is blame avoidance by more or less subtle reinterpretation of the past. The second epigraph to this chapter is a mocking comment on the tendency of blame-obsessed officeholders constantly to rewrite history as the political circumstances of the moment dictate.[8] It has been said that traveling on a backwards-facing seat on a train allows you to see the past ever changing before your eyes,[9] and there are times when observation of official spin machines at work creates a similar impression. Indeed, the modern world of web-based information has created something closely equivalent to the instantly fading ink that the novelist William Thackeray ironically declared to be the best form of ink for letters in the opportunistic and fast-changing social scene he depicted in *Vanity Fair*[10] because it makes inconvenient history so instantly rewritable—and erasable—on government and organizational websites.

Problem denial, by adjusting the facts or their interpretation in a range of ways running from alterations of emphasis through insertion of qualifiers up to outright lying, is the blame avoiders' equivalent of data massage and fabrication in science, and can call for the same degree of ingenuity. But problem denial is not the only form of winning-the-argument strategies for blame avoidance. Officeholders and organizations often deal with blame by accepting that there is a problem and then trying to explain it away or at least to mitigate their own culpability. And following the analysis of the twentieth-century Oxford philosopher John Austin (1956), it is conventional to distinguish between excuses and justifications in arguments designed to limit or avoid blame. Excuses are arguments that are intended to mitigate or deflect blame for a problem that is admitted to exist. Justifications are arguments that are designed to turn blame into credit—for example, by persuading people who think they are losers from some act of commission or omission that they should see the matter in a more positive light.

Like problem denial, excuses that give reasons why organizations or officeholders should escape some or all blame for whatever harm or offense they have caused are commonplace as strategies for blame avoidance. Familiar and standard examples that many readers will regularly encounter from private business and government include "events beyond our control," "unforeseeable circumstances," "teething troubles," "staff shortages," and (the all-purpose information age excuse) "it's the computer/the system's down."[11]

Excuses may be a less risky strategy than problem denial in that the organization or individual making them cannot be later shown to be completely out of touch with the difficulties or hardships being experienced on the ground. Those in the front-line world of blame avoidance discussed in the last chapter may well be driven to make more use of excuses than the top bananas, since problem denial can be a harder position to maintain at the street level (where many kinds of failure will first become noticeable) than in high places. But excuses too can backfire spectacularly, stoking the flames of resentment as well as derision. For example, in Britain, "the wrong kind of snow," stemming from an unguarded technical statement made by Britain's former nationalized rail company (British Rail) to explain massive disruption of rail services in England after a relatively minor snowstorm in the winter of 1991, has become a catch-phrase commonly used to ridicule any particularly lame official excuse.[12]

While excuses are commonly used at the frontline level, they can sometimes be crucial for warding off blame at the higher level too. Often when top public officeholders are in trouble for some adverse outcome, who gets the blame will turn on exactly who knew what and when—that is, the time element we discussed in the first chapter. Thus one very familiar form of excuse by higher-level officeholders consists of denying that they were in possession of some vital piece of information at a particular time—for example, about orders given to front-line troops or operational staff.

Indeed, when blame games start, those top bananas sometimes move from a credit-claiming strategy of portraying themselves as all-knowing managers of their organizations to portraying themselves as hapless victims of a conspiracy of silence, completely unaware of anything untoward that was going on around them in the organization until they read about it in the newspapers. This is where the "no one told me ..." excuse, so commonly invoked by high officeholders after corruption or other foul-ups emerge into public view, comes into its own.[13] Though often used, this approach can be high-risk, since if a "smoking-gun" e-mail or other evidence later emerges that the officeholder did in fact already know about the problem at the time in question (as discussed in the previous chapter), the blame heat will be correspondingly higher. It also invites the obvious blame riposte that someone who claims to know nothing about what is going on in the organization that he or she nominally heads is unfit to hold such a senior leadership position.

Whereas excuses often have that sort of downside as a blame avoidance strategy, successful justifications may sometimes serve to do more than mitigate blame. In contrast to excuses, justifications give reasons why the harm or offense being claimed should really be seen as a benefit or a blessing in disguise. In their most extreme form, they seek to turn blame into credit, or at least to mitigate blame by offsetting arguments as by claiming that pain now will lead to gains later on.

For example, during a rocky political patch in 2006, British Health minister Patricia Hewitt memorably chose to round on the many critics of her government's management of the country's National Health Service (NHS)—at a time when she was presiding over a net deficit of about £600 million, 7000 job cuts, and substantial hospital ward closures in England in spite of an unprecedented tripling of the service's tax-funded budget—by boldly asserting that the NHS had in fact had its "best year ever."[14]

Justification tends to be used more by the top bananas (and sometimes by the middle-level players) than by the frontline troops in the blame worlds discussed in the previous chapter, and in principle they offer a more positive riposte to blame than a string of excuses. But they too involve risk of a blame backlash: Hewitt's claim attracted massive negative publicity, and was even ridiculed by the popular writer Helen Fielding (2006: 7), who had her antiheroine say, "Soon [it] will be like Cold War Russia with cheery government broadcasts blaring out how fabulous everything is, while everyone else sits … hurling empty vodka bottles at the TV." As was mentioned in the previous chapter, finding winning arguments in blame games can demand a reading of public mood and culture, and is not just an exercise in logic.

DRAWING A LINE: CONFESSION TIME

As with the winning-the-argument approach, much presentational strategy consists of contesting responsibility in one way or another, either by denying there is any problem of avoidable harm for anyone to be responsible for or by offering excuses or justificatory arguments, as in the "best year ever" example. But sometimes, especially for high-level officeholders, blame avoidance consists of not contesting either problems or responsibility, and instead involves simply coming out with a preemptive apology calculated to disarm critics and attract sympathy.

The case for the preemptive apology as a strategy of blame avoidance is that it takes the wind out of critics' sails before they can make much headway with a blaming campaign. Such a tactic makes the officeholders or organizations in the frame look as if they are made of different metal from the stereotype of those slippery politicians and bureaucrats who will go on with denials and evasions until every avenue for such tactics has been exhausted and apologies can only be dragged out of them when they are caught like rats in a trap.

So officeholders who choose to apologize early in a blame sequence can present themselves as honest and sincere, acknowledging their mistakes and drawing a line under them before moving on purposefully to repair the damage and face new challenges. Adopting a posture of public contrition, with husky-voiced tearful confessions in TV interviews, may help to head off blame by showing officeholders' soft side. Preemptive apologies present those officeholders' critics with the choice of whether to go on pressing charges, as it were (with the risk that they will be made to look negative and vindictive, thereby unintentionally increasing public sympathy rather than blame for the officeholder), or to accept the apology, drop the charges, and move onto other ground.

Again, perhaps the best known example of this variant comes from Bill Clinton's handling of the scandal over his affair with Monica Lewinsky in 1998. In their analysis of this episode, Ronald Lee and Matthew Barton (2003) show that Clinton encountered strong public disapproval in his early attempts to brush off the scandal as a private matter. They claim that Clinton only managed to limit the blame coming from the media and the public when he shifted from a secular defense based on notions of individual privacy to a "confessional rhetoric" of religious contrition, evoking the penitent sinner on the stool of repentance[15] or some similar place of public confession.

The concede-and-move-on approach—defusing blame by (apparently) picking it up—was a regular weapon in the armory of the propaganda machines of Bill Clinton and Tony Blair in the 1990s and early 2000s. And in the 1990s a former Dutch minister, Ed van Thijn (1998), even coined the phrase "sorry democracy" to characterize the political style of the Netherlands at that time, with public apology taking the place of other, more traditional kinds of public accountability (see also Bovens et al. 1999). In principle, such preemptive apologies are available to any of the sets of players in the blame game that were discussed in the last chapter. But apologies made by the top bananas about their own personal conduct are the ones that get the most attention, and indeed the risk for lower-level institutional players is that apologies can be taken as useful confessions of guilt that invite dismissal by their bosses to cover their own backs.

Sometimes higher officeholders extend the approach to apologizing for things that happened long before—working on the time element of blame by apologizing for things that occurred well before their term of office, such that they cannot be held directly responsible for those faults and failings. Such tactics can often be seen as credit-claiming as much as blame-avoiding, insofar as they portray the apologizer as a person of superior moral sensibilities expressing solidarity with those who have suffered avoidable losses caused by someone else in the past.

Again, this kind of approach seems to be used more by the top bananas in the blame world than other players, and it is not a risk-free move either. The risk of such tactics is that they will be dismissed as insincere or that they will lead to demands for compensatory action rather than token or costless apologies, particularly since these latter-day apologizers often aim for expressions of contrition with no strings attached. A clear example of that is Tony Blair's carefully phrased statement in 2006 that he felt "deep sorrow" about the transatlantic slave trade of two centuries earlier, uttered without any offer of reparations.[16] Indeed, the following year, Brian Mikkelsen, the then Danish culture minister, perhaps took the approach to its limits by expressing regret for the damage that Viking raids and pillage had done to the people of Ireland a thousand years earlier.[17] In neither case did those statements go beyond general expressions of regret.

Neither preemptive apologies nor post hoc expressions of regret can be expected to be a panacea for blame avoidance. If they were, organizations and officeholders would use this tactic all the time, whereas they tend to be used mainly for institutional failures rather than for personal conduct (in which it seems more common to refrain from confession and apology until other options for blame avoidance have been tried). And indeed, like problem denial, apologies, and justifications, such tactics can backfire. They may lead to demands for something more than perfunctory line-drawing over the issue or episode.

"Sorry seems to be the hardest word," as the line goes from the song by Elton John and Bernie Taupin. But as with all such maxims, there are always exceptions. And the drawing-a-line approach of preemptive or after-the-fact apologies clearly has its place in the array of presentational strategies, though the long-after-the-fact apology of the Viking-raid type is right on the edge of blame avoidance as ordinarily understood. The most familiar examples of this approach seem to concern personal misdemeanors or institutional errors from the past, when other people were in charge. And the most favorable conditions for the "sorry-democracy" tactic of preemptive apology perhaps come when blame-shift fatigue has set in—that is, when a long series of blame games featuring "it wasn't me" evasions by the main players have produced a mood more receptive to an apparently less defensive approach.

CHANGING THE SUBJECT: BURYING BAD NEWS AND SHIFTING THE AGENDA

Much presentational activity for blame avoidance consists of getting the words precisely right in the same way that a poet agonizes over every syllable and inflection—going though all those endlessly tricky choices and nice judgments to hit the proper note of contrition, craft the excuse that is powerful enough to silence critics and skeptics, and find the killer argument that can convincingly show that what might be seen as a major loss is really a blessing, or at least is not as bad as it seems. As already noted, much of the study of rhetoric is precisely concerned with ways of finding the right words and putting them over in a persuasive way, and that applies to the first two classes of presentational strategies considered in this chapter.

But sometimes blame can be avoided by presentational strategies designed to alter perceptions and impressions in other ways. As military strategists like the famous Chinese warrior Sun Tzu (1983, originally c. 500 BC: 11) have long pointed out, some potentially powerful forms of persuasion are not verbal at all. They create impressions in other ways, by behavior, activity, images, music, and other nonverbal forms of communication. These forms are not "loquocentric" (using a term coined by Kenneth Minogue [1986]), in that they do not work through words. They rely, in the jargon of modern political science, on impression management or agenda control.

Easily the best known form of this approach is the creation or use of diversions to avoid the spotlight of blame and shift the public agenda onto other issues. Foreign affairs are a traditional standby of politicians trying to escape the focus of blame directed at their domestic activity (Howard Kurtz [1998: 224], in his account of the Clinton presidency, refers to "another week of high-minded diplomacy abroad as a way of muffling lowly scandal back home"). And times when public attention can be expected to be focused on other things (such as big sports events or public holidays) can provide convenient moments for officeholders and organizations to sneak out potentially embarrassing announcements of U-turns or unpopular policies.

That aspect of blame-avoiding presentational strategy became notorious in Britain in 2001, when a fateful "bury bad news" e-mail came to light. That e-mail was written by Jo Moore, then a special adviser to Transport secretary Stephen Byers, and it declared that September 11, 2001 (the day that the World Trade Center in New York was attacked) was "a good day to bury bad news."[18] The bad news that Moore was encouraging her bureaucratic colleagues to bury included announcements of increased allowances and more generous retirement pension terms for local government councillors in England—certain to be deeply unpopular with voters and taxpayers and bound to attract negative media coverage on a normal day.

That "bury bad news" e-mail became legendary and indeed it was wholly counter-productive in that it sparked a strong reaction against the spin of the Blair government, turned the spin machine into the central story, was used as part of a drive to limit the powers of special politically appointed advisers relative to permanent civil servants, and effectively ended Jo Moore's own career in government. But Moore was certainly not the first to discover the use of diversions in the search for blame avoidance. Long before the term spin doctor was created, governments were sneaking out unpopular pieces of information (about politicians' pay raises or reports about policy fiascos, for instance) at carefully selected times, to coincide with other events that concentrate public attention.

Sometimes diversionary tactics can be more subtle than that, and reach well into the world of bureaucracy as well as that of elected politicians. For example, Iain McLean and Martin Johnes (2000: 737–8) argue that Britain's Liberal government used such tactics to deflect blame away from itself after the super-liner *Titanic* sank after hitting an iceberg on its maiden voyage across the Atlantic in 1912, with the loss of 1490 lives. The British government faced potential blame over the disaster for several reasons. The Board of Trade, the relevant government department, had certified the ill-fated vessel as fully seaworthy shortly before the fatal voyage, even though the ship had lifeboats for only 1178 of the 2201 people who were on board for its maiden voyage (the *Titanic* was officially authorized to carry as many as 3500 passengers). In fact, the number of lifeboats required by the Board of Trade for passenger ships over 10,000 tons had had not changed since 1894, even though *Titanic* was over 40,000 tons. And in the face of technological change, the Board of Trade had made no regulations to ensure that all ships in Atlantic shipping lanes had continuous radio watch or that distress rockets were of a different color than other flares.

McLean and Johnes argue that the Board of Trade and the British government of that day managed to create or use diversions that took public attention away from their own regulatory failures over shipping safety.

Attention was focused onto the way the ship had been run by its operator (the White Star line, which was faced with compensation claims by relatives of those who had drowned), onto the competence of the committee of experts who had drawn up the bulkhead requirements applying to the vessel, and onto the behavior of a cargo steamer, the *Californian*, which (it was claimed) had been near to the stricken *Titanic* and could have saved lives if it had gone to the rescue. Indeed, McLean and Johnes argue that the main blame avoidance tactic by the Board of Trade and the British government was the diversionary (and extraordinary) tactic of drawing the official inquiry's attention to the question of vessels that could have given assistance to the *Titanic* before the *Carpathia* arrived on the scene, thus deflecting the inquiry from other potentially more embarrassing matters for government officials.

As that story shows, there is nothing new about the use of diversionary tactics as a strategy of blame avoidance. And the modern media environment presents both challenges and opportunities for the changing-the-subject approach to presentational strategy. The challenge is that the modern internet world of media makes it more possible for those preoccupied with particular negative stories to focus on the dedicated websites that carry such stories, without going through the filter of general news media, which may make diversionary tactics harder to use. But the corresponding opportunity is that a more global twenty-four-hour media world can generate more potential big stories as possible cover for concealment of embarrassing facts, decisions, or documents.

Keeping a Low Profile: Secrecy, Lying Doggo, Working behind the Scenes, and Removing the Messenger

"Silent Cal," a.k.a. Calvin Coolidge, Republican president of the United States from 1923 to 1928, once said, "Never go out to meet trouble. If you just sit still, nine cases out of ten, someone will intercept it before it reaches you" (Fuess, 2007: 497). Coolidge had practiced this tactic of mute nonengagement successfully when he was vice president under President Warren Harding and the Harding administration ran into a series of corruption scandals in the early 1920s (including the Teapot Dome affair, involving shady political dealings at the highest level to promote oil company interests).

The subtypes of presentational strategy for blame avoidance we have discussed up to now all involve active engagement of some kind with the media and the public. Those sorts of activities naturally appeal to those who believe in the adage, "Don't just stand there, do something," and indeed communication professionals have often lauded the virtues of "active media engagement" in one way or another, if only because it creates more work for them. But Calvin Coolidge's maxim points to an alternative form of presentational strategy for blame avoidance, in which officeholders or organizations deal with blame by saying as little as possible and instead use a range of tactics ranging from official secrecy through keeping their heads down (to sit out a blame firestorm until it passes over and public attention comes to be focused on something else) to backdoor methods of silencing critics. The old adage that 'it is better to keep your mouth shut and let people think you are a fool than to open it and remove all doubt'[19] is perhaps the watchword of those who follow this approach to presentation.

Restricting information is one possible way to keep potential blame at bay, and it can come in many different forms, from the traditional kind of official secrecy (see Sulitzeanu-Kenan and Hood 2005: 13) to the tighter central management of potentially embarrassing information that Alasdair Roberts (2006a) found in every case of the democracies he studied that had adopted Freedom of Information Laws. And then there is the tactic of concealing blameworthy information in a sea of dull material or releasing information at the very last minute (and/or for a very short time) before debate in some crucial accountability forum, so that potential blamers will have as much difficulty as possible in spotting the key details to muster their case.

A slightly different tactic, perhaps involving a lesser degree of anticipation than those mentioned above, is that of lying doggo, or choosing to keep silent. That is of course an unheroic stance, and certainly goes against the sort of mindset that equates activity with achievement, but governments and corporations often choose to have no one available for comment just when the news media are baying for someone to defend or excuse some decision or event that has attracted blame, and some British observers see an increasing trend for politicians to behave in that way (see Freedland 2007). Faced with the prospect of going into the ring for a set-piece interview against well-informed and pugnacious critics, officeholders often conclude that keeping a low profile may be the option that attracts the least blame. The countervailing risk is that media shows may damage the officeholder's reputation by "empty-chairing" the individual concerned. (Empty-chairing is the practice of drawing attention to someone's refusal to show up by using a real or metaphorical empty chair, with the implication that absence is to be taken as some sort of tacit admission of guilt.) Alternatively, media show hosts may respond to an officeholder's reluctance to show up by threats to put critics on the show instead, giving a free run to the blame makers over the blame takers.

As with other forms of presentational strategy, the tactic of keeping a low profile can be pursued in several ways. One, familiar in the corporate defensive armory as well as that of government, is to opt for one-way communication—issuing lawyerly statements in writing but declining to elaborate on them by turning up in a live forum where there is a possibility of being ambushed by an awkward question or damaging riposte. Individuals or organizations that go for this approach are choosing to balance the risk of extra blame resulting from being bested in a live interview against the risk of appearing weak or guilty or both. Jonathan Freedland (2007) quotes a comment by Ceri Thomas, editor of the BBC flagship current affairs radio show, *Today*, "If you do a quick statement that will be carried by twenty-four-hour news, why would you submit yourself to the rigour and unpredictability of a set-piece interview?"

A second variant of the lying doggo strategy is to assent to media interviews but only if the questions to be asked are agreed to in advance, something easier to do for print-medium magazine interviews than live broadcasts. In the latter case, a variant of not choosing to appear at all is to show up to the interview but walk out (or threaten to do so) with an air of self-righteous indignation if the questions asked become too loaded, threatening, or off-limits in ways defined by the interviewee. Celebrities and politicians occasionally use this "bolting" tactic for one reason or another—for example, French President Nicolas Sarkozy walked out of a CBS interview on American television in 2007 when an interviewer asked him about his divorce from his wife Cecilia[20]—but it is a weapon that can be hard to use repeatedly.

A further variant, favored by numerous government spin machines and by beleaguered celebrities more generally, is to use the lying doggo tactic selectively, boycotting some unfriendly media outlets altogether and engaging only with those that deal with officeholders on their own terms and in less challenging ways. Sensitive announcements that could be reported negatively can be fed first to those media outlets likely to be friendly,[21] and potential scoops can be given selectively as rewards to favored journalists. Top officeholders can bypass traditional and more challenging interview forums for those in which they are likely to face less challenge. For example, Margaret Thatcher preferred to appear on Jimmy Young's undemanding BBC radio chat show rather than on the more confrontational and demanding *Today* programe, and Tony Blair sometimes made similar choices—for example, in bypassing the heavyweight media to appear on the unchallenging *This Morning* ITV chat show (later the Richard and Judy show on BBC) in 1999 (Campbell and Stott 2007: 363).

Those tactics in turn shade into other covert attempts to fix the media agenda by the use of backdoor threats and inducements to the individuals and organizations involved, rather than engagement through the front door in the process of argument and framing. For example, in a crucial period running up to the 2005 British general election, the Department of Health used consultants to systematically monitor the output of every journalist writing health stories in the major print or broadcast media in that period, coding each piece individually for the degree of positivity or negativity it showed toward government policy (Department of Health 2006). Such analyses are rarely conducted for purely academic enlightenment.

It is a short step from such positivity/negativity surveillance to attempts to lean on "negative" journalists behind the scenes. Indeed, the diaries of Alastair Campbell, Tony Blair's chief press secretary, are full of accounts of various kinds of strong reproofs being sent to journalists and media executives over the tone or content of their coverage. For one instance: "I ... bollocked David Wastell (the reporter)...." For another: "I called Victor Blank, chairman of Trinity Mirror plc, to say I really thought the *Mirror* (newspaper) coverage had been a joke, just not serious." The sort of backdoor pressure that individuals like Alastair Campbell can exert is designed to improve the presentation of policy and conduct, but of course carries the corresponding risk (which did indeed eventually happen) that what can be portrayed as attempts to bully journalists can rebound on organizations and officeholders and increase rather than decrease the level of blame they face.

Going beyond the sort of imprecations and verbal tongue-lashing that the journalists mentioned received from Alastair Campbell is the legalistic approach to deterring or blocking unwelcome claims about government and individual behavior, with actual or threatened legal injunctions or libel actions. The Singapore government has long been noted for its vigorous use of libel actions or threats of such action against attacks by its political opponents, and such tactics belong on the edge of the lying doggo approach and the winning-the-argument approach discussed earlier. Other organizations and individuals facing potential blame can also use the legal route to shut down debate in some cases. Even more heavy-handedly, the government can shut down newspapers or ban certain news organizations from the country, allowing only its own news outlets to operate, as Robert Mugabe's ZANU regime did in Zimbabwe.

Even the ZANU approach to silencing potential blamers, not ordinarily practiced by democratic regimes, runs the risk that the official news organs will be disbelieved and that critical information will still appear on the internet. And, like most blame–avoidance tactics, attempts to silence potential blame makers by legal injunctions and threats of libel actions can backfire. In the former case, the imposition of injunctions may be counterproductive if it alerts media to a potentially important story, especially if—as will often happen—the censored information quickly appears on the internet.[22] In the case of libel action threats, if the threat alone does not succeed and it comes to court actions, the officeholders or organizations will indeed have to produce arguments or evidence to justify their claims of defamation or other legal misconduct by the media, with the corresponding risk that the case may be lost.

A well-known example of that sort of risk is what happened to Jonathan Aitken, who had been a defense procurement minister and later Chief Secretary to the Treasury in John Major's Conservative government in Britain in the 1990s. In 1995 a British newspaper (the *Guardian*) and TV program (Granada's *World in Action*) ran a story claiming, among other things, that Aitken had breached the code of conduct for government ministers by accepting hospitality from Saudi businessmen engaged in an arms deal for a weekend at the luxurious Ritz hotel in Paris in 1993. Aitken responded by saying he was "shocked and disgusted" by these "wicked lies" and issued a writ for defamation against the *Guardian*'s editor and the journalist who had written the story, declaring that he would "fight to cut out the cancer of bent and twisted journalism in our country with the simple sword of truth and the trusty shield of British fair play."[23] However, the libel case collapsed in 1997 after evidence from airline and car rental records was produced in court, undermining Aitken's claim that his wife had been in Paris with him and had paid the Ritz hotel bill, and in 1999 Aitken was convicted and imprisoned for perjury.[24] This case demonstrates how two-edged the sword-of-truth approach to silencing blame through legal proceedings can be.

Altogether, nonengagement may seem a passive and negative approach to combating blame that is out of line with the upbeat image that political and public service leaders like to cultivate as positive have-a-go individuals. But it may come into its own in at least two circumstances. One is when blame incidents are likely to be short-lived and the media are likely to move on to other material. That is what Coolidge believed to apply in most cases, and when it does, this strategy can save emotional energy on the part of organizations and individuals, and prevent their attention being diverted from their other priorities. The other circumstance when this approach seems likely to come into its own is at the other end of the scale, when things have gotten so bad that any kind of argument or excuse by beleaguered institutions or officeholders will tend to become counterproductive, pouring gasoline rather than water on the flames (for instance, in the sort of culture captured in the cynical adage that nothing should be believed until it has been denied by at least two government departments). Sometimes "Don't just do something, stand there" may indeed be the least-blame presentational strategy (Hood et al. 2009: 712).

The Scope and Limits of the Presentational Approach to Blame Avoidance

As noted at the outset, presentational approaches to blame avoidance have a long history. Devices such as diversions and get-out-of-jail excuses are hardly peculiar to the modern age, and spin doctoring was a political and organizational art form long before that particular term was coined about twenty years ago. But how effective are presentational strategies in limiting or avoiding blame?

The high political centrality of presentational strategies and strategists, and all the investment that goes into this activity, suggests that such strategies are widely believed to be effective and necessary for warding off blame. (Later on, in chapter six, we will look at how presentational strategies are institutionalized in modern government and what changes can be detected in the weight given to spin activity.) But like much else in the world of blame avoidance, the evidence that such strategies actually work is fairly limited and much of it is anecdotal.

Much of that evidence comes from qualitative analyses of case studies, such as the analysis by Mark Bovens and his colleagues (1999) of embarrassing revelations that the Dutch police had authorized importation of hundreds of tons of drugs, much of which ended up on the streets, and that the police had financed their investigations with the proceeds of illegal activity. Some of the evidence comes from more general accounts of the development or practice of spin activity in government, such as Howard Kurtz's (1998) work on the Clinton propaganda machine that has been cited several times in this chapter.

A certain amount of evidence also comes from laboratory experiments, such as Kathleen McGraw's (1990) simulation experiments, mentioned in the first chapter, which were designed to explore the relative efficacy of excuses and justifications in blame avoidance. And we are beginning to see some evidence from quantitative analyses, such as an impact intervention analysis conducted by the author with several colleagues (Hood et al. 2009) which coded press stories and government actions over about a hundred days of a blame firestorm, relating the degree of blame in the next day's newspaper stories with what ministers and other officeholders had said or done the previous day.

None of that evidence suggests that presentational approaches are a sure-fire way to avoid blame, though Bovens' work suggests presentational strategies may sometimes be more effective than agency strategies of delegation. McGraw's work (1990: 128) found justifications were commonly more effective than excuses in reducing blame, with some kinds of excuses likely to increase rather than avoid blame. Hood and colleagues' work (2009) suggests that presentational strategies can sometimes have the effect of reducing the blame level in the next day's newspapers, but by no means always did so in the cases they analyzed and in a number of cases had nil or negative effects.

More broadly, some types of presentational activity seem to be subject to the law of diminishing and even negative returns, with short-term successes capable of turning into difficulties further down the line as political credit is used up and chickens come home to roost. For example, the more governments and officeholders use diversionary tactics (by timing the release of potentially embarrassing information to coincide with events that get saturation news coverage), the more news media and watchdog groups will be on high alert for government "story burying" at such times.

Diminishing and negative returns seem to have applied to the media management strategies of Bill Clinton, according to Howard Kurtz (1998: 302): "As Bill Clinton dug in for the long haul [faced with saturation-level negative publicity over his relationship with Monica Lewinsky], one could see, at long last, the limits of spin. When it worked, the coordinated strategy of peddling a single line to the press, of browbeating some reporters and courting others, was stunningly effective. Damage could be contained, scandal minimized, bad news relegated to the fringes of the media world. But each time an administration did that, each time it beat back the negative publicity with shifting explanations and document dumps and manufactured announcements designed to change the subject, it paid a price. The journalists were more skeptical the next time around, less willing to give the Clinton spin team the benefit of the doubt...." Robert Denton (2003) comes to a similar conclusion, arguing that the President's presentational approach diminished the presidency and encouraged public distrust of presidential discourse.

Sir Bernard Ingham (2003), Margaret Thatcher's press secretary, argued that much the same happened to Tony Blair's New Labour spin doctors, who, as has already been noted, used tactics closely modeled on those of the Clinton propaganda machine, putting pressure on journalists who stepped out of line and exploiting the competitive nature of journalism such that only favorites got the interviews, the selectively leaked stories, and the pre-packaged soundbites. But Ingham claims these developments came to have a reverse effect, as blame attractors rather than blame deflectors, leading to a backlash of cynicism, reduced trust, and a tendency for scandals to drag out more than they would otherwise have done. The media world, initially favorable to New Labour, came to feel "like a lover who had been rejected," and turned on the spin doctors with a lover's revenge, seeing everything through the prism of 'spin' and turning the spin-doctors themselves into the central and recurring story (Ingham 2003: 232-9).

If these accounts are to be believed, investment in spin, prebuttal, and agenda management for the purposes of blame avoidance is another of the many kinds of intervention in social affairs that turn out to have the reverse of their intended effect, at least some of the time (Sieber 1981). That suggests a conclusion similar to the famous saying attributed to various business leaders, including the first Lord Leverhulme and the American department store mogul John Wanamaker, that "half the money I spend on advertising is wasted, and the trouble is I don't know which half" (Ogilvy 1964: 59). Increased investment by governments and other organizations in spin doctoring and media management has evidently not had the effect of improving the public's trust and confidence in politicians, government, and many other institutions from the mid-1960s to the mid-1990s, if the evidence about rising disillusionment with such entities over that period, produced by Nye and Zelikhov (1997: 83), is to be believed. Of course, it could be that public trust in government (and particularly in politicians) would have fallen even lower had it not been for the valiant efforts of the growing army of high-level presentational specialists working for high public officeholders. But presentational strategies can be shown to have had reverse effects in some cases and may have had a more general effect on the public's willingness to give politicians and big organizations the benefit of the doubt.

"What works" in presentational strategy for blame avoidance will also depend on attitudes and beliefs in particular times and places. As mentioned in the previous chapter, the sorts of excuses and justifications that will limit blame in one cultural context will be different from those that will limit blame in another. Timing matters too: a public that is tired of excuses may warm for a time to the different strategy of tearful apologies, and vice versa. High-level spin machines that appear formidably effective at one moment—as with the Clinton and Blair spin doctoring discussed earlier—can find themselves apparently unable to do anything right at the next moment as public moods change.

Moreover, as times get really tough for officeholders and organizations in the sense that their credibility with their publics falls so low that nothing they or their spin doctors say is likely to be believed, the emphasis of presentational strategy will need to turn from the first two approaches we discussed earlier—winning the argument and drawing a line—to the second two approaches (changing the subject and keeping a low profile). That is because if a large proportion of the population has come to subscribe to the belief that "you know they're lying when their lips are moving," even public apologies are unlikely to deflect blame. In those circumstances, the creation of diversions or the strategy of non engagement may create less immediate damage to the organizations or individuals in the line of fire.

So what this chapter has shown is that instead of thinking of presentational strategies or spin as a single approach, it makes more sense to think of them as a set of approaches, each of which may tend to produce diminishing or negative returns at some point.

But presentational strategies as a whole are never likely to disappear from the blame avoider's armory, for at least two related reasons. First, for those officeholders who are not in a position to employ agency or policy strategies, presentational strategy will be the only weapon available, for instance in the sort of post-disaster scenario where there is not much they can do but call for an inquiry and praise the emergency services. Second, as we will see in chapter 7, even those high- and middle-level players who in principle can readily deploy agency and policy strategies in the blame game will find themselves relying on presentation after a blame crisis has struck. That is because agency and policy strategies are mostly what we called anticipative types of blame avoidance strategy in the first chapter, requiring action in advance from officeholders to reduce their exposure in the event of blame firestorms, whereas presentational strategies can be adopted after the event as well as before it.

CHAPTER FOUR

Agency Strategies: Direct or Delegate, Choose or Inherit?

> Princes should delegate to others the enactment of unpopular measures and keep in their own hands the distribution of favors.
> —Niccolò Machiavelli 1961: 106

> We trained hard ... but it seemed that every time we were beginning to form up into teams we would be reorganized ... creating the illusion of progress while producing confusion, inefficiency and demoralization.
> —Observation often attributed to Gaius Petronius but not actually contained in Petronius' published work, and seems more likely to be a comment on military organization in World War II by a disillusioned soldier.

BLAME AVOIDANCE BY AGENCY STRATEGIES: A LOGIC OF ORGANIZATIONAL DESIGN

While presentational strategy, as discussed in the previous chapter, is primarily concerned with shaping the perceived loss or harm component of blame, agency strategy is concerned with the perceived responsibility component, namely who or what caused those perceived harms. So we are dealing here with all the attempts officeholders and organizations make to deflect or limit blame by creative allocation of formal responsibility, competency, or jurisdiction among different units and individuals (see Hood 2002: 16). Welcome to the world of agency strategies for blame avoidance.

As explained in the first chapter, agency strategies focus on the arrangement of the organizational deck chairs. Agency strategists aim to craft organograms that maximize the opportunities for blame-shifting, buck-passing, and risk transfer to others who can be placed in the front line of blame when things go wrong or unpopular actions are to be carried out. As we noted in chapter 2, delegation is a favorite agency strategy for high-level officeholders, so that technical advisors, regulators, or executive supremos can take or at least share the blame when things go wrong. Many of their strategies for blame avoidance are variations on Machiavelli's classic maxim, given in the first epigraph to this chapter. Indeed, as was also noted in chapter 2, modern-day equivalents of Machiavelli's prince seem to be constantly searching for that elusive political nirvana in which formal responsibility is defined in such a way that blame always flows downwards or sideways to other actors while credit always flows upwards to them.[1]

Delegation is also an agency strategy open to the middle-level players whose world we discussed in chapter 2, because putting all the responsibility for potentially blame-attracting decisions onto the frontline players can be a way of taking the heat off themselves. And while the simple delegation approach of the kind described by Machiavelli is almost by definition not open to the front-line players, those players can sometimes at least make use of organizational arrangements that help them to spread or shift the blame (such as outsourcing or "partnership working" arrangements that enable them to shuffle off the blame to subcontractors or other organizations with joint responsibility for delivering services). Similarly, they can shift blame to others if they are part of a changing cast of characters dealing with a subject (as in the situation highlighted in the second epigraph), and even onto those they are intended to serve where "partnerships" comprise real or rhetorical compacts or contracts that put obligations onto public service clients or customers.

As suggested in the first chapter, some of what would otherwise seem to be puzzlingly dysfunctional features of government organization make much more sense once we start looking at those arrangements through blame avoidance spectacles. After all, whether or not expensive consultants and business gurus actually offer any worthwhile new solutions to all the complex and perplexing questions of government organization that have baffled the highest intellects over the ages, their often banal ideas can provide useful cover for ways of dissipating blame. Similarly, whether or not privatization, agencification, and outsourcing of public service provision really do cut costs, improve quality, or produce all the other effects that are so confidently and earnestly claimed for them (on the basis of so little hard evidence), what those arrangements *can* offer is the apparent prospect of shifting blame away from politicians and central bureaucrats to private or independent operators. Whether or not partnership working truly produces a new dawn of caring-sharing cooperation across organizations that somehow eluded everyone in less enlightened times, a service provided by a slew of different organizations offers each player the opportunity to blame the others for failure and to direct the army of frustrated callers or complainers somewhere else.[2] And whether or not constant reorganization and accompanying turnover of staff in frenetic and costly management merry-go-rounds contributes in any positive way to effective service delivery, it creates a conveniently moving target to avoid blame directed at previous structures and incumbents.

So when the logic of blame avoidance dominates organizational design, it may lead in directions very different from those suggested by other design principles. In particular, when deflecting or diffusing blame is of the essence, the emphasis typically goes on designing organizations to achieve disconnection among different units and disconnection from past structures—the very reverse of what are ordinarily considered to be desiderata of good public organization. (And, as we shall see in the next chapter on policy strategies, the same sort of logic often leads to adoption of organizational operating routines that involve a heavy focus on back-covering checklists rather than on the interconnection, memory, learning, and intelligent responses to particular cases that the rhetoric of good service delivery tends to emphasize.)

Most of this chapter is devoted to exploring variants of the agency strategy for blame avoidance, and it closes with a brief exploration of the scope and limits of this approach to blame avoidance. If, as we are often told, there are no free lunches in the world of political and institutional choice, what exactly do officeholders have to give up to equip themselves with the protective Teflon coat that delegation or other forms of agency strategy are assumed to offer them? And in what conditions are agency strategies for blame avoidance subject to diminishing or even negative returns?

Types of Agency Strategy

As with presentational strategies, agency strategies come in numerous forms. They comprise a family of approaches rather than a single tactic. And as with presentational strategies, human inventiveness and differences in cultural context mean there can never be a single, all-purpose, cut-out-and-keep approach. But some broad variants can be identified, and four are highlighted in table 4.1, which combines two dimensions. Some blame avoidance agency strategies focus on organizing within a single corporate framework or within executive government as a unit, while others focus on using institutions or agencies beyond the main government institutions to spread or avoid blame. And on the other dimension, some agency strategies can be termed "orderly," in that they are designed on the assumption of some fixed allocation of responsibilities among units in or around government (however fuzzy round the edges that allocation may turn out to be in practice), while others are more disorderly and dynamic.

Combining these elements gives us at least four types of agency strategy, namely blame avoidance through delegation (cell 1), through defensive

TABLE 4.1
Some Varieties of Agency Strategy

	Static or orderly strategies	Dynamic or disorderly strategies
Focus on corporate organization	Delegation of responsibility down the line or out from the center Motto: "The buck doesn't stop here" Example: blame-attracting "czars," flak-catchers, lightning rods	Defensive reorganization and staff rotation Motto: "That was then, this is now" Example: frequent management-merry-go-round reorganizations in high blame services like child welfare
Focus on trans-organizational elements	Partnership structures Motto: "Don't go solo" Example: public-private partnerships, intergovern-mental projects and other multi-agency arrangements	"Government by the market" Motto: "Don't blame me, blame the market" Example: use of "market forces" to absorb blame, e.g. in executive remuneration systems

reorganization (cell 2), through partnership working (cell 3), and through "government by the market" (cell 4). As in the previous chapter, we will discuss each of these types in turn, but we will devote the most attention to delegation strategies (cell 1), because this form of agency approach gets the most attention in political science.

DELEGATION: THE KEY TO BLAME AVOIDANCE?

The first epigraph to this chapter reminds us that Machiavelli noted four hundred years ago that a crucial and basic choice faced by every office-holder or corporation is whether to direct or delegate. That choice is typically discussed in economics and managerial literature in terms of what will produce the greatest effectiveness or efficiency in the organization and much of the public administration and public management literature or delegation is also concerned with factors other than blame avoidance, such as credible commitment (see Gilardi 2002: Thatcher 2002; Elgie

2006). But seen from a blame-avoidance perspective the delegation issue is like choosing whether to be the coach or the chair of the board of a sports team. To be the coach (or captain or manager) means to be close to the action with hands-on control, personally directing the players from day to day and framing the team's strategies for each individual game. To be the chair of the sports club involves more distance from operations on the sports field, but includes the responsibility for hiring and firing the coach. Being the chair means reflected glory and the role of praising and rewarding the coach when things are going well. Equally, when the team is doing badly and the fans or investors are disappointed and angrily calling for someone's head to roll, the chair can try to shift the blame by criticizing, warning, or firing the coach.

Now both of those roles can be appealing sometimes. Top officeholders often find credit-claiming opportunities in the team manager approach, taking direct command of crucial operations in a crisis, or appearing to do so. They assume voters or other constituents will give credit to a leader who is seen to take charge, not dithering on the sidelines blaming everyone else, but boldly overcoming the obstacles that would defeat, or have already defeated, lesser mortals. And of course there are plenty of photoops that can be linked to the holding of crisis meetings or appearances on the front line of operations clad in hard hats or protective jackets or track suits as the event demands. After all, such images have become a cliché of modern politics and indeed of behavior by organizational leaders more generally. For instance, Chancellor Gerhard Schröder's surprise re-election in Germany in 2002 (when he had been trailing his conservative challenger Edward Stoiber in the polls but came from behind to win) has been explained in part by his successful exploitation of serious floods on the river Elbe in the middle of the election campaign, which gave Schröder the opportunity to obtain favorable TV coverage as he waded through the flood waters in his rubber boots and green raincoat to offer aid and succor to flood victims.[3]

But equally in other conditions high officeholders judge that by placing themselves at a safe distance from problematic day-to-day management or delivery operations, it is better to sidestep blame by casting themselves in a more arms-length role as target setters, performance monitors, commentators, hirers and firers of managers, and critical inquirers into managers' conduct and decisions after the event. A notable example of such self-casting is the case of Colonel Muammar Gaddafi, de facto ruler of Libya since 1969, who nominally gave up all his official posts in 1979 as part of a move to make Libya a 'state of the masses,' and could therefore concentrate his energies on blaming everyone else for whatever went wrong.[4] And of course officeholders often use the sort of presentational skills we noted in the last chapter to morph from the appearance of the club chair to that of the team coach according to whether things are going well or badly. At that point agency strategies and presentational strategies start to blur, in intersection (d) of the blame strategy circles depicted in figure 1.2.

As noted earlier, the standard literature of management and economics treats the direct-versus-delegate choice in terms of which of those approaches can be expected to lead to greater efficiency or effectiveness, of the organization as a whole, or which is more likely to promote the general economic welfare of society, in providing the greatest quality or quantity of service at the least cost. But when we look at the problem from a blame avoidance perspective, concerns about individual blame risk may dominate concerns about organizational effectiveness, and corporate blame avoidance imperatives may trump collectivistic searches for social welfare. That does not mean that the logic of effective management or economic welfare maximization can never run together with a logic of blame avoidance. But equally those different logics may come into conflict, as we shall see later.

Machiavelli's idea that potentates should delegate unpopular tasks and perform popular ones directly represents a long-running theme in political science. In explorations of what shapes the architecture of executive government, the notion of lightning rods and flak-catchers repeatedly appears amid the more functional accounts of the direct-versus-delegate issue. The term "lightning rods," used in the title of Richard Ellis's (1994) account of the organizational strategies of American presidents, denotes individuals who are intended to deflect blame away from higher office-holders in the way that a lightning rod conducts electricity from a lightning strike away from a building into the ground.[5] And the term "flak-catchers," apparently dating from 1960s American slang, uses the analogy of anti-aircraft gunfire to denote bureaucrats who are there to take the blame from angry callers or protesters.

A conventional rational-choice approach to institutional design assumes that in making the choice between direct control and delegation of policy or operations, legislators and other elected politicians have to trade off credit and blame risks. Direct control—acting as the team coach or manager—is assumed to be a high-risk, high-reward option that brings credit if outcomes turn out to be positive but blame if the reverse occurs. On the other hand, delegation of responsibility to others—acting as the chair of the sports team rather than the team coach—is assumed to be a risk-averse strategy that limits blame if outcomes are adverse but equally limits credit if those outcomes are positive.[6] Table 4.2 maps out those basic choices and the assumed blame and credit outcomes according to whether the policies or operations in question turn out well or badly.

TABLE 4.2
Delegation and the Risk of Political Blame: Conventional Analysis

	Outcomes or Performance	
Strategic choice	*"Benign"* (positive outcomes)	*"Malign"* (negative outcomes)
Direct	(1) Credit: high Blame: low Result: credit-claiming	(2) Credit: low Blame: high Result: blame attraction
Delegate	(3) Credit: lower than (1) (partly deflected by delegation) Blame: low Result: credit slippage	(4) Credit: low Blame: lower than (2) (partly deflected by delegation) Result: blame avoidance

Source: adapted from Hood 2002: 19.

Table 4.2 summarizes some of the trade-offs that modern-day equivalents of Machiavelli's princes have to make. It also highlights one of the basic problems with Machiavelli's classic statement about delegation, namely that the maxim ignores the risk problem and assumes that potentates can reliably identify in advance what will count as unpopular or as favors. That may be easy enough in some cases—such as firing people from their jobs or handing out lavish honors and prizes. But in many cases the direct-versus-delegate decision has to be made in conditions of less than certain knowledge about how worthy of blame or credit any particular action or project will turn out to be. After all, some policies that are expected to be popular can unintentionally turn out to be blame magnets, and vice versa.

A classic example of the former is the ill-fated Millennium Dome once eagerly espoused by Tony Blair's New Labour regime in the late 1990s. The Dome was a vast temporary exhibition building on an expensively cleared site on the Greenwich peninsula in London. Tony Blair and some of his key ministers saw the Dome to celebrate the millennium as a potential temple to the wonders of New Labour rule and an iconic emblem of what was then (without irony) being dubbed "cool Britannia." Shortly before it opened, Blair hubristically claimed that the Dome would be "a triumph of confidence over cynicism, boldness over blandness, excellence over mediocrity."[7] Instead, the ill-fated Dome turned into a running sore for the government and a soft target for the many critics of the regime's political vanity and mismanagement. The venture cost over £800 million, ran into endless financial and management problems, attracted only half the number of visitors that were officially expected, and lay derelict for some six years after the millennium exhibition at a reported cost of over £1 million per month[8] while the government struggled to dispose of it to a respectable buyer (Jennings 2004). Big sports programs like the Olympic Games pose exactly the same kinds of blame risk.

Where risk complicates Machiavelli's simple maxim, negativity bias, as discussed in the first chapter, once more comes into the picture. We might expect delegation to be a dominant strategy in the choices depicted in table 4.1 if officeholders themselves exhibit negativity bias in their risk preferences over political blame and credit—that is, if they value possible losses more highly than potential gains of an equivalent amount. Delegation may also be the choice of those who follow what is known as a minimax strategy in decision theory (von Neumann 1928, von Neumann and Morgenstein 1944)—that is, minimizing the risk of maximum loss.

In table 4.1, the maximum potential loss is found in cell 2, when officeholders choose to direct and outcomes turn out to be malign—exactly the unwelcome position that Tony Blair and several of his ministers found themselves in over the Millennium Dome. To minimize the risk of ending up in cell 2, the minimax position involves delegation, which means giving up the possibility of high credit associated with the strategy of direction (cell 1) in exchange for the lower level of blame associated with the worst outcome under the delegation strategy (cell 4).

That conventional analysis is useful as a starting point. But it leads us to wonder why higher-level officeholders and government organizations should ever choose to assume direct responsibility for operational action, except in societies where blame avoidance somehow does not matter. And there are at least four possible answers to that.

One is that it all comes down to individual personalities, with those who wish to expose themselves to as little downside blame risk as possible tending to follow the minimax approach and those who are more disposed to gamble over blame risk making different choices. A second explanation, going beyond personality differences, is that the assumption that delegation can shield the delegator from blame may simply not be valid in all cultural or institutional settings. The more or less explicit assumption behind the delegation approach as it applies to high-level officeholders is that blame events are often of fairly short duration (before something else comes along to capture public attention), such that organizational arrangements that at least serve to muddy the waters about the agency component of blame during that short window of time when a blame episode dominates news media will be sufficient to do the work of blame avoidance.

But that assumption may be invalid for lower-level officeholders. It may also not apply to circumstances where blame is not counted in terms of obloquy in the news media. It may be invalid in cases where blame turns out to be a long-drawn-out event rather than something ephemeral in its claims on public attention. And in some cases, as Murray Horn (1995: 46) claims, blame shifting through delegation may be more diffi-cult in parliamentary systems than in systems of divided government (though, as we shall see later, that claim is contestable). In circumstances like those, officeholders may find themselves facing blame if they *fail* to take direct control of policy or operations and are seen to tolerate or preside over muddle or incompetence in operations directed by or shared with others. Delegation as a form of agency strategy for blame avoidance reaches its limits when delegation or sharing of responsibilities will attract as much blame as direct control by a single officeholder, if not more.

In those conditions, where there is no risk-free agency option, "calling in" powers, conducting high-level summits, and being seen to take per-sonal charge of high-profile government efforts may be a better option for avoiding blame as well as claiming credit. And that may help to ex-plain why it is far from unusual for prime ministers to take over particu-lar ministerial portfolios themselves on occasion or effectively to call in powers by personally leading government operations in some particular domain. Such personal direction does not have to be forever, and in a crisis, credit-claiming or blame avoidance is often aimed at by temporary assumption of command, shouldering others aside, to give an impression of resolution and "buck-stops-here" responsibility without indefinite com-mitment. For example, Tony Blair took "personal charge" of his govern-ment's efforts to deal with a serious epidemic of foot-and-mouth disease in cattle for a short period during the run-up to the British general elec-tion of 2001, at a time when his government was being heavily criticized for seriously mishandling the crisis.[9]

What such examples show is that, even if it worked most of the time, there may be some circumstances where delegation can attract as much or more blame as direct control, perhaps particularly where it is done "on the hoof" rather than reflecting long-established arrangements, or in con-ditions where an officeholder is expected to take direct charge (for ex-ample where delegated arrangements have clearly failed). That means another tricky blame-risk calculation for would-be blame avoiders.

Third, in other conditions officeholders may be able to escape from the trade-offs portrayed in table 4.1. Sometimes they may be able to have the best of both worlds of delegating blame and retaining credit—for example, by creating separate authorities to mount high-profile sport events so that they can blame the delegatees if things turn out badly but still appear center stage for smiling photo-ops if the events are successful. Even when that sort of variable credit-blame institutional geometry is not attainable, top officeholders may still be able to disavow responsibility while keeping control in practice by behind-the-scenes intervention and arm-twisting. Why accept a trade-off when you can have it both ways?

Examples of such behavior are hardly far to seek. After all, the semi-independent public corporation form of organization that became widely adopted for many public service functions in both developed and developing countries, particularly from the 1930s to the 1960s, in principle offers the opportunity for ministers and governments to disavow responsibility for operational matters when errors occur or unpopular decisions are made (for instance, when fares or charges go up), without in practice surrendering much power to call the shots. For instance, France's former state-owned oil company Elf-Aquitaine, created out of a merger of other organizations in 1965 under Charles de Gaulle's presidency, was often seen in practice as an instrument of French government policy in Africa up to its privatization amid corruption scandals in 1999 (Godoy 2003). And in the corporate world, remuneration committees (supposedly autonomous entities drawn from outside the organization to decide pay levels for top employees) are often in practice far from independent from corporate management.

Indeed, there is a further class of organizations that go beyond the public corporation or state-owned-enterprise form and which consist of bodies that are nominally independent of government, even though the reality may be very different. While he was president of the Carnegie Corporation of New York, Alan Pifer (1967) coined the term "quasi-nongovernment organization" in the 1960s to denote this sort of nominal but more or less phony independence from government officeholders. The term "quango" later came to be used more or less as a synonym for statutory boards and other official bodies (see Barker 1982), but its original meaning denoted a form of organization that is common in the cloak-and-dagger worlds of diplomacy, unconventional warfare and espionage, and sometimes comes into other policy domains as well.

Terms such as "plausible deniability," "black ops," "unacknowledgeable means," and "front organization" are only some of the many official euphemisms for ostensibly independent companies and other forms of organization that are in practice agents of government but are constituted as separate bodies, to avoid diplomatic incidents, political embarrassment, or formal military confrontation. This form of organization has a long history as a means of trying to keep the heat off core government officeholders and shift the blame. It is almost invariably used for the murkier types of back-door foreign intervention, such as assassination, sabotage, engineered coups d'état, even propaganda efforts designed to shift public opinion in another country (for a dramatic case, see Macken-zie 2002). But it can also figure in domestic politics as well, as in the case of those regimes that deploy unofficial death squads for internal opera-tions or unacknowledged state-sponsored militias (as explored by Mitchell (2004) for civil wars and other kinds of conflict).

This form of organization—notionally but not actually independent from government—can also be found in more mundane areas of activity. For example, in the 1930s the Irish government ran a sweepstake based on horse races to help finance its hospitals, and because the domestic pop-ulation of Ireland was too small for the lottery to raise sufficient funds for the purpose, many tickets were sold to emigrant Irish populations over-seas, particularly in the United States and Britain (three-quarters of the tickets were sold in Britain in the early days, and the Irish Sweep seems to have cornered the market for foreign lotteries there in the 1930s) (see Coleman 2005: 201). But lotteries were generally illegal in the United States and Britain at that time, so to avoid diplomatic incidents the sweep-stake was formally run by a private company up to the time of its final demise in 1986 (Coleman 2005: 218).

But there are of course risks associated with the back-channel approach to delegation, either to supposedly independent public bodies that can be informally controlled by governments or to nominally private or inde-pendent bodies that are creatures of the delegator. After all, if backdoor influence or the provenance of nominally independent organizations comes to light, the blame consequences may be as bad as, or worse than, the blame that accrues when adverse outcomes result from direct government control or decision-making.

Moreover, the issue of whether to direct or delegate is not always a yes/no institutional choice in the simple way presented in table 4.1. There are many different ways of delegating. After all, in everyday life you can del-egate some or all of your responsibilities to someone else; you can dele-gate irrevocably or in ways that enable you to take back the reins at some point; you can delegate to people you personally appoint and can dismiss, or to people or organizations outside your control. In the analysis of del-egation arrangements such as the independence of central banks from core executives, there is in principle a spectrum or ladder of levels of au-tonomy, as various authors have sought to show. Of course any such analysis is complicated both because there are multiple dimensions of for-mal or statutory independence and because informal links can cut across formal ones (see, for example, Forder 2001).

Developing this point, table 4.3 indicates two dimensions on which delegation arrangements can vary. One of those dimensions is the degree

TABLE 4.3
Hard and Soft Delegation: Two Dimensions

	Clarity of delegation	
Distance between delegate bodies and core of government or high officeholders	Clear-cut An identifiable delegatee body is permanently responsible for conducting all of the relevant activity	Fuzzy An identifiable delegatee body is responsible for some but not all of the relevant activity, or only at some times
High (delegation to entrenched agencies like law courts or elected authorities)	(1) Hard delegation Blame shift credibility: high Control loss: high	(2) Mixed delegation Blame shift credibility: mixed Control loss: mixed
Low (delegation to bodies whose composition the delegator can readily determine or alter)	(3) Mixed delegation Blame shift credibility: fairly low (dependent on visibility of links) Control loss: low	(4) Soft delegation Blame shift credibility: fairly low (dependent on visibility of links) Control loss: low

of clarity or fuzziness in delegation—for instance, whether it involves all of the activity or policy responsibilities in question or whether some but not all of the relevant activity is the responsibility of delegated bodies and part is retained by others, such that the allocation of responsibility is not visible at a glance. The other dimension is the degree of social or institutional distance that exists between the delegators and the delegatees. On this dimension we can distinguish a scale running from weak forms of delegation with little formal distance from the individuals or organizations whose powers are being delegated (for example, nonelected or nonjudicial bodies whose composition the delegator can readily determine or alter), through agencies with statutory independence that requires legislative time to reverse, to constitutionally entrenched agencies (like law courts or elected authorities) that need even bigger legislative coalitions to dislodge or alter. If other things are equal, the latter kinds of delegation will be more costly or difficult to revoke than the former type.

If we put those two dimensions together, the hardest type of delegation will be that shown by cell 1 in table 4.3, while the softest type can be expected to be that shown by cell 4, and the other two will be more mixed types. The blame shift credibility of cells 3 and 4 is likely to depend on how obvious it is that the delegatee organizations are in practice creatures of the delegator, as in the case of the quasi-independent class of bodies discussed earlier.

The most blame-risk-averse officeholders and organizations with the strongest negativity bias will be drawn toward the 'hard' type of delegation shown in cell 1, which in ordinary circumstances will have a high element of public credibility but carry for officeholders a corresponding risk of loss of control.[10] But for the least blame-risk-averse officeholders and organizations, the type of delegation shown in cell 4 may be attractive, since it offers the beguiling possibility of a having-it-all strategy that avoids a choice between credit-claiming and blame avoidance and leaves open the options as to whether to take charge or disavow responsibility in a blame crisis. Organizations and officeholders whose level of blame risk aversion comes between those two extremes are likely to go for more mixed forms of delegation, of the type shown in cells 2 and 3, whenever they are in a position to make such choices as opposed to taking the institutional arrangements they work within as given and fixed. So whereas delegation is sometimes treated in the literature on the subject as if it were an on-off or yes/no decision, it turns out to involve a range of fine-grained institutional choices when we look at the issues in more detail.

Moving-Target Approaches

Delegation, whether formal or informal, is the form of agency strategy for avoiding blame that has attracted the most attention in the literature of political science from Machiavelli four centuries ago to more recent writers such as Morris Fiorina (1982), Richard Ellis (1994), and Fabio Franchino (2007). But there are forms of agency strategy for blame avoidance that do not involve delegation down some line of authority. One such alternative, comprising cell 2 in table 4.1 and highlighted in the second epigraph to this chapter, is the strategy of moving the blame target. Attempts to move the target include the practice of defensive reorganization and a merry-go-round of staff changes that will ensure that an institutional system and the officeholders within it are always one jump ahead of those who want to direct blame at it, or even to understand it.[11]

The moving-the-target approach works at the intersection of the agency and time elements of blame that were discussed in the first chapter. It consists of making the structure of responsibility so messy, uncertain and ever-changing that those seeking to level blame at the institutions concerned can always be answered by the counterclaim that the critics have not understood the complexities of the system or that they are hopelessly out-of-date and whatever faults they are highlighting belong to an older system whose faults have now been overcome in the latest round of reorganization. If partnership working (to be discussed below) is the equivalent of making smoke, this approach is the institutional equivalent of zig-zagging by warships or military aircraft to shake off their pursuers—often the key to survival in that sort of conflict, as it is in the natural world for those creatures who try to shake off predators by moving about rather than keeping still.

Obviously there is a fine line between natural or functional turnover in complex organizations and deliberately contrived defensive restructuring, but adverse events or the expectation of such events often serve to produce such changes. The moving-the-target approach is something that can be actively pursued by the top and middle-level officeholders whose blame worlds were discussed in chapter 2, and is often passively exploited by front-line troops as well, even though the latter cannot usually initiate such activity.

An example of the moving-the-target approach is given by Nobuhiro Hiwatari (2000: 129-33) in his account of the break-up of Japan's once-all-powerful Ministry of Finance in the late 1990s. Hiwatari argues that the break-up is better understood as a product of blame–avoidance maneuvers among rival political parties over the passage of unpopular measures to bail out collapsed banks at public expense than as a product of interest-group pressure, the ministry's incompetence, the party-political color of the government, or other factors. That is because the break-up occurred when the Liberal Democratic Party (LDP) was either in coalition with other parties or ruling as a minority government, and the reorganization was a way for the other parties collaborating with the LDP in the unpopular bank bailout policy to claim credit for bringing about a new regime and to avoid blame by distancing themselves from the regime that had brought about the bank failures.

Reorganization of the type discussed by Hiwatari is commonly found in government. When services are exposed to high levels of blame, reorganization and changes of names and titles offer one way of confusing potential blame makers and distancing the current regime from the previous one (see also Reder and Dundan 2004). Other ways of achieving a similar moving-target effect include changes in procedures rather than organograms (which we will discuss in the next chapter as a policy response) and changes in personnel. In any organization where there is a high level of turnover among the staff, the current incumbent can always blame his or her predecessor for mistakes or adverse events.

Indeed, one of the frustrations that many readers are likely to have experienced when they are in "customer service hell" dealing with large organizations is the sense of never dealing with the same individual twice, or finding that everyone associated with the adverse event they are concerned with has now conveniently moved on, leaving a new team who disclaim all responsibility for the events of the past. From ministerial reshuffles in cabinet government systems that mean few ministers stay in office long enough to face the blame consequences of their errors of commission or omission to the frequent turnover of operating staff in some service organizations, this variant of the moving-the-target approach can deprive all but the most determined of their blame quarry and in some cases even allow the organization to disavow all knowledge of the event in question.

PARTNERSHIP STRUCTURES: BLAME AVOIDANCE THROUGH SHARED RESPONSIBILITY AND ORGANIZATIONAL COMPLEXITY

While reorganization and staff rotation are ways to deal with the agency dimension of blame by constant motion, a further agency approach consists of complex collaborative structures composed of several organizations or institutions, such that would-be blamers cannot easily identify which one of a group of organizations is responsible for any given blame event. Partnership approaches aim to deflect blame by the ultimate application of the so-called many hands approach to responsibility (that is, cases where individual agency is hard to trace, an issue much discussed by accountability scholars such as Thompson [1980 and 1987]). For example, Tom Gill (2005: 208) commenting on services for the homeless in Japan, finds "a threadbare patchwork of systems, with responsibility contested, divided and diffused at every level [of government].... The net result is to make it radically unclear who is in charge." The success of such approaches as blame avoidance devices depends on being able to make the allocation of responsibility among the various actors and organizations in a partnership structure so complex and uncertain that no ordinary person can ever hope to figure out who exactly is responsible for what.

The partnership approach to blame avoidance can play out at several levels. One, which is on the boundary line between agency and policy strategies (sector f in figure 1.2), is the exercise of responsibility through board or committee structures rather than single-headed authorities, which we will discuss in the next chapter. Though many have argued against board or committee structures for the conduct of executive functions because such structures offer so many opportunities for each individual member to blame the others for an unpopular decision, some sort of cabinet structure (or its equivalent) is to be found at the top of most government systems. Board structures are similarly adopted in many other institutions, producing rich scope for efforts to shift or at least share blame.

Another variant of the partnership approach consists of horizontal partnerships among organizations. Indeed, frustration with the common experience of public bureaucracies and other organizations that fail to cooperate over all the many problems which fall between the cracks in their jurisdictions or which cut across their areas of expertise has led to much official enthusiasm for more cooperative arrangements in the name of "joined-up government" (see, for instance, Bogdanor 2005), and that has translated itself into institutional arrangements that make several separate organizations jointly responsible for a project or service. Some such arrangements operate among public organizations—for instance, in the Children's Trust Boards introduced in England to coordinate actions for the protection of children after social services had failed to prevent the tragic death of a victim of child abuse (Victoria Climbié) in 2000 (and which included police, probation services, local authorities, various healthcare providers, and several other organizations).[12]

Moreover, it has become common for such partnership arrangements to go beyond public sector organizations to extend to partnerships between public organizations and business or between government and independent bodies. Such arrangements have a long history in various forms. Just one example is the famous Dutch East India Company (*Vereenigde Oost-Indische Compagnie*, or VOC), claimed by some to have been the world's first mega-corporation (see Ames 2008: 102–3). The VOC was founded in 1602 as a trading company and originally given a twenty-one-year monopoly by the States-General of the Netherlands for activities that included the ability to wage war, negotiate treaties, coin money, and establish colonies. But partnership activity that mixes public and private players (though usually in rather less dramatic forms than the VOC case) has come into high fashion and prominence since the 1990s, with the term "partnership" displacing the word "privatization," which had begun to have negative connotations. Public-private partnerships or private finance arrangements have developed in numerous countries, and the model has become much favored by international agencies as a recipe for the developing world as well as a familiar way of running international sporting events (see Heald and Georgiou 2008). The standard official defense of such arrangements is that they enable public services to be provided at lower cost or higher quality than would apply to direct provision by any one government body, and to draw more heavily on outside and business expertise than any single-organization project can easily do. But those arrangements also have the convenient political effect of creating a structure of "no-one-in-charge government" (Bryson and Crosby 1992) and giving each "partner" the opportunity to blame the others if—or when—things go wrong.[13]

The next level up in the 'partnership game' is of course that of intergovernmental arrangements, including partnerships across levels of government within a single country and international collaborations of various kinds, ranging from very specific partnerships (such as the Channel Tunnel Safety Authority, created by a 1986 Treaty between France and the United Kingdom) to the forbidding institutional complexities of the European Union. Such arrangements also have the convenient property of diffusing blame for adverse decisions or outcomes internationally among the various governments and producing the characteristic and familiar features of the EU blame game, in which each individual national government claims that its views have been overridden in the decision-making process, despite its valiant attempts to fight its corner on behalf of the nation's voters. While it would no doubt be rash to interpret the whole development of the EU and other systems that resemble it as a case of blame avoidance institutional architecture, its convenient blame avoidance character may well be a key factor in that development.

The partnership approach is perhaps the agency equivalent of herding strategies for survival in the animal world, and it is closely linked to some decision procedures inside organizations to be discussed in the next chapter. It does not make the perceived loss element of blaming disappear, and it serves more to spread blame than to make it disappear. But it makes the agency element fuzzy, such that the partners can blame one another (openly or by leaks and innuendoes) and leave potential blamers nonplussed by the complexity of the organizational arrangements.

Government by the Market: Blame Avoidance by Impersonal Forces

The late Peter Self (1993) once used the term "government by the market" to denote the stress laid on privatization and outsourcing that went with the mood of "economic rationalism" or public choice economics in numerous government systems in the 1980s and 1990s. But the market as an institution can also furnish the basis for another set of agency strategies for avoiding or mitigating blame. After all, in the private corporate sector, "market conditions" commonly figure among the reasons given for unpopular decisions, such as service cutbacks, price increases, plant shutdowns, mass layoffs—or for high salaries, bonuses, and payoffs obtained by higher-level directorates even at times of apparently poor performance. If corporations can arrange matters such that these things can be claimed to be the inexorable product of supply and demand in labor and product markets, they can shift the agency element of blame to the impersonal forces of the market rather than to the individual greed, rapacity, or stupidity of their own leaders.

Although governments are not firms trading in markets in the orthodox sense, they too can use market forces and institutions as an agency approach to blame avoidance, which perhaps can be considered as a special kind of delegation. One area in which such an approach can be applied is the often sensitive subject of the reward packages for top public officeholders such as politicians and civil servants (see Hood and Peters 1994; Hood, Peters, and Lee 2003). Given the political difficulties in any democratic or egalitarian setting of paying top public officeholders at levels far above what ordinary voters earn, it has become common for those officeholders' rewards to be linked to "markets" through comparability exercises conducted by arms-length bodies whose decisions they cannot overrule (linking the delegation strategy to the market strategy). The resultant reward packages are thus designed to emerge as simply the going rate for such high-level talent, with choice somehow precluded by the working of the labor market.

For instance, the very high salaries paid to top civil servants and politicians in Singapore—whose prime minister for a long time was paid substantially more than the U.S. President—can be said to be a product of "market conditions" insofar as those salaries are institutionally linked to the salaries of the topmost professional and corporate earners in the island-state (see Quah 2003). But of course there are some significant hidden premises in any invocation of market forces in such circumstances, notably the presumption that most elected politicians possess the sort of executive talent that would fit them to run multinational corporations or that the appropriate "market" comparator is really that of top corporate lawyers or the highest level executives in multinational companies rather than other much more modestly paid "talking professionals" like teachers or social workers.

Apart from accounting for executive remuneration, market forces can be used in other ways to blunt the agency dimension of blame in government and public services, if administrative structures can be set up in such a way that the working of the market contrives to preclude potentially blame-attracting choices. For instance, if one country's currency is pegged to another (as in the case of the Hong Kong dollar, which has been pegged to the US dollar since the mid-1980s), then any fiscal or monetary measures needed to maintain such a peg are simply a product of "market forces." Similarly, if government or public service organizations use insurance companies to cover third-party risks for public services rather than self-insuring their operations, then restrictions, closures, and onerous exclusions come out as a product of the insurance "market." The "market" can even be used as a way of governing the operation of security systems in a sense. For instance, the frustrations associated with airport security measures that most readers will have experienced as air travelers (the long lines, the false, confusing, or contradictory information, the indignity that may go along with low-intelligence screening processes) can be blamed on "market forces," if the numbers and competence of screening staff available are determined by what commercial airlines or companies running airports are prepared to pay for. What else can you expect, in an age of cheap flights and budget airlines undercutting what used to be a more oligopolistic structure of a few major carriers and dominant airports?

"Government by the market" as an agency approach to blame avoidance can be considered both as a variant of the delegation strategy (for example, the fixing of interest rates by autonomous central banks is a mixture of both of these approaches) and as an approach which borders on presentational strategy. Insofar as effective blame avoidance by this method requires a culture in which market forces are seen as both impersonal and legitimate, this approach, like soft forms of delegation, borders on the intersection of presentational and agency strategy—section (d) in the overlapping circles in figure 1.2. And as with the other delegation approaches discussed earlier, officeholders may well be attracted to variable-geometry applications of the "government-by-the market" approach, trying to claim credit for themselves in the good times by invoking their own sagacity and trying to avoid blame in the bad times by blaming adverse outcomes on the ungovernable workings of global markets. Indeed, that was precisely the approach being vigorously pursued by politicians and regulators the world over to fend off blame for the financial collapse of the late 2000s as this book was being written.

THE SCOPE AND LIMITS OF THE AGENCY APPROACH TO BLAME AVOIDANCE

The approaches to the agency strategy for blame avoidance sketched out earlier give us a way of understanding aspects of organizational architecture and reorganization processes in government and public service providers which are not otherwise readily explicable—for example, why projects and programs so often get bogged down in an alphabet soup of multiple organizations that tend to pull against one another in practice, in spite of upbeat rhetoric about cozy and harmonious partnerships, and why public organizations so often seem to be engulfed in an endless and expensive process of deck-chair rearrangement, in an apparently fruitless search for a perfect pattern that only confuses and demoralizes most of the people who work in and with them.

Of course, institutional devices incorporating the four variants of agency strategy discussed in this chapter—delegation, reorganization, partnership, and government-by-the-market—are always formally justified by "functional" claims that such arrangements lead to lower costs and more effective administration. But such outcomes invariably turn out to be contested and remarkably hard to demonstrate clearly. In the final chapter we look further into the claim that such devices (and other blame avoidance strategies) lead to better government, and in chapter 6 we explore what if anything might be changing about the agency strategies pursued by officeholders and organizations in their constant search for ways to shield themselves from blame. The question at issue here is whether such approaches are really effective in mitigating or avoiding blame.

It would be surprising if officeholders and organizations put so much effort into delegation and fine-tuning of organization charts and government machinery if such efforts had no effect on public attribution of blame and credit at least some of the time. And indeed, political and organizational scientists have produced some evidence of such effects. For instance, in a well-known comparative study, Christopher Anderson (1995) found that institutional dispersion of responsibilities was associated with less blame for economic failures being leveled at governments by citizens in a set of developed democracies.

Similarly, in an analysis of protest activity over wage arrears in Russia in the late 1990s, Debra Javeline (2003: 113-4) found that the more specifically the respondents in her survey could identify the actors and institutions responsible for those arrears, the more likely it was that they would be involved in active protest. In the corporate sector, Warren Boeker's (1992: 418) study of sixty-seven organizations over two decades showed that chief executives were often able to buffer themselves from responsibility for poor corporate performance on their watch by shifting blame onto their top management teams and replacing top managers. George Boyne and his colleagues (2008a, 2008b) found similar outcomes in a study of English local authority managers in the 2000s. Such findings suggest that agency strategies can help protect officeholders from blame at least some of the time.

But, just as with the presentational strategies discussed in the last chapter, the efficacy of agency strategies for blame avoidance can reach the point of diminishing returns. A logic of diminishing returns means that credibility will tend to fall the more officeholders try to get themselves out of trouble in such ways. Indeed, as has already been noted, in some conditions such strategies may even be counter-productive, producing negative and not simply diminishing returns, as officeholders come to be blamed as much for trying to shuffle off responsibility as for any substantive failings in services or government action. (The parallel with presentational strategies as discussed in the last chapter is the case where spin activity becomes self-defeating when it becomes a blame magnet.) So if they were rational calculators, we might expect officeholders to apply the delegation approach up to the point where blame from not taking command equals that of avoiding command—the point at which they are equally damned if they do and damned if they don't.

The efficacy of agency strategies for blame avoidance will also depend on the kind of culture and governmental system in which they are applied. In the early nineteenth century, Alexis de Tocqueville (1946: 113) seems to have thought that under the type of democracy he observed in America at that time, the elected rulers would be less able to shuffle off blame to advisers or agents than the monarchs of an earlier era, who could invoke the convenient constitutional doctrine that the king could do no wrong, so it was only the monarch's advisers or support staff who could officially err. If he could be spirited back to life today, Tocqueville might be surprised by the academic attention that has been paid to lightning rods (agents and delegatees intended to conduct blame away from presidents and other officeholders) in American political science over the past sixty years or so (see Herring 1940; Fenno 1978; Ellis 1994), and might conclude that the political culture had changed since his observations. He would also find that there has been periodic and somewhat inconclusive debate among political scientists over that time as to whether blame avoidance through delegation is more easily pursued under a separation-of-powers governmental system of the American type or under parliamentary regimes.

Indeed, two of the leading luminaries of political science in the United States and Britain in the 1940s, Pendleton Herring and Harold Laski, were on the opposite sides of an argument as to whether blame avoidance through delegation was likely to be easier to achieve in one or other of those two types of political systems. Laski (1940) argued that the tendency of a presidential system to personalize political responsibility sharply limited the practical ability of presidents to pursue the Machiavellian approach to blame avoidance set out in the first epigraph to this chapter. Herring (1940), on the other hand, saw the all-purpose party control associated with parliamentary systems as less propitious ground for delegation approaches to blame avoidance.

Again, both of those departed eminences might be surprised by the institutional complexity of blame avoidance arrangements operating in both of those systems today, though Christopher Anderson's work, as mentioned earlier, seems to bear out Herring's view of the matter rather than Laski's, and indeed the former seems to be more commonly accepted today. In fact, one of the major developments for those European democracies over the seventy-odd years since Herring and Laski were writing is the creation of the European Union and its regulatory regimes that involve such a complex mixture of EU-level activity, national government activity, and activity by special-purpose bodies and sub-national government that no one who is not thoroughly steeped in such matters will be easily able to identify the agency element of blame with any accuracy when adverse events occur.

More generally, Anderson's study is mainly concerned with what we earlier called hard rather than soft delegation (see table 4.3 above). It is concerned with constitutional or quasi-constitutional arrangements that are relatively costly to change, such as federal versus unitary government. But can we read across from elected politicians' ability to achieve blame transference over that sort of delegation to conclusions about the efficacy of the softer and more short-term agency strategies for blame avoidance that we discussed earlier, such as partnership working, permanent reorganization, or attempts to make market forces take the blame?

If we combine our earlier analysis of the direct-or-delegate dilemma (see table 4.2) and the distinction between hard and soft institutional arrangements, we might expect the political efficacy of agency strategies for blame avoidance to be greatest when they involve hard rather than soft and easily revocable institutional arrangements, simple rather than complex delegation, and delegation to elected rather than appointed officeholders. So all the agency approaches discussed in this chapter present officeholders and organizations with the sort of credit-blame trade-offs that we discussed for the delegation approach, even though they will naturally always be searching for a have-it-all approach.

After all, when the political climate around officeholders and organizations becomes skeptical, the revocability of soft institutional arrangements leaves ample room for questioning and counter-allegations about where the true location of responsibility lies. The fuzziness of complex delegation invites debates about fudging and lack of transparency. And delegation to nonjudicial and nonelected bodies invites debates about "democratic deficits" or a "lack of public service ethos" if private operators are involved. We might therefore expect the efficacy of agency approaches to depend on a combination of the prevailing blame climate, the nature of the institutional arrangements adopted, and the extent to which agency approaches have been pursued toward the point of diminishing or negative returns.

Finally, as we have already noticed, agency strategies must have their limits in other ways, or else why should other types of institutional arrangements ever be used and why should bureaucratic and political officeholders ever take direct control of anything? As noted in chapter 2, there are some parts of all our lives that effectively can't be passed out to or shared with others. Top-level political officeholders often hand over formal control of their personal financial affairs to others in blind-trust arrangements (though there are inevitably ragged edges to such arrangements, which are often the source of embarrassment), but they cannot very well conduct their love lives through others, except in bizarre circumstances. And the sort of relentless self-publicists who often tend to gravitate toward high office will rarely be inclined to delegate responsibility for their own publicity and spin operations to truly arms-length operators. So when blame comes their way over the conduct of their private financial dealings, their amorous affairs, or their own self-promotion activity, they are likely to find themselves in the same position as lower-level officeholders in the media blame spotlight (such as teachers accused of having inappropriate sexual relations with students or police accused of belonging to fascist organizations). Such officeholders will therefore have to rely on something other than agency strategies of delegation, complexification, or the other approaches discussed here to get them out of trouble. Accordingly, we now turn to a third broad family of blame avoidance approaches, namely policy strategies.

CHAPTER FIVE

Policy or Operational Strategies

> Excuses kill. Fit a smoke alarm.
> —British fire safety advertisement early 2000s

> You don't know nothing and you can't do nothing and you can't say nothing.
> —Protestor to San Francisco poverty office bureaucrat in Wolfe 1970: 116

"If You Can't Be Good, Be Careful"

If your mother tried to teach you that honesty is the best policy, she might have told you that the best way to avoid being blamed is not to do anything wrong in the first place.[1] After all, if you manage to live a life of spotless virtue, you are much less likely to have to resort to agency strategies to try to pin the odium of blameworthy actions onto someone else, or presentational strategies to try to make blame disappear by smoke and mirrors, or the other rhetorical arts.

And indeed, a third main strategy that can be found in the literature of blame avoidance is precisely that of choosing the least-blame policy, procedure, or method of operation, as in the fire safety advertisement in the first epigraph. Installing that smoke alarm and keeping it in working order will help to protect you from blame if a fire breaks out, and indeed may also protect you from lawsuits on the grounds of negligence or from having your compensation claim rejected by your fire insurance company. And in the same way, you cannot be blamed for greed, self-indulgence, or hypocrisy if you choose to follow the sort of hair-shirt, ascetic lifestyle that leaders such as Mahatma Gandhi have followed and that the great German sociologist Max Weber (1958) saw as central to the early development of western capitalism.

Below that demanding standard are numerous ways of limiting or avoiding blame by making evidence of failure hard to find, by avoiding cases or problems with a high blame risk, by filling out a checklist ("box-ticking," in British parlance), or by showing some form of due diligence—a term that originally derives from a famous clause relating to equity investments in the U.S. Securities Act of 1933, and is widely used today to denote any official or legal defense based on the claim that all reasonable precautions and steps have been taken to avoid causing harm or committing an offense (see Lawrence 1994).

So a third set of blame avoidance approaches, to which we earlier gave the label of policy or operational strategies, comprises the various attempts by officeholders or institutions to avoid or limit blame by what they do or how they do it. While agency strategies, as discussed in the last chapter, work mainly on the agency perception dimension of blame and presentational strategies operate on the loss or harm perception dimension, policy or operational strategies work on either or both of those dimensions, by choosing the course of action that minimizes likely blame, by reducing the chances of avoidable losses occurring, by reducing the chances of blame being detectable, or at least by showing that agents did all they reasonably could have done to foresee and prevent those losses. And as we shall see later, that means some variants of policy strategy focus on being good, in the sense of eschewing potentially blameworthy activities altogether (such as total abstention from alcohol). But others concentrate more on procedural devices (such as safe drinking, which follows official recommended practice in observing prescribed limits for drinking and driving, not drinking at the workplace, or limiting alcohol consumption to not more than so many prescribed units a week). The old adage, "If you can't be good, be careful," perhaps sums up that second approach.

Just as with agency and presentational strategies, policy strategies for blame avoidance turn out to be everywhere once you start to look for them, though it would hardly be surprising if examples of being careful turn out to be more plentiful than examples of being good. In the early 1990s, for instance, 'business process re-engineering' (BPR) was one of those catch-phrases of corporate management that become invoked to the point of cliché and are advocated with evangelistic fervor by management consultants, bureaucrats, and corporate managers. The BPR movement began with a 1990 article by Michael Hammer arguing that too many firms were using the IT developments of that time simply to automate what they already did, rather than to use those developments to reorganize their businesses to eliminate non-value-producing activity (see Hammer 1990; Davenport et al. 1990). But the same era also saw many public and private organizations in practice following a different kind of BPR, namely 'blame prevention re-engineering' (Hood, Rothstein, and Baldwin 2001: 163n11). Blame prevention re-engineering has the same initials as business process re-engineering, and what it focuses on—the detailed organization of a work process carried out by various players—is the same as well. But what this type of BPR is designed to strip out are potentially blame-attracting elements.

As with agency and presentational strategies, there are several different approaches to policy or operational strategy, and this chapter aims to delve into variants of this form of blame avoidance. Most of it is devoted to exploring four BPR approaches to blame avoidance. At the end we explore the political-risk issue of credit-claiming versus blame avoidance that surrounds the choice of defensive as against more expansive approaches to policy and procedure, and explore the scope and limits of the policy strategy of blame avoidance. What is the evidence that policy strategies are effective ways of avoiding or limiting blame, and is there a point when things get so bad that policy strategies start to take blame as a given and focus on personal survival?

Some Varieties of Policy and Operational Strategy

To give an indication of some of the varieties of the policy or operational approach, but again without making any claim to comprehensiveness, four variants are explored in the next few sections. They are summarized in table 5.1. One, which is very familiar in the literature about matters bureaucratic, is what can be called the protocolization or standards approach. This approach comprises attempts to avoid blame by following rules or best-practice guidelines or routines and procedures that are blessed by hierarchic or scientific authority. A second is the herding approach of always doing things in groups in some way, so that no one individual or organization can be singled out for blame as deviant, and potential blame takers can find strength in numbers. A third is the opposite, in the sense that it individualizes blame by finding ways to blame users, operators, or

TABLE 5.1
Some Varieties of Policy Strategy

Abstinence	Protocolization
Motto: "Just say no"	**Motto:** "Stick to the rules"
Example: closure of advice or recreational facilities	**Example:** defensive medicine through best-practice protocols
Individualization	Herding
Motto: "Let the buyer (or operator or user) beware"	**Motto:** "Stay with the group"
Example: mission statements that profess highest ethical standards	**Example:** collective assessment of child safety or pedophile risks

victims, protecting some (such as managers or service provider organizations) by putting the blame onto others who may be less well-resourced or nimble when it comes to dodging the bullets. And a fourth is what might be called the abstinence approach of simply not pursuing certain policies, keeping certain records, or providing certain services if they are seen to involve too great a risk of blame.

PROTOCOLIZATION: PLAYING IT BY THE BOOK

One of the commonest types of policy or operational strategy for blame avoidance is that of protocolization, in various forms, as shown in the top right quadrant of figure 5.1. We have noted a few instances of this follow-the-rules approach in earlier chapters. Rather than allowing common sense or ad hoc professional judgment to govern what is to be done, appropriate behavior is stipulated by formulae, algorithms, computer programs, best practice guidelines, or other kinds of rules, turning human functionaries into some approximation of robots. That is perhaps the standard government-bureaucracy reflex when issues of blame are to be faced, and it is a frequent standby of private companies too.

Indeed, the essence of traditional bureaucratic decision-making, as expounded by many classic authors on the subject (such as Max Weber [1948], Charles Perrow [1972] and Victor Thompson [1975]), is that it is built on routines for consistently putting cases into categories on the basis of enacted procedural rules and documented facts. That way of doing things has often been justified by its advocates on grounds such as efficiency or predictability—getting the job done in some technical sense, as in a famous simile of machine-like precision that Max Weber used to characterize bureaucratic functioning.[2] But it can also and equally be understood as a way of limiting blame for the faulty exercise of discretion. That is because this method of working substitutes rule-of-law procedures for seat-of-the-pants decision-making and so makes it harder for the functionaries concerned to be blamed for arbitrariness, favoritism, corruption, double standards, or poor personal judgment.

The protocolization, playing-it-by-the rules approach can be followed by all three kinds of institutional players whose blame avoidance worlds we briefly sketched out in chapter 2. It is often associated more with the behavior of the middle and front-line players than that of the top bananas, but the latter players can use it on occasion too. Indeed, the protocolization approach is to policy strategy what delegation is to agency strategy, in that it involves much the same sort of blame-credit trade-off that we discussed in the last chapter and summarized in table 4.2. That is, if the players choose to follow rules rather than exercise discretion, blame can be expected to be lessened if outcomes turn out to be malign, but political credit will be correspondingly reduced for benign outcomes.

If negativity bias dominates such calculations, it will create a thrust for ever more protocolization of work processes at every level and in every domain. The logical limit of that process is the point at which (as in the old joke about Mussolini's Italy) everything that is not prohibited is compulsory (Larsen 1980: 54).[3] And as we will see in chapter 6, many commentators think that is precisely what is occurring for front-line operations in spheres with high blame risks such as medicine, social work, and policing, and at middle and higher levels of organizations, too, in fields such as employment law, corporate governance, security, and information handling.

Such developments have plenty of critics. Indeed, it is nowadays common for would-be reformers who are keen to inject more dynamism into government to dismiss the traditional style of bureaucratic rule-of-law decision-making as hopelessly old-fashioned and out of tune with the flexibility that modern organization, private and public, is often claimed to need in a fast-moving environment. Indeed, "From red tape to results" (the catchphrase of the "reinventing government" program introduced by Bill Clinton and Al Gore in the early 1990s (NPR 1993), or wording to that effect, is one of the most frequently invoked slogans of management reformers over the last generation. And one of the commonest sources of frustration with government and public services—now often satirized in art and literature—arises from tickbox procedures and the like that seem to be more driven by the imperatives of blame prevention re-engineering than by any other considerations. Familiar examples include police or social workers who seem to be buried under paperwork designed to protect themselves from blame and living a mainly screen-based existence in their offices defensively ticking procedural boxes rather than actively pursuing criminals or helping vulnerable clients.[4] Often the private sector is held up as a model of preferring 'results' to 'process' that government should follow.

But in spite of such recurring frustrations, the do-it-by-the-rules approach shows little signs of having retreated in the supposed age of "new public management" and indeed is often found to be extending in the very business sector that is held up as the shining example of results-oriented management by public sector reformers. For example, a decade or more ago, Michael Power (1997) pointed to widespread tendencies for public and private organizations to develop elaborate audit-trail procedures that establish a paper trail of due diligence in the face of possible blame or challenge, in fields such as risk management, health and safety management, environmental practices, security, and corporate governance. Power argues there is no evidence that such procedural "rituals," typically cranked up in the aftermath of every high-profile fiasco or collapse, make much difference to the incidence of corporate failure. But those rituals serve as tombstones to past disasters, and—more to the point for our analysis here—provide procedural armor against blame.

It is therefore perhaps not surprising that protocolization often figures large in policy domains with high blame risk, such as the handling of pedophile sex offenders on their release from custody or the protection of children from abuse by their parents or guardians. In a study by this author and his colleagues (Hood, Rothstein, and Baldwin 2001), the bureaucratic response to the UK's 1997 Sex Offenders Act was found to place heavy emphasis on formalizing the procedures for risk assessment. The study noted: "The ostensible purpose of these procedures was to improve decision-making, particularly in allocating scarce resources. They also served the important purpose ... of limiting blame, giving the ... bureaucracies a procedural excuse if registered offenders committed further offenses ...' (Hood, Rothstein, and Baldwin 2001: 158). And more recent work on social workers in England and Wales dealing with the protection of children also reveals a similar heavy emphasis on protocolization to limit exposure to blame, with the whole work process dominated by elaborate IT-driven documentation of quantitative risk assessments to be produced within tightly specified times of initial case referral of children in potential danger (see White et al. 2009).

Discretion can be removed from officeholders or operators by physical or electronic mechanisms as well as by rules, codes, or guidelines. Indeed, the logical conclusion of the protocolization approach, far from uncommon in the front-line blame avoidance world that we discussed in chapter 2, is to build the rules into machinery or computer software physically such that humans cannot readily override them. Such an approach relies on what Lawrence Lessig (2000) terms "architecture" as a mode of control. Designing decision processes that way produces systems that are "no hands" in a literal sense: if decisions are made by machines rather than by the exercise of human judgment, it is harder to attach blame to human agents (other than the usually anonymous system designers). Automatic fail-safe devices in transport are one example of such technical architecture, such as the "dead man's handle" that has been fitted to certain types of locomotives and subway cars since the 1880s and which causes a train to stop if the driver is not actively pressing on the handle. Other examples include devices that prevent the driver from starting a train if sensors detect someone leaning on the doors and physical systems designed to reduce medical error (so-called technoregulation). Thus single-use needles serve to prevent infections, and couplings are designed to prevent the wrong things from being connected—for example, to make it impossible to accidentally administer vincristine via the intrathecal (spinal) route, which is fatal (see Yeung and Dixon-Woods 2010).

Similarly, as was noted in chapter 2, software systems that do not allow users to leave blanks, enter contradictory information, access certain internet sites—even in some cases perform other tasks until deadlines have been met for unfinished tasks in hand—are among the growing number of ways in which discretion can be limited through information architecture. Another example, mentioned in chapter 1 and much developed over the past few decades, is the shift in grading students from an older system of judgment calls about their creative compositions or overall performance to computer-marked multiple-choice tests of academic proficiency, language ability, or factual knowledge. Assessments of the latter kind may or may not have pedagogical advantages over traditional forms of testing that rely on qualitative assessment by examiners—opinion will always be divided on that issue, with strong views on both side of the argument. But taking the human element out of quality assessment makes the results less vulnerable to blame and litigation about alleged bias, discrimination, or error.

While protocolization is the policy strategy equivalent of delegation in removing the possibility of blame for an individual's judgment (and is often used by front-line or middle-level players for whom delegation is not possible), it has the same sort of limits as the delegation approach to agency strategy. If blame avoidance is achieved by this approach, it comes at the price of loss of control by the players concerned, which may be inconvenient or worse in some circumstances—for example when it is impossible to reuse a single-use medical device (such as a needle) and nothing else is available. Similarly, a vehicle that will not let you start the engine unless the driver is wearing a seat belt might seem like a good idea for avoiding blame over those occasional slips or memory lapses that all mortals are subject to, but what if the seat belt is broken and the vehicle is urgently needed for some life-or-death mission?

The "nuclear option" of blame avoidance by building discretion out of control or decision systems is prone to producing such outcomes, because there will always be some individual cases in which a better outcome might have resulted if the rules had not been followed. Examples include those cases in which road accident victims would have been safer if the vehicles they were traveling in were not fitted with airbags (see Wiener 1998: 40n7) or patients would have survived if the standard medical care protocols had been departed from in their particular cases (for example, if a blood transfusion had been given even if two nurses were not available to take part in the procedure).

Protocols and automated decision procedures therefore reach their limits as blame avoidance devices when organizations or individuals come to attract as much blame for the inappropriateness of the rules they follow as they would for exercising their own "common sense" judgment. For instance, if protocolized systems such as the ever more elaborate security arrangements that have developed for air travel in recent times are pushed to the point that they are seen to be counter-productive, their blame avoidance potential may come to be lost.

Herding: Safety in Numbers

A second common type of policy or operational strategy consists of collective decision-making or group styles of working—staying with the herd, such that no individual's neck is ever on the block when things turn out badly. This approach is the procedural equivalent of the partnership approach in agency strategy discussed in the previous chapter. It is the basis of traditional cabinet-government systems of pooling political risk, following the principle (in a phrase commonly attributed to Benjamin Franklin) that "we must all hang together or we shall hang separately." Indeed, the blame-spreading potential of collective decision-making caused the utilitarian philosopher Jeremy Bentham to see boards as "screens." In his famous *Constitutional Code* (begun in the 1820s and left unfinished at the time of his death), Bentham argued for "functionaries no more than one" in each official situation, on the grounds that having more than one individual with decision-making authority readily enabled the actors to shift blame onto others and to evade blame for any unpopular decision by purposely absenting themselves from or not participating in the relevant meetings (Bentham 1983: 173–4). "On the present footing," he declared, referring to the pervasive system of management by boards in Britain in the early nineteenth century, "no one is responsible for any thing that he does' (Bentham 1983: 180).

The risk-reduction approach of safety in numbers can be followed at all levels and is therefore open to the top, middle, and frontline players in the risk avoidance worlds discussed in chapter 2 (and arguably to the noninstitutional players as well). Variants of it are commonly found within the world of bureaucracy as well as that of cabinet ministers and high-level board members. Sometimes it takes the form of informal clearance and consultation systems to ensure others are "on board" for some course of action that might attract blame down the line. Sometimes it consists of "benchmarking" of what the organization does so that it can be claimed to be following best practice (even though some heretics argue that benchmarking is all too apt to mean corporate mediocrity and conformity in practice [Frederickson 2003]). And sometimes it works through formal and elaborate collective decision procedures.

An example of the latter is the long-established practice of *ringi* in the Japanese bureaucracy. *Ringi* is the traditional convention that policy initiatives as they go up the line are signed off by all the relevant officials, starting with the most junior one at the bottom, such that everyone in the group is committed to the idea. A somewhat similar convention applied in the former Soviet Union (see Hood and Jackson 1991: 109), and it can be found in less elaborate forms in other bureaucratic organizations. Herding procedures of this kind comprise an intra-organizational variant of the partnership working agency strategy that we discussed in the previous chapter and thus verges on agency strategy. But where it differs is that procedural herding does not need to involve partnerships of several organizations or any delegation of responsibility to separate units.

Nor is the herding approach confined to high-level politicians or to the policy bureaucracy. Variants of it can often be seen on the front line and in specialist professional spheres as well, and when decisions cannot literally be made by machines (the extreme form of protocolization, as mentioned in the previous section), the herding approach of seeking safety in numbers offers an alternative route to dealing with blame. An example is the common practice of professionals undertaking group assessments of the risks faced or posed by individuals where the stakes can be high, as in the case of children at risk of abuse or in the case of pedophile offenders released from custody.

As mentioned in the previous chapter, the response to the difficult (and blame-loaded) problem of assessing how to deal with pedophile offenders released from custody in the UK after the passage of the 1997 Sex Offenders Act took the form of a partnership approach spanning a range of different organizations. The "policy strategy" equivalent of that approach within a single organization is to do all the difficult decision-making in teams. Academic practices that border on this territory and which will no doubt be all too familiar to student and scientific readers include the use of boards of examiners rather than a single professor to grade student performance, and in its extreme form the so-called double-blind multiple-reviewer approach to academic grading (meaning variously that reviewers and reviewed and/or different reviewers are made anonymous to one another). This approach is widely used for journal paper submissions and applications for grant funding, as well as for student examinations in some countries. A system of this type that mixes anonymity with multiple participants means that no single individual takes the blame for decisions that create losers, for example when laboriously written papers are rejected for publication, key examinations failed, prestigious prizes not awarded, high-stakes grant funding applications turned down. It can thus be seen as the herding equivalent to the no-hands computer-grading approach discussed in the previous section.

Staying with the group to avoid blame comes in other forms as well. One is to avoid any difference in policy or practice among potential rivals, or to follow the policies of previous officeholders (a tactic that works on the time element of blame that was mentioned in chapter 1). Some twenty years or so ago, Richard Rose and Terence Karran (1987) interpreted the common reliance of British governments on the tax policies of their predecessors as a blame avoidance strategy, and the continuing prevalence of so-called stealth taxes that follow this pattern suggests that Rose and Karran's analysis remains valid.[5] If negativity bias means that losers from any new tax measures will tend to be more active than the beneficiaries, the government-by-inertia route of simply following existing taxes with minor and non-transparent modifications may prove to be the least-blame policy option (especially where mechanisms such as fiscal drag can increase the tax yield with no apparent tax increases).

The same goes for reduction of welfare benefits. For instance, in his analysis of cutbacks in Swedish welfare benefits in the 1990s, Anders Lindbom (2007) has shown that those who were chipping away at the famous Swedish welfare model at that time also tended to avoid obvious changes of direction. Rather, the cuts took the form of small-print, non-transparent changes that could have large effects (such as letting inflation reduce the value of non-indexed benefits, manipulating the price index according to which welfare raises were calculated, changing the calculation of what counted as the "normal" wage on which benefits were based, and altering the details of qualification rules). He quotes a telling comment from a journalist who said, "It is hard to imagine a banner in a May 1st [Labor Day] demonstration with the text 'Supplementary wage benefits should be included in the basis for the calculation of sickness payment'" (Lindbom 2007: 136). He interprets these cutback strategies as largely shaped by blame avoidance considerations, since cutting welfare benefits that way did not visibly break with established entitlements and thus reduced the perceived harm element of blame.

In some cases, too, official or unofficial coalitions among otherwise competing political parties may be formed to push through potentially blame-attracting measures, from war mobilization to policies that benefit the political class as a group, such as parliamentary pension or pay increases. While the political science literature on blame avoidance over welfare state retrenchment (following in the wake of Paul Pierson's [1994] landmark study of American and British welfare cutbacks in the Reagan-Thatcher era of the 1980s) has argued that parties in government can find ways to avoid punishment from voters for welfare cutbacks without the need to form grand coalitions, that option is nevertheless sometimes taken. And informal collaboration over potentially blame-attracting measures is widely observable too, in several of the blameworlds we discussed in chapter 2. Well-known examples include those cases where transportation companies, banks, or energy utilities mysteriously all choose to raise their fares or charges at the same time, such that blame is faced collectively rather than individually. Herding does not remove blame, but it may blunt it by collectivizing it.

INDIVIDUALIZATION: BLAME THE OPERATOR, USER, OR VICTIM

The opposite of an all-for-one herding approach to blame avoidance is the scapegoat approach of individualizing blame rather than allowing it to be attributed to systems, powerful organizations, or those who direct them. As with the group strategy, that does not make blame disappear but rather works on the agency dimension to shape the distribution of blame and put the onus of blame onto some individuals and groups rather than others. It is about shifting rather than reducing or preventing blame.

As with herding and protocolization, this approach can take various forms. Familiar in the business world, but with many close relatives in the world of government, is the "disclaimer" device of putting the onus on users or operators of a product or service to inform themselves about its risks and to take appropriate precautions. We discussed this issue in chapter 2, in connection with the conflict between the fourth world of blame avoidance and the other, "official" worlds. Here the presumption is that if you as a customer did not carefully read and digest all the tortuous and legalistic clauses in that six-point mauve font on your cell phone contract or insurance policy, did not wear the recommended space suit for applying the pesticide product you innocently purchased, did not consult a medical practitioner before starting that diet or wonder exercise regime you saw advertised, did not realize that by clicking your mouse on a particular spot on your computer screen you were committing yourself to a legally binding twenty-five-year contract that could lose you your home, the blame and legal liability of any adverse effects on your health and wealth are all yours.

Where the liability of the user or purchaser ends and that of the supplier or manufacturer begins is much contested in the law, as we noted in chapter 2. (Those who believe in strict liability argue that manufacturers or providers should not be able to blame users or operators for not taking adequate care to mitigate their legal liability for harms caused, while critics of that view argue that it encourages users to bring lawsuits against providers for mishaps caused by their own carelessness [see Posner 1986:

160–7]). But in the wider world of blame, it is common for organizations and officeholders to try to find ways of pinning fault onto individuals in some way. For example, the European Union turned increasingly in the 1990s to approving pesticide products with elaborate user conditions attached, such as the wearing of protective clothing or the observation of buffer zones between the spray area and watercourses, rather than requiring manufacturers to make products that were safe to be used by ordinary error-prone mortals without doctoral degrees (see Hood, Rothstein, and Baldwin 2001: 120). Thomas Keefer, one of the characters in Herman Wouk's (1951) great novel *The Caine Mutiny*, describes the U.S. Navy as "a master plan designed by geniuses for execution by idiots." Blame individualization tactics often seem to imply a reversal of this approach.

Similarly, professionals and other workers can shift the blame for ill-advised treatment or service by putting their clients in the position of choosing among options, so that they later have only themselves to blame—for instance, if they opt to deal with a toothache by antibiotics rather than by extraction or vice versa. "Choice" can be a route to blame individualization too.

Perhaps the logical extension of the blame individualization approach is what can be called "blame for blame." That means putting the blame on the individual client or customer for any unpleasantness in his or her dealings with an organization, should voices come to be raised in the course of complaining about poor service. Of course, in authoritarian bureaucratic regimes those who make complaints about powerful organizations will automatically be branded as politically motivated troublemakers. But organizations can find ways of blaming the blamers in other contexts, too; as we noted in chapter 2, some organizations make it a policy not to tolerate any verbal or physical abuse of their staff by customers or clients. On the face of it, such policies seem unexceptionable, but if they are used to define almost every complaint as verbal abuse, the effect can be to make the individual client or customer take the blame for any organizational encounter that goes sour, however unreasonably those clients or customers have been treated and whatever obvious lies they have been told.

Closely related to the approach that puts the onus of blame onto the individual user or client is that of blaming frontline workers or operators for errors or malfunctions rather than those who design, control, or preside over the systems within which those operators have to work. In chapter 2, we noted this approach as a common way for the denizens of the first two blame avoidance worlds (top bananas and middle-level players) to shuffle blame for adverse events onto the front-line staff, even if the difficult conditions in which the latter have to work might be put down to acts of commission or omission by the higher-level corporate people.

A modern variant of this approach is the organizational mission statement, a corporate fad that began in the United States in the late 1980s and later came to be applied across the organizational world, from cathedrals to sandwich bars. Mission statements are commonly dismissed by skeptics as just another example of management-speak twaddle, insofar as they often involve impossibly sanctimonious or hyperbolic aspirations that no mere mortal could ever live up to. Holier-than-thou aims like total commitment to customer satisfaction or highest ethical standards will often contrast sharply with what happens on the ground, particularly when front-line staff are subject to importunate pressure from higher corporate levels or have to face stresses such as chronic understaffing, under-training, or dysfunctional software systems. But when something is done that attracts blame because it falls short of loftily proclaimed aspirations, the blame spotlight can be directed onto individual employees rather than onto the organization that professes its mission in such unexceptionable terms.[6]

Blame can be individualized within organizations in other ways as well. For example, it once seems to have been common in the British armed forces for young recruits to have been blamed for their illicit homosexual love affairs with those in higher ranks, as if the senior, more experienced officers were merely helpless victims of their subordinates' allure.[7] Equally, blame can sometimes be individualized in the other direction, when the bosses have to take the hit for the failures of others. Perhaps the most extreme example of "upward individualization" of blame is the traditional Chinese practice under the various imperial dynasties of blaming the emperor for natural disasters and other failures. That meant that the system of rule escaped blame while the individual at the top absorbed it (Hood 1998: 79). But while egalitarian pressures to blame the bosses of powerful organizations in the public and private sector are commonly observable in today's world, in the day-to-day playing of blame games, top bananas and middle-level players are likely to take vigorous steps to deflect blame downwards as well.

ABSTINENCE: JUST SAY NO

A fourth variant of policy strategy can be summed up as "just say no," to borrow a famous slogan used in the American war on drugs in the late 1980s and early 1990s. But in this case the abstinence comes from bureaucrats or politicians. That means choosing not to operate or provide facilities or services (including record-keeping) that attract blame or have the potential to do so. After all, if protocolization offers one route to blame avoidance, one logical alternative is to avoid keeping records, such that evidence of culpability becomes elusive. For instance, blame for the loss of seven of the eighteen men involved in the Burke and Wills expedition to cross Australia from south to north in 1860–1 was hard to pin down because Robert O'Hara Burke, the leader of the expedition, kept no regular journal and chose not to give written instructions to his officers. That made it difficult for those officers to later substantiate their blame-shifting claims that Burke had given them unsatisfactory or contradictory orders (see Moorehead 1963: 191).

Similarly, simply not providing services may sometimes attract less blame than any alternative. We have already noted that organizations and governments often find themselves in the line of fire for cutting down on what they provide, meaning they need to find low-visibility ways of shrinking benefits or cutting back on services. But sometimes the boot is on the other foot, and the policy route to blame avoidance may be seen to lie in abandonment or non-provision of services.

Even though we are often said to live in an age of hyperactive politicians and managers, blame avoidance considerations do sometimes dictate a "just say no" approach. In the commercial world, a familiar example is that of airlines withdrawing flights to destinations they deem to be too dangerous (and may be unprofitable as well, such that shutting them down saves money as well as the blame that may come from skyjacking or hostage-taking). The same goes for politics and public policy. When delegation or partnership is not available as a way of deflecting blame, it is far from unusual for governments to avoid altogether or give up activities that are seen as attracting too much blame from a significant body of voters.

For example, in 1838 the British government stopped collecting taxes (tithes, the traditional church tax) to support the established Protestant and Episcopal church in Ireland, as a result of nationalist and Roman Catholic resistance to a tax earmarked to benefit only a small minority of the population. The collection of this tax was also finally abandoned in England and Wales nearly a century later after a long period of protest, particularly by Welsh nonconformists.[8] Abandonment of official rationing systems for goods in short supply and the lifting of the requirement for compulsory vaccination of infants in the UK after World War II are other cases in point. More recent examples are the West Australian government's efforts to stop providing any services to the former asbestos-mining town of Wittenoom by closing down its approach roads and cutting off electricity, water, and telephone lines,[9] and the UK Met Office's abandonment of quarterly seasonal weather forecasts in 2010 after heavy criticism of its spectacularly inaccurate seasonal forecasts for the summer of 2009 and the winter of 2009/10.

Similarly, in a crisis, the provision of advice and information about such things as the safety of drinking water or travel facilities often turns into a potential blame minefield. In those conditions, organizations' established routine announcements have to be abandoned, and when the blame risk of giving false information has to be balanced against the blame risk of saying nothing at all, the latter option is often chosen. That is what is highlighted by our second "can't do nothing and … can't say nothing" epigraph from Tom Wolfe about poverty bureaucrats beleaguered by the radical activists of the 1960s.

Why do it if it is simply going to attract blame? Well, apart (of course) from all the frailties of human nature, what will obviously limit this "just say no" approach is the possibility of blame coming from the opposite direction. A government that avoided blame by not collecting any taxes would find itself being blamed for not being able to act or spend when there were pressing reasons for doing so. Politicians who avoided blame from irate taxpayers by not drawing any salaries or allowances for themselves from the public purse would still have to hold body and soul together somehow, and might find themselves blamed even if they begged on the streets, let alone took other jobs or accepted handouts from wealthy corporate or individual backers. A pacifist government that never sent any troops into battle would certainly escape blame for avoidable deaths in ill-judged military operations, but it might find itself in the dock for avoidable tragedies caused by lack of armed intervention (for example, to prevent genocide such as that occurring in Rwanda in 1994 while the rest of the world looked on).

Likewise, a government that never forcibly took children away from their parents or guardians would escape blame for the harm caused by all those false positives when such actions are based on mistakes or the unlucky children come to a worse fate in official care. But it would be unlikely to escape blame for failure to act to prevent tragedy when children are killed or damaged by abusive parents or guardians. Even those leaders who follow a simple doing-without way of life (to avoid blame for living off the fat of the land at the taxpayers' expense) can find themselves under fire from some quarters for bringing their office or their country into disrespect by an excessively mean or modest lifestyle.

To capture this blame-blame problem we can adapt a figure from John Graham and Jonathan Weiner's (1995) analysis of the "risk protection frontier," to produce a "blame avoidance frontier" (BAF), as shown in figure 5.1. This analysis is based on the assumption that for every source of blame there is a countervailing form of blame (such as blame for sins of commission versus sins of omission). In such conditions, the choice of policy strategies for blame avoidance is a matter of finding the optimum point on a production possibility frontier (a concept taken from microeconomics to mean the combinations of alternative goods—in this case blame avoidance gambits—that can be provided with efficient use of the

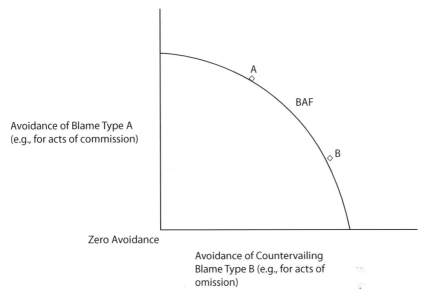

Figure 5.1. Policy Strategies and Their Limits: The Blame Avoidance Frontier (BAF). Source: Adapted from Weiner 1998: 43.

finite resources available). This analysis is of course simplified to a two-dimensional world in which there are only two possible sources of blame.

In a world of the type represented in figure 5.1, where the no-blame policy option is lacking, the logic of blame avoidance implies a search for the least-blame policy option rather than a no-blame outcome. A policy strategy has to be selected somewhere along the BAF shown in that figure, weighing up the relative importance of avoiding blame for any given action against that of the countervailing action at that particular point in time. So in principle we might expect each policy approach (protocolization, herding, individualization, abstinence) to be pursued up to the no-win point[10]—i.e., to the point at which any further development of the policy approach to avoid blame from one quarter will attract an exactly equivalent amount of blame from another quarter. When that no-win position is indeed reached, we reach the limits of being careful as well as being good.

THE SCOPE AND LIMITS OF POLICY STRATEGIES FOR BLAME AVOIDANCE

Considered as a blame avoidance enterprise, the design of policies and operational procedures involves a balancing of upside and downside political risk that is equivalent to that involved in the delegate-or-direct decision that we discussed for agency strategies in chapter 3. From a conventional rational-choice perspective as developed by the Chicago school of government theorists[11] in the 1960s and 1970s, politicians are assumed to select policies for what government should do or how it should do it according to support-maximizing electoral calculations, with support weighed both directly in terms of likely votes and indirectly in terms of campaign contributions and other support. Given that any potential policy or operational procedure is likely to involve winners and losers, officeholders are assumed to make a calculus of votes and other political benefits to be gained and lost from alternative policy choices they could make. They weigh up the expected gratitude of the likely beneficiaries from each option as against the expected vindictiveness of the likely maleficiaries, and pick the policy option with the greatest expected benefit.

In making such calculations, elected politicians are conventionally assumed to take into account the ease or otherwise with which those various beneficiaries or maleficiaries can mobilize organized support or opposition. The ease or difficulty of mobilization is expected to depend on factors such as whether winners or losers are socially or geographically diffused or concentrated (Wilson 1980: 357–74), whether the loss or gain to each of the parties involves high or low stakes, and how visible or transparent those gains or losses are to beneficiaries or maleficiaries. The latter two factors are directly related to the harm perception dimension of blame, and as we saw earlier, the transparency of losses and gains is central to Anders Lindbom's account of how cuts in Swedish welfare state benefits were made in the 1990s. Such transparency can change over time, as is shown by Charlotte Twight's (1991) study of Congressional policy on the use of asbestos over the course of a century. Twight argues that the changing policy stance of the legislature in this domain (from an original position in support of the risk creators—the asbestos industry—to a later position in support of risk victims) was crucially governed by the way information about the dangers of asbestos to health became more widely known and the policy losers became more informed about their losses, with consequent effects on group mobilization.

Even starting from such relatively simple (many will say simplistic) rational assumptions that portray political choice as a sort of computer program rather than a product of habit or ideology, the necessary calculations needed to choose policy under those assumptions are often exceedingly complex and difficult, particularly once we factor uncertainty into the process.[12] Moreover, as with the direct-or-delegate decision over agency strategies, considerations of risk immediately further complicate any such computation. After all, as we saw in the first chapter, policies can have unintended outcomes as they are implemented, meaning that who wins and who loses may be far from easy to tell in advance. And gratitude, in politics as everywhere else, does not necessarily translate into actual votes or other forms of political support. Beneficiaries may just silently pocket their gains or even bite the hand that feeds them.

Indeed, once negativity bias enters the picture, the potential blame losses in any calculus of political gains and losses under alternative policy choices may need to be weighted more heavily than the potential credit benefits. That means that, as with the direct-or-delegate decision that we discussed for agency strategies in the last chapter, a defensive (blame-avoiding) approach to policy will often dominate more expansive (credit-claiming) approaches, and the sorts of defensive policy strategies we have discussed earlier will be pursued, irrespective of the welfare effects on voters at large.

A parallel can be drawn with the phenomenon of defensive medicine, which came into everyday language in the USA to denote the behavior of medical practitioners after the judicial liberalization of the rules governing the law of medical practice in some states in the 1960s. With the relaxation of earlier requirements for expert testimony in court and reinterpretation of the statute of limitations, it was easier for patients to prove malpractice by their doctors (Duke Law Journal 1971: 941).[13] That produced a situation in which doctors and other health professionals often felt they had to choose methods of diagnostic testing or treatment primarily according to what would minimize the risk of liability or compensation suits being subsequently brought against them. Defensive medicine is controversial, because as well as sharply raising overall costs of health care, it may mean taking courses of action that have no medical benefit or that may cause actual harm to the particular patients that doctors treating, as in cases of unnecessary medication or surgery.

Defensive medicine has its parallels in many other fields of policy. Indeed, the greater the real or perceived negativity bias in the population at large, the more policy selection in general is likely to move toward a defensive approach to choosing procedures, goals, and service provision. Such moves are intended to protect institutions or individuals against blame in what is assumed to be a threatening environment, rather than an expansive interest-aggregative stance (designed to produce a winning coalition at the expense of policy losers). That is what can account for some of the otherwise puzzling observations that we noted in the first chapter.

If we think of policy defensiveness as a ladder, we will find weaker forms of the approaches discussed in this chapter on the lower rungs. Examples might include soft best-practice guidelines (for protocolization), relatively informal consultation (for herding), unexceptionable mission statements (for individualization), and marginal policy and procedure changes such as not making any announcements in a crisis (for abstinence). Somewhere on the middle rungs may be found approaches such as more formulaic decision rules, *ringi*-type practices, disclaimers, and medium-scale service or policy abandonment. The topmost rungs comprise automatic decision systems that humans cannot override (the blame-avoiders' equivalent of the chastity belt rather than the vow of chastity), all-for-one committee decision-making with unanimity rules, and wholesale abandonment of services or other fields of activity that are perceived as magnets attracting more blame than credit. As the going gets tough, we can expect organizations and officeholders to move to higher levels of defensiveness in their choice of policy and operational strategies.

But do policy strategies for blame avoidance actually work? What is the scope of such strategies and what are their limits? What side effects or reverse effects can they have? Systematic tests of the efficacy of such strategies are few and far between. But, as we have seen, scholars such as Power (1997, 2007) and McGivern (2007) have suggested that protocolization and checklists or box-ticking can provide organizations with defenses against blame. Political scientists such as Rose and Karran (1987) and Lindbom (2007) have argued that a herding approach that involves only apparent small-print tinkering with previous practice can help elected governments to avoid being punished by voters for tax increases or retrenchment of welfare benefits.

Much of this work is qualitative, dependent on accounts of selected cases. We lack evidence anywhere approaching the randomized trials standard, and the political science work mostly does not tell us about the efficacy of policy strategies for avoiding blame in the middle-level and front-line blameworlds discussed in chapter 2.

Nevertheless, it seems safe to draw three broad conclusions about the scope and limits of the policy approach to blame avoidance.

Damned If You Do and Damned If You Don't: When Blame for Commission Equals Blame for Omission

First, the limits of policy strategy are reached when we arrive at the blame-blame frontier in figure 5.1—the point at which damned-if-you-do and damned-if-you-don't reach exactly equal levels of damnation for organizations and officeholders and there is no longer any no-blame or low-blame option available. For instance, if you follow exactly the same policy as everyone else, you may escape being singled out for particular blame, but the corresponding price you pay is that of being blamed for being as bad as all the others, tarred with the same brush, and seen as part of some culpable system or establishment. If you do everything by the book, you may also avoid standing out as guilty of irregular conduct and no one can throw the book at you. But the price you pay is that of at best being seen

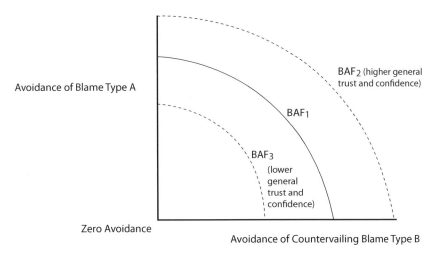

Figure 5.2. Movable Frontiers of Blame Avoidance. Source: Adapted from Weiner 1998: 43.

as mediocre and unadventurous, at worst as being at fault for failing to resist the dictates of an unconscionable regime. Somewhere in the middle is the prospect of being blamed for failure to use discretion and common sense when the rules you have chosen to stick to are patently inappropriate to the situation in hand—as when police clamp the wheel of ambulances that have stopped in a no-parking zone in a serious emergency, or when banks refuse services to individuals with no arms because they cannot produce a signature or thumbprint,[14] to take two cases that came into the news while this book was being written.

Now the production-possibility frontier analysis that we drew on in Figure 5.1 is conventionally used in economics to make the point that if more efficient or productive methods can be developed, the whole curve can be pushed outward so that more of good A can be produced with less corresponding sacrifice of B or vice versa. In principle, the same thing applies to the blame-blame problem represented in figure 5.1, and that is shown in figure 5.2. After all, if officeholders or organizations can improve the level of trust and confidence that the population as a whole places in them, they may indeed be able to push out the blame avoidance frontier in an analogous way, as is shown by the BAF_2 curve in figure 5.2, so that the blame trade-offs become less restrictive. But of course the reverse can also apply, in that if general trust and confidence fall, the blame avoidance frontier may move inwards, with officeholders attracting blame at lower thresholds, as is shown by the BAF_3 curve. They hit the damned-if-you-do-and-damned-if-you-don't point at a lower level.

When Policy Strategies Have Unintended Side Effects
or Reverse Effects

A second general conclusion is that policy strategies aimed at reducing blame can produce numerous unintended side effects or reverse effects, such as increasing public cynicism. For example, herd approaches to dealing with blame on the part of political parties or high officeholders (in the form of bipartisanship over sensitive issues like pay or the following of existing policy frameworks so that current officeholders can lay the blame on their predecessors) may only serve to fan the flames of public disillusion and disaffection with politics and government in general. If that happens, such policy strategies may unintentionally help to encourage anti-system plague-on-all-your-houses political parties in politics, a growth in "none-of-the-above" public attitudes toward politicians as a group when it comes to voting, and general disaffection with all forms of public authority among the citizenry.

Such developments are indeed a notable feature of politics in many democracies in recent years, with voting turnout tending to decline over time, apparently falling public respect for politics and government, and a growth of anti-system parties that challenge the establishment (such as the anti-immigration party formed in the Netherlands by Pim Fortuyn, who was assassinated in 2002 on the eve of a general election, Jean-Marie Le Pen's Front National, which reached the final round of the 2002 French presidential elections, and Jorg Haider's Austrian Freedom Party, which won substantial numbers of votes from the established Social Democrats and Conservatives in the late 1990s). Such developments may be an ironic and unintended effect of the very blame-avoidance strategies that the political class and administrative elite have developed to ward off criticism.

When Things Get So Bad That Defensive Medicine Turns
into Defensive Driving

Third, the limits of blame-avoidance policy may come when things get so bad that personal survival rather than avoidance of blame becomes the main consideration for the players involved. Earlier we likened blame-avoiding policy and operational strategies to the practice of defensive medicine, where treatment is driven by the overriding aim of avoiding blame and litigation. But at a certain point of hostility, the practice of defensive driving may come to be a more accurate analogy. The idea of defensive driving, a term said to have originated as far back as the 1920s, when phrases such as road rage had not yet been coined, normally refers to behavior that is primarily designed to ensure the survival of the driver in what is assumed to be a hostile and dangerous environment.[15] Defensive drivers are trained, among other things, to always assume the worst in other drivers, to maintain an exit route in all circumstances, to use bulky four-wheel-drive vehicles rather than flimsier cars to provide themselves with greater protection against collision, and to avoid road rage by not having tinted windows or other distinctive features on their cars that might provoke anger or resentment from other road users. To protect themselves against the downside risks, such drivers give up potential upside advantages of other ways of getting from A to B (such as time saving at least in the short term, the lower cost and possibly green advantages that might come from using lighter vehicles, and maybe the psychological gratification that can be gained from letting emotions out, or being the center of attention).

As with driving, there is a point at which defensiveness in policy moves away from blame avoidance altogether and officeholders start to concentrate on ensuring their own physical safety and that of their families, regardless of the blame they may incur. That can happen in those crisis or disaster situations when those who are responsible for providing the coping services (such as the crew and other operators of emergency services) choose to concentrate on saving themselves and their families regardless of the blame that may come to them. It can happen when officeholders start walling themselves and their families off from the population at large, living and working in bunkers or other heavily fortified buildings to protect themselves from attack from their enemies, and trading what they believe to be personal safety for blame avoidance. After all, the ultimate defensive driving strategy is to drive a tank and stop worrying about what other road users think—up to the point when everyone else *also* starts driving tanks, of course. So blame-avoiding policy strategies are evidently not adopted in all situations, particularly when we move outside democratic politics or into life-or-death emergencies. It is only when physical survival does not have to be traded against avoidance of public censure that blame avoidance is likely to drive policy.

CHAPTER SIX

The Institutional Dynamics of Blameworld: A New Teflon Era?

> The Western world has lost its civil courage, both as a whole and separately, in each country, each government, each political party, and of course in the United Nations. Such a decline in courage is particularly noticeable among the ruling groups and the intellectual elite, causing an impression of loss of courage by the entire society.
> —Extract from Alexander Solzhenitsyn's address to Harvard University's Class Day Afternoon Exercises, June 8, 1978[1]

> Ce bureaucratisme tâtillon et formaliste, cette Administration papassière ... (this finicky and formalistic bureaucracy, this form-filling administration)
> —French Comité du Plan 1936, quoted in Legendre 1968: 43

Introduction: Arrows or Circles?

The last three chapters delved into the three broad strategies for blame avoidance that were identified in chapter 1. If you believe, like the famous nuclear physicist Ernest Rutherford,[2] that "all science is either physics or stamp-collecting," you can think of those chapters as a sort of stamp collection, since they catalogue an assortment of types of blame avoidance and some variants around each of the three basic strategies. And blame avoidance is after all a domain in which even the most basic kind of stamp collecting is hard enough, never mind anything approaching physics.

Still, there are clearly questions to be asked about the general direction of travel in blameworld. Are we moving ever more deeply into a Teflon age in politics and bureaucracy, with blame becoming more difficult to pin down as the agency, presentational, and policy strategies sketched out in the previous chapters become more deeply embedded in organizational routines at every level and taken to new levels of slippery sophistication? Or is blame actually harder for individuals and organizations to avoid in modern information-rich societies with the rise of blame entrepreneurs or fear entrepreneurs (Frank Furedi's term, as noted in chapter 1), a declining propensity to attribute adverse events to acts of God rather than human agency, and twenty-four-hour news media desperate to fill space and attract viewers? Is blame a greater risk in societies with a commentariat that picks over every politician's and government's statement, as if it can be taken for granted that in such utterances nothing is ever quite what it seems? Or again, is blame better seen as a case of *plus ça change, plus c'est la même chose* (the more things change, the more they remain the same), where the fundamentals of the blame game remain fairly constant?

At first sight, all of these ideas have some plausibility. If we start with the *plus c'est la même chose* idea (as a null hypothesis, in scientific language), everything turns on what exactly we choose to count as fundamentals and unchanging. If we take the contrasting idea that blame avoidance is changing (with blame becoming either more difficult or easier to avoid for some or all of the institutional players discussed in chapter 2), we find that hard evidence is in much shorter supply than loose assertions. That problem has its equivalents in many other areas of social life, where "circle theories" about change or persistence vie with "arrow theories."[3] Arrow theories, such as the late Alexander Solzhenitsyn's doom-laden diagnosis of a long-term loss of courage in the western countries as quoted in the first epigraph, posit a one-way street in development. Circle theories of the *plus ça change* ... variety posit patterns of recurrence and return, with no single or unilinear direction of travel. And after all, as the second epigraph reminds us, there is nothing new in complaints about formalistic paper-chasing bureaucracy.

There are many possible variants of both circle and arrow patterns in blameworld. For instance, some of the players we identified in chapter 2 might experience more circle-like or arrow-like changes than others. But rather than spelling out all those possible combinations, this chapter looks at the three types of blame avoidance strategy discussed in the previous three chapters, identifies what might be changing over time in the way each of those strategies are institutionalized in modern government and corporate life, and explores what the implications are for the four sets of players we discussed earlier.

PRESENTATIONAL DEVELOPMENTS: MASTERING THE MEDIA UNIVERSE
  OR RUNNING TO KEEP UP?

Is the presentational approach to blame avoidance (as discussed in chapter 3) one of those constants in political and organizational life, or something that has changed beyond recognition over the last generation or so? And have the spin doctors of the information age gotten more powerful weapons for deflecting blame than their predecessors of a few decades ago?

As to the first question, the answer seems to be: both. There are obviously some constants. After all, Aristotle was spelling out the fundamentals of the rhetorical arts nearly two millennia ago. Dodging blame by weasel words and impression management has no doubt always been central to politics and institutional leadership, even though the curious English term "weasel words" to denote deliberate imprecision of language designed to mislead readers or listeners seems to date back only about a century (see Hart and Ferleger 1989 [1941]: 645). Indeed, as was shown by the example given in chapter 3 about blame avoidance for the heavy loss of life when the liner *Titanic* sank in 1912, there is nothing new about tactics such as the creation of diversions to take public attention away from other matters, or about backdoor pressure on news media. The term "spin doctor" may be a recent coinage but much of the activity it connotes is far from new. Anyone who thinks that government by spin is a new phenomenon needs to recall earlier instances such as Josef Goebbels' notorious Ministry of Propaganda and National Enlightenment in Nazi Germany seven decades or so ago (see, for instance, Broszat 1981: 115) and its counterparts among both the Allied and other Axis states. Indeed, Bernard Ingham (2003: 40), Margaret Thatcher's chief press secretary, points out that the World War II Ministry of Information in Britain employed far more people (over 6000 at its peak) than any government in the modern so-called age of spin.

But there are clearly at least three elements that are new as well. One is the much discussed expansion of the number of media outlets over the last generation—from the 1970s world dominated by newspapers and a few, mostly nationally specific, TV and radio channels operating on a daily news cycle, through the cable TV era, into an ever expanding universe of new communications channels from traditional print media to text messaging and the internet world of websites, podcasts, and the "blogosphere"—the so-called 24/7 media world with many more players and in continuous operation. Such developments may mean that sometimes less may hang on performance on any single media outlet than in the past, but they also mean that presentational blame avoidance wars have to be fought across a much longer frontier than before.

Second, the same new world of information technology produces new kinds of blame risk in the form of new sources of blameworthy action or incidents. Such sources include those indiscreet texts or e-mails that can be much more easily misdirected and rapidly broadcast to the world at large than their paper or telephone age equivalents—so often a feature of embarrassing revelations about personal indiscretions by the great and the good or about the conduct of policy (as with the 2001 "bury bad news" e-mail discussed in chapter 3). In that sort of communications environment, top officeholders have to be careful about using the trusty "no one told me" excuse. The sources of potential blame today include a range of organizational websites far more easily scanned and searched than their paper-age equivalents for inconsistencies or other kinds of potentially embarrassing information. Another common information-age source of potential blame is loss or abuse of individuals' digitized personal data by carelessness, malice, corruption, or by all those computer foul-ups and software failures (for example, over payment systems or screening systems) that can make some kinds of public services go off the rails more quickly, dramatically, and comprehensively than in a pre-digital age.

Third, those same developments produce new opportunities for presentational blame avoidance and credit-claiming activity as well. After all, more media outlets operating on a twenty-four-hour cycle offer more potential routes for the creation of diversions and more competitors to be played off against one another, to say nothing of the possibilities offered by today's technology for governments and officeholders to put out their message directly to individuals rather than having it filtered by news media. The presentational tactic of attacking individual journalists rather than unfriendly newspapers or the media at large, said by Craig Crawford (2005) to be a new departure in U.S. presidential spin tactics dating from the first Reagan term (though an ever-present phenomenon in authoritarian regimes) may be facilitated by greater competition among journalists.

As we noted in chapter 3, the age of modern communications also offers convenient new ways for instant rewriting of history by removing suddenly embarrassing material from official websites, and new technology for keeping groups willing to use it "on message" in the sense of being able to give the same account of events (see, for instance, Norris et al. 1999). It may present new opportunities for behind-the-scenes control of potential sources of blame—for example, by slowing the speed of the internet (by apportioning less bandwidth to internet connection providers) to put difficulties in the way of critical bloggers and hostile activists, as the government of Iran was said to have done in the face of protests following its contested election in 2009.[4] And indeed modern technology offers new kinds of potential excuses as well; after all, the "it's the computer" excuse and the infinity of modern variants thereon (from the wrong version of a file being inadvertently chosen to various forms of "system down" excuses) were not available to our great-grandparents' generation.

Against that background, we might expect to find greatly increased numbers engaged in presentational activity in the corporate and governmental world over that generation, and the development of new institutions or techniques for monitoring and managing the media world to keep blame at bay. There has indeed been much discussion of such developments in media control, polling, and focus-group activity in political management over the past two decades, as noted in chapter 3. And Alasdair

Roberts (2006a and 2006b) found that in many of the government systems he studied in a comparative analysis of the impact of Freedom of Information laws across a set of developed democracies, there were attempts at institutionalizing substantially tighter central control of politically sensitive information. That control took the form of more rigorous central clearance and risk classification systems than before, contrary to the rhetoric of 'a new culture of openness' that tended to accompany those laws.

Government's presentational activity seems to have changed in size and shape over recent decades, though getting a firm analytic grip on the relevant numbers can be difficult. For instance, in the 1950s Dwight Eisenhower's media and public relations staff amounted to just three professionals—barely one per cent of the White House office staff at that time. By the time of Bill Clinton in the 1990s, there had been a more than thirteenfold increase to over fifty such staff—comprising well over ten per cent of the total White House office staff, and indeed as much as a third by some estimates (Hess 1998: 751). Those numbers had risen further to over sixty working for Barack Obama in 2009.[5] The accommodation within the White House that was given over to dealing with the media grew over that time from a space no larger than a typical hotel room on the edge of the West Wing lobby to a substantial briefing room that was central to the operations of the presidential machine.[6]

The numbers dealing with the media for the Prime Minister in No. 10 Downing Street have also increased substantially over that period, from a handful of people to well over thirty at the height of Tony Blair's spin phase, if special advisers (political civil servants) are included in that category (Ingham 2003: 244).[7] Indeed, the sharply rising costs of the No. 10 Press Office were often criticized by political opponents during Tony Blair's premiership as evidence of the emphasis placed on spin doctoring by that regime, though, needless to say, the numbers turn out to be elusive and ever-changing.[8]

But more broadly, the overall number of staff working on communications in the UK central government does not seem to have risen greatly—or possibly at all—over the last thirty years (though various changes in the administrative basis of counting over that time make exact comparisons impossible, of course).[9] Indeed, it might be argued that the high point of the British central government's media management effort came not so much in the much-vaunted spin world of the last few decades as in the general strike of 1926, when the government went to the length of producing its own national newspaper, the *British Gazette*, to put across its viewpoint on the strike, or during the World War II period, when government's secret war operation (the Special Operations Executive) undertook "black" (unacknowledged) propaganda designed to change American public opinion about neutrality in the war (Mackenzie 2002), and it employed heavy-duty machinery to both gauge and shape domestic public opinion (Ogilvy-Webb 1965). What seems to have changed in the more recent period is a move of communications people away from a central government-wide agency toward location around the prime minister, cabinet ministers, and other top executives in government and more deployment of those communications staff in blame-dodging activity over politically embarrassing stories. More of the top-level communications staff had become political or quasi-political appointees rather than regular career civil servants of the traditional type. They had become more highly paid and more politically weighty in policy and operations within government, too (see Oborne 1999; Jones 1999).[10]

How general such developments are is not easy to tell (for instance, little or no growth seems to have taken place in the establishment of the German federal chancellor, whose press corps seems to have been more stable in numbers and funding for decades, perhaps reflecting continuing reluctance to follow anything approximating the Ministry of Propaganda in the Nazi era). How we interpret those developments is debatable too. After all, even in those areas where the numbers of staff clearly did increase markedly, such as in the White House, it is not clear whether the growth amounted to more than (or even as much as) running to stand still, given the growth of the media frontier along which blame attacks could come, as discussed earlier. That twentyfold increase in the presidential PR staff over fifty years has to be set against the growth of the media over that time from a handful of newspapers to a world of hundreds of cable or internet channels drawing stories from a burgeoning blogosphere, and an environment in which reporters had to work with extreme speed to avoid being scooped by another source. In the face of those developments, it might well be argued that government's presentational capacity is barely keeping pace with the expansion in the number of media points from which blame can originate, and might even have declined in relative terms.

AGENCY DEVELOPMENTS AND DELEGATION:
GROWING, DECLINING, FLATLINING?

Chapter 4 showed that agency strategies for blame avoidance—particularly through delegation—have a long history both in theory and practice. As noted there, Niccolò Machiavelli wrote about such delegation in the sixteenth century, Jeremy Bentham wrote about boards as screens for blame in the late eighteenth and early nineteenth century, and in the 1930s William Robson (1937: 59, quoted by Flinders 2004: 744) commented,

"Politicians of every creed, when confronted with an industry or a social service which is giving trouble ... almost always propose the establishment of an independent public board."

But it is often assumed or implied that there is something new about delegated bodies and quangos as ways of shielding high officeholders from blame. For example, Gary Marks and Liesbet Hooghe (2004: 15) open a discussion of multi-level governance by asserting a general tendency across the EU countries for formal authority to be dispersed from central states both up to supranational institutions and down to regional and local governments over the 1980s and 1990s. Within the UK, the campaigning NGO Democratic Audit claimed a decade or so ago that there had been a "huge explosion of unelected, untouchable, and often invisible activity" in the shadow of government (Hall and Weir 1996: 80), and in the 2000s similar claims were being made about the development of intergovernmental organizations (see, for instance, Vibert 2007). Such claims would imply that something arrow-like rather than circular was going on in the use of delegated bodies, whether to shield officeholders from blame or for other reasons.

In fact, if we look back, we can find similar claims being made over a long period. In Britain, the same refrain about rampant growth of quasi-government bodies diffusing political responsibility away from elected officeholders can be found in the 1918 report of the Haldane Committee on the Machinery of Government and in the report of the Anderson Committee on the Machinery of Government, established in 1942 (see Lee 1977). Writing in 1950, Arthur Street (1950: 159) referred to "a proliferation of quasi-government bodies of all kinds—boards, authorities, commissions, councils, committees, corporations, and executives.' A decade later, Lord Reith, the first Director-General of the BBC, who in his early years had championed the quasi-autonomous public corporation as a recipe for nonpartisan public service with effective leadership, thought this form of organization had been turned into a mechanism for blame avoidance.[11] The same perception that such bodies were growing uncontrollably and being used to undermine accountability can be found in the 1970s and 1980s, after the term quango had been coined.[12]

Now for an arrow theorist, the recurrence of such claims over more than half a century might suggest that we are indeed witnessing a one-way street in the development of blame-avoiding quasi-government bodies, if every generation perceives a growth in their incidence. But a circle theorist might argue that the persistence of the growth story over time merely means that there have always been a lot of such organizations around, albeit taking different institutional forms over time. Can we resolve that puzzle by turning to numbers about change over time?

Only up to a point, it seems. Indeed, the available numbers prove to be far less clear-cut in supporting an arrow story than some of the claims about explosive growth in such institutions might lead us to believe. Nineteenth century physicists like Pierre-Simon Laplace and James Clerk Maxwell invented "demons" or hypothetical beings that had the power to gather data that could prove or disprove key theoretical claims that were beyond the measurement capacity of scientists of that time (and still are, in some cases). Likewise, a quango demon that could help us to resolve whether the resort to delegated bodies for blame avoidance or other purposes was a circle or an arrow phenomenon would need to know at least three things. It would be able to distinguish the cosmetic from the substantive, and to identify organizations that look as if they are private or independent but are actually creatures of government (the original meaning of quango). It would be able to reliably divine the conscious or semiconscious political motives for the creation or maintenance of organizations in and around government. And it would be able to trace change over time, seeing through or around the numerous changes in the statistical basis of official counts or classifications of types of organization. A hypothetical observer of that type could readily resolve the circle-vs.-arrow issue.

The problem is that neither official nor nonofficial estimators come even close to possessing such knowledge. Political scientists are ingenious at developing comparative indices of many aspects of government and politics, but as yet we have no well-developed index of deliberately contrived autonomy in the organization of executive government that would answer the question as to what is happening to delegation for blame avoidance. So conclusions about long-term changes in the number of such bodies, and in the spending and patronage power they represent, depend heavily on what and how you choose to count.[13]

For example, in the UK there is a yawning gap between the claims made by opposition parties or campaigning groups and what official statistics say about changes in the number of so-called non-departmental public bodies at the national level since figures were first collected on that subject some thirty years ago. And that gap is not a nice difference of a few percentage points that could be ignored by anyone except the expert number-crunchers who make a living out of wrangling over such things: the numbers differ by a factor of ten or so and show diametrically opposite patterns of change.[14] If you look at the official numbers, you will be prompted to ask, "Where have all the quangos gone?" and to conclude that British politicians must have become less risk-averse over that generation and consequently more inclined to direct rather than delegate. If you look at alternative sources, you will arrive at exactly the opposite questions and conclusions.

We might think that such uncertainty as to whether formal delegation in government is growing, declining, or flatlining was a peculiarly British mess,[15] reflecting the characteristically indefinite nature of British institutions. And indeed there are some countries where the administrative system can be reliably traced over time, as in Norwegian studies that seem to show a discernable increase in the number of autonomous state bodies from the 1940s to the early 2000s.[16] But for many other countries it seems to be equally hard to find clear-cut numbers for the changing incidence of delegated bodies over time. Though much academic effort has been put into attempts at comparison, Christopher Pollitt and Colin Talbot (2004: 28, 45) observed some years ago in a book whose title referred to a "Global Trend to Agencies and Quasi-Autonomous Bodies" that while it is frequently claimed that there is a long-term trend to increasing delegation from the core of government to other bodies in a range of countries, that trend is more often asserted than carefully demonstrated. The problem is that any such demonstration has to rest on observations of administrative data over time or on periodic surveys, and both methods have severe limitations.

Analyzing administrative data to try to get at change over time presents at least three problems. First, such data rarely correspond to the analytic categories that our imaginary quango demon would be able to discern. For example, they will by definition tend to leave out quangos in the original sense of bodies that are nominally private or independent but are in fact agencies of government, as in the case of front companies often used in the cloak-and-dagger world of security and intelligence. And indeed if what we are trying to get at is organizations that are instruments of government operating at arms-length, there will inevitably be "coder bias" issues in what we take to be an instrument of government. For instance, should religious and charitable foundations be counted as delegated bodies in some sense,[17] or as independent bodies that may sometimes share purposes with government? Administrative data will rarely reflect such important nuances.

Second, official statistics are seldom recorded in a consistent enough form over time to allow long-term developments to be charted reliably. And even if such data did not present the first two problems, anyone trying to gauge the incidence of such organizations serving as instruments of government over time has to wrestle with how to cope with institutional mergers, conglomerates, and re-badging exercises. Are conglomerate organizations to be taken as a single unit or as multiple ones? If what is officially taken as a single conglomerate at one point in time is taken as multiple separate units at another, should we try to recreate the original units, or take the change in the counting method as reflecting a change in political reality? How do we deal with mergers, shifts in formal status, and moves from one level of government to another? Such judgment calls are pervasive and difficult, and can have major implications for the numbers any count will throw up.

The alternative to trying to wrestle with historical series of administrative data to get at population numbers for such instruments of government is to take a survey of such bodies at a given point in time, and that has been done for several countries. But that approach is far from problem-free too, because any such survey will be contaminated by the omission of "deaths" in the bureaucracy unless it involves recurrent analysis over time, and that is hard to do. For example, a picture of unambiguous growth in numbers of quangos in the Netherlands throughout the second half of the twentieth century is painted by Sandra van Thiel (2001), drawing on a survey of national-level independent public bodies conducted by the Netherlands Court of Audit in the early 1990s and a longer-term historical study by the Scientific Council for Government Policy a decade earlier. But both sets of data rest on analyzing the composition of a set of organizations in existence at a particular point in time, and then ascertaining their date of creation. So, as van Thiel herself acknowledges, such data will inevitably have a growth bias, since they necessarily exclude the deaths along the way. It is like ascertaining population changes by taking the current population and dividing it up by dates of birth, without taking account of those who died before the census date. Even if the population was not actually reproducing itself, let alone increasing in numbers over time, such a method will paint a potentially misleading picture of growth.

Three conclusions might be drawn from this brief foray into the world of the quango-counters. First, growth in numbers of delegated bodies and institutions of "multi-level governance" is widely believed to have taken place across several countries. But commentators often seem to be readier to explain what they assume to be a pattern of explosive growth or to discuss an assumed erosion of democracy than to get into the messy and frustrating business of trying to count up the numbers in a consistent way.

Second, when we do get into those numbers, hard evidence for the arrow view of developments turns out to be surprisingly elusive, and indeed it may be that part of the appeal of delegation is the ease with which naive counting can be thrown into confusion. Perhaps one day we will have reliable and comparable panel data that will make all talk of quango demons out of date and provide solid evidence that will allow us to test the arrow theory against the circle theory. But until then we can only conclude that, whatever might be the true figures for the changing incidence of quangos, their use as blame avoidance devices in government has shown remarkable tenacity, with new examples discernible in every decade.

Third, whatever might be the true figures for the changing body count or other indices of the incidence of delegated activity over time, there are several more qualitative developments over the recent past that do point to new applications of agency strategy for blame avoidance. We can obtain some telling pointers to such developments from several different literatures.

One such development is the emergence of new multi-level governance arrangements, most dramatically in the European Union, which offer fertile opportunities for blame avoidance. Stephanie Mudge (2006), for instance, has argued that the EU in the 1990s played a central role in national-level blame avoidance politics, with unpopular welfare reforms blamed on the EU by national politicians from left and center-left parties. Similarly, unpopular aspects of environmental and safety policies could be blamed by national governments on the standards set in Brussels, with no single government being accountable to voters for the whole regulatory regime (Hood, Rothstein, and Baldwin 2001). Indeed, the EU itself has been called 'a political system without a principal' (Dehousse 2007), referring to the lack of any single authoritative source of power from which delegation can take place. That can be considered the *ne plus ultra* for blame avoidance architecture: there is no central point in the system to which blame can revert, while there are ample possibilities for every major player in the structure to blame every other.

Moreover—carrying the logic of blame avoidance to the next stage— the EU itself created a number of autonomous agencies to carry out various regulatory tasks in the 1990s and 2000s, such as the European Aviation Safety Agency and the European Agency for Reconstruction (distributing EU money to the former Yugoslavia). Only two such agencies existed before the 1990s but there were twenty-eight or so by 2007 (see Dehousse 2007: 1–2). Such developments enable national politicians and even the core EU institutions to distance themselves from responsibility for the decisions made by such bodies, producing an even more labyrinthine world for would-be blame makers to navigate when trying to pin down the agency dimension of blame.

Another development is the apparently worldwide growth over more than a decade of what are claimed to be independent utility, financial, and network regulators (mostly consisting of pale imitations of the independent regulators set up in the United States in the late nineteenth century). One of the five global trends that Jacint Jordana and David Levi-Faur (2006) detect in their analysis of regulatory capitalism is an increase in delegation of regulatory power to relatively autonomous units responsible for managing utility markets once commonly dominated by public enterprise (see also Levi-Faur 2005). While like all such changes this development can be portrayed as a functionally rational development, it can just as plausibly be seen as a way of allowing elected politicians to shift blame for rising prices, interest rates problems, and service issues that would once have been more directly under their control, while in many cases continuing to exert influence behind the scenes.

In several countries, too, reforms of the New Public Management type that took place in the 1980s and 1990s contained attempts to delegate operational responsibilities to appointed public servants, at least in some jurisdictions, and involved the idea of transferring risk, blame, and responsibility to quasi-autonomous public managers (see Savoie 1995), regulators, or private entrepreneurs. Those 'agency' reforms seem to have been commonest in parliamentary systems with Westminster-type traditions of ministerial responsibility, though even there the styles and extent of the reforms varied, ranging from New Zealand writing such delegation to public servants into statutory form in the 1980s to the UK adopting a softer and more reversible style of delegation in its central-government agency reforms in the 1990s (see Pollitt and Talbot 2004).

To those developments we can add the development of the international consultancy industry, which produces a continuous stream of proposals for reorganizing the executive machinery for politicians and other high officeholders. Though derided by some as a new way of "plundering the public sector" (Craig and Brooks 2006), the work of these professional consultant-reformers creates a new institutional basis for strategies of recurrent reorganization that were discussed in chapter 4.

Finally, we can observe at least a new generation of partnership arrangements for providing public services (with partnerships between public and private organizations, or between different kinds of public organizations, as well as arrangements with individuals in which 'co-production' between individuals and officials is stressed, as in health and policing). As was argued in chapter 4, partnership arrangements have a long history, but public-private partnerships have been taken to new lengths in recent years in several countries, with the UK's development of its "private finance initiative" from the 1990s, earlier developments in some Francophone and Spanish-speaking countries, and later developments in other countries, producing a policy boom that has often been commented on and which strongly resembles the privatization policy boom of the 1990s. As with the reorganizations and the quasi-independent regulators, such developments may offer new ways of spreading the blame when things go wrong.

So even if the numbers of delegated bodies over time are hard to interpret, the many examples of new institutional forms suggest that human ingenuity in devising agency strategies for dodging blame at least shows little sign of diminution and indeed seems to have extended in some directions over the recent past.

POLICY DEVELOPMENTS: TOWARD HYPERDEFENSIVENESS?

Is a pattern of change or stability discernible when it comes to policy and operational approaches to blame avoidance? Are we moving toward a world in which blame-avoidance considerations are forcing public organizations and those who deliver public services into increasingly defensive stances? Are we moving away from a red-tape world into one whose players are more exposed to blame? Or is nothing much changing?

From the prevailing rhetoric of public sector reform in many countries, to which we referred in the opening chapter, we might at first sight assume that defensiveness was in retreat, because reformers so often fulminate against risk aversion by public officials and stress the need for a shift from an emphasis on bureaucratic rules and procedures to a focus on results in public policy and a more entrepreneurial approach to public service management. One well-known example of an initiative intended to drive administration in the direction of less form-filling defensiveness is the 1980 Paperwork Reduction Act introduced under the Reagan presidency in the United States (and renewed in 1995). The Act stated its first purpose was to "minimize the paperwork burden" for individuals and other organizations resulting from the collection of information by the federal government. Another, already mentioned, is the 1993 National Performance Review under the Clinton presidency (Gore 1993), which included in its very title the phrase "from red tape to results." Indeed, many governments today have some administrative unit dedicated to stripping out needless paperwork and procedural rules.

But (as with any law or policy initiative), the existence and recurrence of such reform attempts might equally be used to support a quite different conclusion, namely that policy defensiveness is an ever-present tendency in executive government and public services or even that it has been on the increase. And indeed, as we have seen in earlier chapters, we do not have to look far to find examples of new "follow the rules" procedures in public services—many of them now embedded in unforgiving computer software, "required fields" in online forms, and the like, rather than paperwork in the old-fashioned literal sense. Even—or perhaps especially—when private or independent organizations become providers of public services as a result of privatization or outsourcing strategies, the intensity of procedural rules rarely diminishes and often seems to increase. Part of what happens in such cases is that contractual terms tend to be spelled out more explicitly to establish liability and new oversight regimes are established, both of which may increase the intensity of rule-bound behavior aimed to offload blame and liability onto others. The same results can follow if public organizations go from self-insurance against third-party or other risks to external insurance arrangements.

If quango-counting is difficult, policy strategies offer even less for number-crunchers to go on, and it is even harder to find metrics of changes over time. But one relatively "countable" indicator of the strength of blame avoidance policy strategies that was highlighted by Kent Weaver (1988) two decades ago is the extent of formula funding in public budgets that remove discretion from individual officeholders. Weaver argued that there had been a long-term shift from discretionary to formula budgeting in the United States, which he attributed to blame avoidance factors. And indeed the trend to which Weaver drew attention in the United States has markedly continued since he was writing, with the percentage of the federal budget composed of discretionary spending steadily falling from over 70 percent in the early 1960s to less than 40 percent in the early 2000s. Moreover, that percentage is projected to fall further in the period up to 2012, according to projections from the Congressional Budget Office.[18]

Now some of that change may be due to a broader tendency in many western countries over the past fifty years or so for certain types of domestic spending, particularly on health, to grow faster than defense, the biggest component of discretionary spending, and that might be attributable to the general preferences of voters rather than blame avoidance. But the fact that formula funding is a notable feature of those welfare areas is itself notable, and (as Weaver also observed) moves toward no-hands policy "automaticity" are not confined to funding formulae. In the domain of monetary management (perhaps an area on the borderline between agency strategy and policy strategy), many European countries abandoned their formerly separate currencies for the Euro and its accompanying standard rules in the 2000s. Many Asian and Middle Eastern countries (such as Malaysia after the Asian financial crisis of 1997) chose to peg their currencies to the U.S. dollar in the 1980s and 1990s.

Policy procedures such as protocolization that give due diligence protection to individuals and organizations in the event of blame or liability also seem to be widespread in modern government and public services, producing a not-so-brave new world of defensive policy provision in fields such as education, health, and social work. The paradigm case is perhaps the notion of defensive medicine, which was referred to in the previous chapter and which has been around in the United States for forty years or so.

The term is conventionally used to denote two types of behavior by medical professionals. One is "avoidance behavior," when medical practitioners choose not to participate in high-risk procedures or deal with high-risk patients. The other is "assurance behavior," when medical practitioners choose forms of diagnosis and treatment primarily for the purpose of deterring their patients or their relatives from raising malpractice suits against them (Duke Law Journal 1971: 942).[19]

As with the issue of how many quangos there are and how they are changing over time, the incidence of avoidance and assurance types of medical defensiveness is hard to put into numbers. We do not have anything approximating an authoritative coefficient of medical defensiveness over time, and such numbers as there are can usually be interpreted in more than one way. For instance, if the number and costs of medical malpractice suits and similar litigation have gone up over recent decades, as is indeed the case in the United States and the UK, does that mean the environment in which health-care workers operate is changing in a way that forces them to be ever more defensive in diagnosis and treatment, with the consequence that health care costs go up and patients who are the subjects of assurance-type defensive behavior may be exposed to risks that they would otherwise not face?[20] Or could the rise in the costs of litigation possibly mean that medical professionals have become less defensive and more inclined to take risks?

Qualitative evidence seems to point to the former rather than the latter conclusion. Such evidence includes the observable increasing tendency of American doctors to locate themselves in states with less rigorous malpractice regimes, the observable increase in malpractice insurance premiums, and developments such as the collection of databases on malpractice lawyers by medical practitioners (Parker 2004). But it seems likely that such change would be irregular rather than smoothly incremental.

Defensive medicine is perhaps the paradigm case, but very similar claims about a tendency to increasing defensiveness have been made about the practice of policing, social work, volunteer work, and many aspects of education, from testing to school discipline. The relative incidence of avoidance and assurance behavior being highlighted in such discussions seems to vary from one domain to another. In the case of policing and law enforcement, both types of behavior are commonly discussed. Police and other enforcement officials are often said to have an incentive to focus on petty or routine violations by tractable offenders (avoiding more difficult cases), particularly if that sort of avoidance behavior can help them to meet clear-up or arrest targets of the kind associated with modern quantitative performance regimes. And certainly in the UK there has been much discussion of growing assurance behavior by police in the form of ever more paperwork and associated procedures (such as recording interviews) designed to counter accusations of intimidation or brutality with suspects (see, for example, Flanagan 2008: 50–3; Wintour 2003).[21]

For social work and voluntary work, too, defensive policies and procedures have often been said to have been on the increase in attempts to protect practitioners from blame. In the case of voluntary and community work, avoidance behavior takes the form of abandonment of risky activity (for example, in the light of the toll taken by rising third-party insurance costs and more onerous government regulation on limited resources) and also of decreasing willingness of individuals to take leadership roles in the face of blame risks and ever-increasing regulatory paperwork. In the case of social work, avoidance behavior is on the face of it difficult to practice for organizations dealing with individuals and families at the end of the line (though there can be ways of doing that in practice).

But there is more obvious scope for assurance behavior in the form of increasing preoccupation with paper trails or their digital-age equivalents as defenses against blame. Work by Sue White and her colleagues in Britain (2009), already noted in the previous chapter, has pointed to developments over a generation, in response to repeated child-death tragedies, that include moves to close control of workflow by inflexible software that demands early risk assessments for every case within strict deadlines, and an increased tendency by social workers to spend most of their time working on the due-diligence paper-trail aspects of their jobs on computers in their offices rather than out in the field visiting problem families and individuals (the social work equivalent of the police paperwork phenomenon).

We can even discern moves toward defensive education practices. Compared to the sort of schooling depicted in some nineteenth-century novels like Charles Dickens' *David Copperfield* (1850) involving summary beatings and arbitrary assessments by (to say the least) idiosyncratic teachers, defensiveness in modern education takes various forms, comprising both avoidance and assurance behaviors. Avoidance behavior includes attempts on the part of schools to exclude or expel difficult pupils (though that response may be easier for autonomous schools than public schools, which may be limited by caps on exclusions imposed by higher authorities). It also includes restrictions on activities that might attract blame or liability, such as school excursions and expeditions or potentially hazardous playground games.

Assurance behavior in education, as discussed in the previous chapter, includes moves away from in-the-round qualitative assessments of essay compositions to multiple-choice testing, restrictions on teachers being alone with students, ever more formal and explicit risk assessment systems, formal reporting procedures, and legalistic due-process procedures for discipline. The more elaborate testing regimes for students that have developed in many western countries in recent decades can also be seen as a form of assurance behavior, providing 'evidence' of educational progress to be used by various players in the blameworlds sketched out in chapter 2 to counter charges of falling standards and dysfunctional schooling. As in medicine, the world of defensive education is one in which rigid adherence to standard best practice protocols is far less risky than bespoke responses. There is an old saying, normally attributed to Plutarch's *On Listening to Lectures*, that "students are candles to be lit, not vessels to be filled,"[22] but in today's defensive world of education any kind of naked flame would be unthinkable.

Though the evidence is anecdotal and circumstantial, claims of increasing defensiveness are commonly found across the whole field of government and public services, and to some extent across the organizational world more generally. Take the case of escape clauses and disclaimers. Such phenomena are hardly new developments in organizational policies and operations. After all, signs that declare, "The management takes no responsibility for ... [anything]" can be found displayed in car parks and cloakrooms in many countries. But in today's internet world similar disclaimers now appear on every website and on most business e-mails too. Language itself may provide some clues to the direction of change: the creation of terms such as "defensive medicine" and "flak-catcher" in the United States in the late 1960s (as already discussed) and 'jobsworth' in Britain at about the same time may have some significance. (The latter term is said to have first appeared in a popular song in the late 1960s to denote officious and inflexible following of petty rules, mainly at low levels of administration,[23] although the phenomenon itself was no doubt widely observable before then.) The same might be said of the development of 'blame avoidance' itself as a term and an academic subfield from the mid-1980s, as noted in the first chapter.

Other pointers to increasing awareness of policy or procedural approaches to blame avoidance over the last decade include Michael Power's (1997) analysis of new audit systems as a version of institutional assurance behavior, Onora O'Neill's (2002 and 2006) attack on "transparency" as a response to falling trust in professionals that provided in practice only a debased and low-intelligence form of accountability, and the emergence of academic literatures on "box-ticking" and "standards" in the 2000s, for instance in the work of Gerry McGivern and Ewan Ferlie (2007) and Olivier Borraz (2007), respectively. For Michael Power, the growth of audit systems such as official standards, inspection, and quality assurance arrangements reflected a society in which there was a greater need for "symbolic reassurance." Even though the efficacy of such systems is at best unproven (some would say that the international financial crisis of the late 2000s definitively demonstrated their ineffectiveness), this trend could be understood as the assurance form of policy defensiveness, in that they provide due-diligence defenses when things later go wrong.

O'Neill sees the development of a lower-trust, higher-blame environment for professionals as leading to formalistic but ineffective accountability systems involving only one-way defensive communication (for example, through websites) rather than intelligent and frank conversations. Box-ticking as analyzed by McGivern and Ferlie similarly provides a shield from blame without intelligent engagement with the issues to be faced. The "standards explosion," analyzed by Olivier Borraz, and the related development of benchmarking across many public and private organizations that was noted in the previous chapter, may well be considered parallel developments having a substantial defensive or blame avoidance dimension even if they may serve other purposes as well.

An Overall Perspective

As noted at the outset of this chapter, an arrow theorist might expect to see ever-growing use of agency, presentational, and policy strategies for blame avoidance. A circle theorist, by contrast, might expect blame avoidance to be more of a constant—albeit taking different forms as technology opens up or closes down strategic options, as new variants are invented and older ones become too familiar to be credible. The evidence is too fragmentary to allow us to firmly dismiss either of these theories (so we are in a rather similar position to that of those nineteenth-century physicists mentioned earlier, who had to specify what they knew they did not know). But it seems likely that both arrow and circle processes are at work in blameworld.

That is, blame avoidance approaches seem to be frequently mutating into new forms as technological and social invention produces new weapons for organizations and individuals to use in their efforts to fend off blame. But there is also evidence for growth in the number and influence of presentational staff at the top of government in several countries and for a worldwide growth in semi-independent regulatory bodies for utilities and for some other functions. There are many instances of growth of intergovernmental arrangements, certainly for the EU countries and in other parts of the world as well, and several notable new developments in organizational routines and procedures that provide new opportunities for assurance varieties of defensive behavior (and perhaps to a lesser extent avoidance varieties).

Indeed, for those sociologists such as the late Samuel Huntingdon (1971: 286) who think "social modernization" means a long-term shift away from primordial ties (for example, to place and family) and belief in supernatural power or traditional religion (see also Giddens and Griffiths 2006: 405), it would not be surprising if blame avoidance by the sort of strategies sketched out in the preceding chapters did not come to take on more significance as "modernization" in that sense proceeds. A weakening of primordial ties would imply that all institutions become more shallowly rooted in civil society than before. Attachment to such organizations becomes more a matter of lifestyle choice and individual cultural bias than something determined by birth and family ties and linked to long-standing associations with a particular place.

Given such conditions, the behavior of organizations and their officeholders could be expected to be increasingly judged with a degree of critical detachment by a greater proportion of the population at large and perhaps even of their own membership, rather than attracting knee-jerk support or criticism from friends and enemies on the basis of unchanging and well-understood tribal loyalties or traditional forms of class solidarity. Such conditions might be expected to produce a more unpredictable blame environment for such officeholders, meaning that personal skill in extricating themselves from blame when adverse events occur may count for more than in the past.

Similarly, declining belief in traditional religious values and beliefs would imply ever less scope for adverse events and mishaps to be attributed to fate, evil spirits, or acts of God rather than to human acts of commission or omission. Accordingly, the export of blame to the supernatural sphere or the inexorable workings of fate could be expected to be less credible over time, with a corresponding need to find more (literally) down-to-earth modes of blame avoidance.

But against that "arrow" view of what social modernization might mean for blame avoidance, it should be noted that some authors (such as Therborn 2000) argue that modernization is a term that has no "specific intrinsic content" and has been used to denote contradictory traits of social change by different modernization theorists (see also Margetts 2010). Indeed, Jean Monnet (1978: 259), the architect of the European Union, famously stated that "Modernization is not a state of affairs but a state of mind." And indeed there are plenty of reasons for expecting circle processes to be prominent in the dynamics of blame avoidance as well, in the form of back-and-forth movements as times and fashions alter, and the balance shifts among different blame cultures of the kind discussed in chapter 2. For instance, when the dominant mood is egalitarian, the blame avoidance gambits that will resonate most effectively with the potential blame makers will be different from the measures that will hit home when the dominant mood is hierarchist or individualist.

Further, the developments in presentational, agency, and policy strategies discussed in this chapter are likely to play out differently for the various players in blameworld. As noted earlier, much of the development of high-level spin capacity and information control over recent decades has taken place around the top bananas and the upper to middle corporate levels, and has been more about controlling whistle-blowers than protecting the frontline players from blame. When it comes to agency developments, some of the changes described earlier can be interpreted as serving the blame avoidance needs of top officeholders, while defensive reorganization, complex outsourcing, and partnership arrangements can also provide scope for middle-level and front-line players to dodge the blame by shifting it onto partners, contractors, or other front-line players. For policy and operational strategies, many of the changes discussed earlier, such as protocolization and some types of herding, seem to be as amenable to protecting the frontline players as those at higher levels. Both agency and policy developments have also brought in new possibilities for directing blame at the fourth category of player, namely those outside the conventional institutional machinery of executive government, who can come into the frame of blame as "partners" or through blame-the-victim policy strategies.

But that of course leaves open the question as to how effective blame-avoidance strategies can be, whether there are regular sequences in which the various types are deployed by beleaguered officeholders and organizations, and whether blame-avoidance activity contributes to good governance or detracts from it. Accordingly, the next chapter explores issues of sequencing, and the chapter following that explores blame avoidance from the angle of effectiveness and good governance.

PART THREE

Living in a World of Blame Avoidance

CHAPTER SEVEN

Mixing and Matching Blame-Avoidance Strategies

> Any port in a storm
> —Old proverb, said to be Scottish

INTRODUCTION: THE SEQUENCING AND COMBINATION PROBLEM

As explained in chapter 1, this book began by naming the parts of blame-avoidance strategy. Having named the parts, a next step (in chapter 6) was to look at broad developments and institutional changes over time in blameworld. The aim was to explore whether we should think of blame avoidance as a constant of political and institutional life or as something peculiar to our own times, and the conclusion was that both of those propositions—the arrow approach and the circle approach—seem to apply to some extent.

This chapter looks at the dynamics and deployment of blame-avoidance approaches from a rather different angle. Instead of looking at the broader social picture that we dealt with in the previous chapter, it explores how individual officeholders and organizations can mix and match the various strategies and approaches in their attempts to avoid blame. When can those different approaches be combined to work together, providing defense in depth for beleaguered would-be blame avoiders, and when do they clash with one another? What sequencing strategies do organizations and officeholders use to string those various approaches together over time?

To get an insight into the problem, imagine you are an officeholder facing a blame firestorm or feeding frenzy about some alleged personal or institutional misdemeanor. Anyone in that situation will face some hard choices about how to deploy the various approaches to blame avoidance described in the previous chapters. For instance, as we saw in chapter 3, when it comes to presentational strategies, you can try to win the argument or you can try to keep a low profile (by trying to keep things secret or pursuing various forms of nonengagement tactics), but you cannot easily do both at once. Indeed, one of the things that often leads to much corporate and individual agonizing in dealing with blame is precisely which of those two approaches to follow at any one point in a blame episode. But while would-be blame avoiders have to choose between such approaches at any given moment, they can switch between those approaches over time, following one at one point in the blame game and turning to another later on. Moreover, some of the different approaches to blame avoidance sketched out earlier can be used at the same time without difficulty. For instance, you may be able to keep a low profile and change the subject by diversionary tactics at the same time, or to simultaneously change the subject and draw a line, perhaps by preemptive apologies.

Those were exactly the kind of choices that faced former British prime minister Tony Blair and his chief spin doctor, Alastair Campbell, a few months after the landslide electoral victory that brought his New Labour government to power in 1997, when the first of what turned out to be a succession of "sleaze" stories hit the headlines. That first major blame episode took the form of an embarrassing question about party funding. The issue involved a substantial donation (later revealed to be one million pounds) to the Labour party from Bernie Ecclestone, the head of the Formula 1 motor racing organization. The newly elected Labour government had initially exempted Formula 1 racing from a ban on tobacco company sponsorship of sporting events, and though it later had to execute a swift retreat from that position, the question inevitably arose as to whether there had been some improper connection between the donation to the party and the government's initial policy over tobacco sponsorship. That issue was particularly embarrassing given that New Labour had come to power after repeatedly making high-minded attacks on what it had claimed to be the sleazy style of the previous Conservative government, and had promised to bring the most rigorous ethical standards to its own administration.

The diary of Alastair Campbell gives an account of the arguments that went on in No. 10 Downing Street as to how to handle this tricky issue (Campbell 2007: 257–62). Faced with the conflict-of-interest accusations, what was the best way to duck, limit, or redirect the blame? Was it to follow the Calvin Coolidge strategy of just lying low and hoping other news stories would soon replace that one as a hot topic? Or was it to take a more proactive drawing-a-line approach in the form of immediate disclosure of the size of the donation accompanied by sorry-democracy noises of contrition? In the early days when the story began to break in the media, the presentational strategy that Tony Blair's office chose to follow was to combine a low profile (saying little and not revealing the size of the donation made by Ecclestone to the Labour party) with diversionary tactics (notably persuading the press to run a story about a leading member of the Conservative opposition having pressed for a knighthood for Bernie Ecclestone (Campbell 2007: 260)). Only when that initial combination of lying-low and changing the subject had failed to stem the tide of media blame did the presentational strategy shift to drawing the line, in the form of a carefully crafted TV apology by the Prime Minister (the apology, when read carefully, turned out to consist of an expression of regret about the way the issue had been handled in presentational terms, rather than regret over the decision to accept the donation itself).

That example concerns choices among different sorts of presentational strategy for blame avoidance, but similar mixing-and-matching issues arise in the choice of agency and policy strategies. For example, you cannot easily combine hard and soft delegation of responsibility for the same matters at the same time, even though you can seesaw between them over time, as expediency demands, if you have sufficient political power, time, and patience to change the formal structure of organizations. But you may be able to link up delegation, partnership, defensive reorganization, and government by the market in creative ways. Indeed, much modern institutional architecture in public services provision does precisely that, as we saw in chapter 4.

Likewise, when it comes to blame prevention re-engineering by policy strategies, you will find it hard to combine extreme forms of policy abstinence with the protocolization (do-it-by-the book) approach, or to follow individualization and herding approaches to blame avoidance at the same time. But protocolization can be readily combined with herding or with individualization. And similarly, there can be creative combinations of presentational, agency, and policy strategies, such as mixing group rather than individual decision-making over case assessments in high-blame domains (such as pedophile release) with an agency strategy of constant defensive reorganizations (meaning that by the time the next scandal arrives, the organizational structure that produced it will already have been superseded by a different one).

To explore the sequencing and combination of blame-avoidance approaches, this chapter starts with the "statics" of the mixing-and-matching issue. That is, it looks at the logic and social processes involved in combining different blame-avoidance approaches at any one point in time, when organizations and officeholders are faced with choices about where to put the overall emphasis, what combinations to use, and what hybrids to avoid. After exploring three statics issues involving the linking up of different approaches to blame avoidance, the analysis turns to the "dynamics" of the mixing-and-matching problem—that is, the ways would-be blame avoiders can move over time from one blame-avoidance approach to another. What choices about how to sequence the approaches are they faced with: what approaches can they be expected to use first and what will they tend to keep in reserve for later stages of the blame game?

LINKING PRESENTATIONAL, AGENCY, AND POLICY STRATEGIES: THE JOINED-UP APPROACH TO BLAME AVOIDANCE

Mixing blame-avoidance strategies together can be thought of as a search for a winning combination, like getting all the lemons in a line to win the payout from a gambling machine, finding the elusive group of numbers that open a combination lock, or finding that ultimate recipe for a perfect chocolate soufflé. As in culinary matters, much human ingenuity and creativity is devoted to combinatorial connection in the search for ways of avoiding blame. And, just as with cooking, what works in some settings will not necessarily do so in others, with all the imponderables of public mood and popular culture interacting with the individual character of each officeholder—his or her personality, risk appetite, and life experience.

So any generalization about combinations must necessarily be limited. But three broad propositions about such mixing-and-matching processes can be advanced. First, the more that the heat of blame is perceived to be on, the more blame-avoidance activity will tend to be self-consciously joined up. Second, group culture (in the sense of shared attitudes and beliefs) will shape the kind of emphasis that goes on blame avoidance. And third, as we have already noticed, not everything can be readily matched with everything else. Some combinations make more sense than others.

The More Blame Heat Is Perceived, the More Blame-Avoidance Strategies Are Likely to be Joined up

At first sight this first proposition might seem almost like a tautology. It merely states that the greater the pressure they feel themselves to be under, the more beleaguered officeholders and organizations will tend to use all the main blame-avoiding strategies together in an orchestrated way. The more the heat goes on, pressure will grow for everything an organization does to be Teflon-coated in a tightly coordinated way. So the spin machinery that delivers rebuttals (or "prebuttals" in the sense of anticipative retaliation) will be dovetailed with the shaping and reshaping of the organogram to ward off blame and with policy strategies such as protocolization or team working that similarly make the act of decision by any identifiable individual as hard to pin down as human ingenuity can make it.

In fairly benign—that is, low-blame—conditions, the various parts of government machinery, (or different parts of any organization) that deal with presentational matters, the structuring of the organizational machinery, or the crafting of policies and operations might be expected to be autonomous to some extent, each going its own way. In that sort of calm environment, media relations and communications people are likely to be found working in one part of the corporate or bureaucratic forest, management structure experts and consultants in another, and policy and operations people in yet another (usually comprising various places and levels from high strategy to front-line health and safety). In the jargon of organizational sociology (Perrow 1972, 1984), the structure of blame-avoidance organization will be low in integration, and those elements will be loosely coupled, in the sense that failure in one of them will not immediately impact on the others or the organization as a whole. But when the blame pressure is perceived to be on, integration can be expected to increase, and these various operations will come to be linked together more tightly. And for reasons that were given in chapter 2, it is likely to be the top bananas who will be in the best position to join up those strategies, because the middle-level players will often tend to be too divided, and some or all of the necessary levers will normally be out of the reach of the front-line troops.

Such a linking together of presentational, agency, and operational strategies can be expected to come about by both anticipative and reactive blame-avoidance activity. For the first, the heightened defensiveness surrounding any issue or domain that is expected to become a blame minefield in the future (because of a bad track record, or anticipated public disapproval) can be expected to lead to high-level involvement that brings all three strategies into play simultaneously as all the various ways of keeping the heat at bay are urgently pursued from the top. The same can be expected to work reactively. Any organization or policy domain that has attracted high levels of blame in the past for its errors or policy failures is also likely to be a theater for joined-up blame avoidance, as the process of defensive mopping up from the problems of the past means looking at the operation as a whole, either by a new top management team or by those who have managed to survive the previous blame episode.

However, while that sort of organizational logic seems plausible at first sight for institutions under pressure, in some high-blame conditions there seem to be imperatives that work against any such joining up, and this may apply particularly in the complex institutional world of modern government, with its multiple delivery agencies and elaborate outsourcing arrangements. Take two cases that we have already referred to on several occasions in previous chapters, namely the handling of the risks of re-offending by convicted pedophiles after release from custody and the care of children at risk of abuse. Both cases raise issues that have become increasingly sensitive to public concern over recent decades—indeed, the now widespread term "pedophile" to designate the danger is itself a fairly recent entrant into common linguistic usage (Hood, Rothstein, and Baldwin 2001: 93n5). Both are domains in which case decisions are unavoidably tricky, involving awkward encounters with difficult and devious people who have very strong incentives to conceal important information, and the consequences of error in making such case decisions can be fatal. Moreover, both are domains in which the kind of negativity bias we discussed in chapter 1 tends to figure strongly. That is, the successes of the police and social services authorities when they make correct judgment calls on such cases normally tend to be invisible outside a small circle of professionals. All the public and media attention goes onto the failures of the system—for example, when known pedophiles reoffend or children are tragically killed or injured as a result of the public authorities' failures of commission or omission.

Such domains also present little scope for putting much reliance on presentational strategies when errors occur. After all, excuses will understandably tend to ring hollow when avoidable child deaths occur or known pedophiles reoffend, even if the judgments of the public agencies responsible are correct in the great majority of cases, or if those agencies are heavily understaffed and under the most severe work pressures, as indeed they often are. Justifications of the no-gain-without-pain variety are even less likely to cut any ice in dealing with blame over such issues. The scope for diversionary tactics can also be severely circumscribed when media attention is heavily focused on a human tragedy involving an innocent child harmed by bureaucratic error. Drawing-the-line preemptive apologies can be tricky too, because of the issues of legal liability that can arise over admission of guilt. So in most cases, lying doggo or empty-chairing may be the least-worst presentational approach available, and the whole domain is rather barren ground for the more active types of spin doctoring.

That means elected officeholders—particularly the top bananas at the upper levels of government—have the strongest incentive to rely on agency strategies that distance themselves as far as possible from any responsibility for individual case-handling decisions in such areas. They will prefer to cast themselves as global resource allocators and after-the-fact scrutinizers and commentators rather than real-time managers. So there will be less need to join up policy and presentational strategies from the top if the upper-level officeholders aim to define their role wherever possible as one of criticizing the professionals for their avoidable errors, on setting up high-profile inquiries into what went wrong when adverse events occur, and on otherwise expressing concern about the plight of innocent victims. What they will never want to do is to closely direct social services operations on the ground.

Even so, front-line professional and bureaucratic actors in such situations have possible ways of redirecting some of the blame onto the middle and top levels, as was noted in chapter 2. For instance, they may choose to see danger everywhere, putting such high risk ratings on every released pedophile and problem family that they can then blame top-level actors for under-resourcing their activities (see Hood, Rothstein, and Baldwin 2001: 158). They may be able to blame middle-level actors for having either approved their operations (for example, by citing recent audit or inspection reports giving their operation a clean bill of health or by having copied back-covering e-mails to their superiors to prove that those upper levels knew what was happening on the ground) or obstructed their work in some way, as by managerial bullying, contradictory instructions emanating from the top, or resource starvation of the organization's front line. Indeed, all of those claims tend to figure large in the blame games that take place in the aftermath of serious error or malfunction in such services.

Those middle-level actors will in turn be looking for ways of individualizing the blame and pinning it onto the front-line workers so that adverse events can be held to be the product of wrong calls by those in the front line rather than arising from a dysfunctional system produced by higher or middle management. But the front-line workers can resist the threat of blame individualization if they follow or accept a variant of the defensive-medicine assurance policy of strict protocolization of operating routines. They can also counter blame individualization by following practices of case decision-making by groups rather than individuals, such that no single person is responsible for any decision.

Such strategic tensions among the various players in the blame game, combined with the complexities of delivery structures in public services, can therefore complicate the idea that organizations closely join up blame avoidance strategies under pressure. But some agency and policy strategies may serve to protect the interests of several groups at once. For example, abstinence policy strategies involving avoidance rather than assurance may serve the interests of front-line, middle-level, and top-level players at the same time. A case in point is that of those local authorities in England in the 1990s who chose to deal with the blame risks associated with handling pedophile ex-offenders by simply refusing to take any responsibility for resettling those offenders in their communities or for providing any housing facilities for them (see Hood et al. 1999: 158).

Partnership working among agencies may also be a way of handling potential blame that serves the interests of players at different institutional levels as well as in different organizations. That was the response of British police and social services agencies to the 1997 Sex Offenders Act, which laid on the police the statutory responsibility to maintain a register of the names and addresses of certain types of convicted sex offenders who had been released from custody. Working together with other agencies in assessing the risks of individual cases meant that the various players both in the front line and at middle levels could share blame and limit the risk that other organizations could pin the blame on them for not passing on crucial information when a released pedophile reoffended with tragic consequences (Hood et al. 1999: 158).[1]

So the joined-up blame-avoidance proposition—that organizations in a high-blame environment will always tightly link up the various elements of blame-avoidance strategy through pressure from the top—evidently has its limits. It will not apply when organizations have a highly individualistic *sauve qui peut* culture. It will not apply when top-level officeholders can successfully step away from the hot seat by delegation strategies. And it will not apply in those cases (usually at the lower levels of the institutional food chain, as noted in chapter 2) where would-be blame avoiders are not in a position to bring policy, agency, and presentational strategies together easily. Accordingly, the sorts of organizations that might be expected to fit the joined-up blame-avoidance proposition are those which cannot easily delegate their activities further and whose heads have autonomous resources for deploying spin and determining policy—indeed, precisely the more managerial organizations of modern government that have been highlighted by the ideas of New Public Management in the recent past. But even then, and even when the pressure is on the top where the various threads and levels might be expected to come together, there may still be forces that stand in the way of a combined operations approach to blame avoidance that we shall come to later.

Blame-Avoidance Mixtures Reflect Ethos or Culture

Like joining up under pressure, the idea that blame-avoidance mixtures will reflect group culture in the institutions or organizations involved at first sight seems to be no more than a statement of the blindingly obvious. It is the way the mixtures come about and the different patterns that emerge that need to be traced out.

One of the oldest themes in social science is the observation that worldviews—ways of seeing the world and corresponding notions of social organization—tend to vary among individuals, groups, and institutions. And different worldviews will be reflected in the way blame avoidance plays out. For example, some organizations and groups will be predisposed to close ranks in the face of blame, while others are programmed to throw some of their members to the wolves (as it were) to safeguard the rest, and still others will split into warring groups or individuals publicly pointing the finger at each other for error and failure.[2] A notable case of the tendency to close ranks was the marked reluctance of American doctors to give evidence against other doctors in medical malpractice suits (the so-called conspiracy of silence), which was the main impetus for judicial changes in various state courts in the 1960s that made it possible for individual litigants in malpractice suits to use medical textbooks or other sources of evidence instead of the expert testimony that had been required for success in litigation up to that point.[3] A contrasting tendency is to throw someone to the wolves: in the business and municipal organizations studied by Boeker (1992) and Boyne and his colleagues (2010), second-tier managers were made to take the bullet for organizational failures to save the chief executive's skin (perhaps a modern equivalent of the old political and legal doctrine that a king can do no wrong).

One well-known way of classifying different worldviews is that of the cultural theory advanced by the late Mary Douglas (1970; 1982; 1990) and her followers, and which has more recently been recast into a more general "way of life theory" by Michael Pepperday (2009). Douglas identified four main ways of life typically associated with corresponding worldviews, which she derived from two basic analytic dimensions of "grid" and "group" in her original scheme (according to Pepperday [2009] those ways of life can be derived from other social bases and imply three rather than two basic dimensions). The link with blame avoidance is that Douglas explicitly saw those distinct worldviews and ways of life as embodying different ways of handling and attributing blame.

That is, in a hierarchist worldview, blame attaches to those who do not follow the rules, do not follow established procedures, or do not pay attention to established expertise. In an egalitarian worldview, blame attaches to those who ignore popular opinion or do not have group support. In an individualist worldview, blame attaches to those who are considered personally inept or maladroit, and failure will be attributed to lack of individual ability. In a fatalist worldview, blame outcomes will be capricious and hard to predict, not necessarily following any clear social logic.

Reverting to the blame-avoidance worlds we considered in chapte 2, this analysis implies that top bananas will find blame avoidance hardest in egalitarian social settings, while those at the organizational front line (and many of those in the fourth world, outside the organizational apparatus of government and public services) will find blame avoidance hardest in individualist settings. The middle-level institutional players are likely to find blame avoidance hardest in hierarchist settings (where they can be caught by organograms and rules created by those above them), and those in the fourth world, of civil society, are likely to find blame avoidance hardest in a mixture of individualist and fatalist settings, where system blame is either pervasive or difficult to assign.

Similarly, each of the worldviews is likely to fit better with some of the variants of blame-avoidance strategies discussed earlier than they do with others. Table 7.1 aims to sketch out some of the matches, showing how the four ways of life identified by cultural theorists link to variants of the three types of blame-avoidance strategy discussed in chapters 3, 4, and 5.

As table 7.1 suggests, hierarchist societies or organizations seem likely to be most attuned to policy strategies emphasizing protocolization, because in that sort of cultural setting the way to avoid blame is to be able to show that whatever is done follows the appropriate rules or good practice

TABLE 7.1
How Cultural Worldviews Link to Variants of Blame-Avoidance Strategy

Culture Bias or Worldview	Type of Blame Avoidance Strategy		
	Presentational Strategy	Agency Strategy	Policy Strategy
	Congruent forms	Congruent forms	Congruent forms
Hierarchist	Winning arguments (by appeal to rules or authority)	Delegation of responsibility down a line of command	Protocolization
Egalitarian	Winning arguments (by appeal to popular will or justice for the disadvantaged) "sorry democracy" expressions of public contrition	Partnership structures	Herding tactics
Individualist	Winning arguments (by appeal to superior or inferior skill or sagacity)	Government by the market	Individualization of blame
Fatalist	Keeping a low profile; any attempts to win arguments likely to be framed in terms of fate/karma/act of God excuses	Staff rotation	Policy abstinence

certified by recognized experts. The delegation forms of agency strategy are also likely to have an impact in a hierarchist setting, since fine distinctions between different types of organizations or officeholders will count for something in such contexts. As for the presentational approaches, the best fit of the winning-the-arguments variety will be those that appeal to the judgments of technically qualified authorities following the correct procedures or best practice guidelines at any given time.

Egalitarian societies or organizations, by contrast, seem likely to be most attuned to policy strategies emphasizing herding (group modes of decision-making such as collective cabinet solidarity and its equivalent in many other organizational settings) and agency strategies emphasizing partnership structures, popular consultation, or both. As for the presentational strategies, the winning-the-arguments form most likely to appeal to egalitarians is the claim that whatever was done reflected the views or wishes of the work group or the population at large and was done in the interests of the disadvantaged rather than the powerful. Justificatory arguments seeking to avoid blame on the grounds that sacrifices have to be made for more egalitarian outcomes are also likely to count for more among egalitarians than they do in other kinds of social settings. And in addition to arguments, sorry-democracy expressions of public contrition by errant officeholders are perhaps also more likely to appeal to egalitarians than legalistic justifications based on fine points of procedure, definition, or organizational status.

For the individualist worldview, the agency strategy that seems most likely to resonate is that of government by the market, as discussed earlier. When it comes to policy strategies, we can expect blame individualization to figure large in such a cultural setting, with a *sauve qui peut* approach overriding any kind of solidarity. From an individualist perspective, those who operate or consume services are expected to be able to make complex risk judgements for themselves and live (or die) by the *caveat emptor* (buyer beware) principle. So for presentation strategies, the winning-the-argument form most likely to appeal to individualists is of the blame-the-victim sort, which asserts that those who show insufficient sagacity or skill in operating markets or otherwise advancing their interests are to blame for the bad things that happen to them.

Fatalists are generally not likely to see blame as avoidable except by luck or chance. So from this worldview the preferred presentational approach is likely to be the passive tactic of keeping a low profile, staying out of the limelight in the hope that something else will turn up to overshadow the adverse event in question. If any form of winning the argument is likely to be particularly important for fatalists in the blame game, it will involve excuses that emphasize the part played in adverse events by fate, act of God, or bad karma that could not be reasonably anticipated or fully understood by the players in the game. If there is any preferred policy approach for fatalists, it would perhaps be the abstinence approach (on the grounds that whatever you do has a chance of attracting blame, so it is perhaps best to do as little as possible). Fatalists are likely to set little store by agency strategies, but a context of continuous chaotic reorganization and redeployment of people is perhaps most likely to fit into a fatalist worldview insofar as they create conditions in which everyone can shuffle off blame on the grounds that they do not really understand the structures in which they are operating and that whoever was here today will be gone tomorrow.

The general point is that the optimum mix of blame avoidance strategies that we referred to at the beginning of this section—that elusive key that opens the combination lock to release organizations and officeholders from blame—is not likely to be uniform. Rather, it will be culturally variable in space and time. The sort of keys that beleaguered blame takers reach for to open the lock will depend on their worldview, and whether the keys those actors choose actually fit the lock of blame avoidance is in turn likely to depend on the worldview of the blame makers. Where the worldviews of the blame maker and the blame taker are congruent, the latter's blame-avoidance strategies are more likely to succeed. Equally, when there is a cultural mismatch—for instance, when officeholders respond with individualist or hierarchist blame-avoidance strategies at a time when the public mood is egalitarian—the strategies are more likely to fail.

Some Ingredients for Banishing Blame Don't Work Together

While mixing and matching is no doubt a key to creativity in blame avoidance as with many other things, there are also likely to be limits to the scope for mixing and matching different approaches.

Some of those limits follow from the working of overall ethos or culture, as we have just seen. If the sort of blame-avoidance strategies that are likely to resonate most strongly will differ from one worldview to another, crafting presentational, agency, or policy strategies that will fit all of the four basic worldviews at once will usually be challenging.

Even more broadly, some combinations of blame-avoidance strategies are likely to fail to work together simply by lack of coherence. For instance, when it comes to the argumentative forms of presentational blame-avoidance strategies, it is incoherent to claim simultaneously that nothing blameworthy has happened and that it is all someone else's fault, or to make excuses while at the same time claiming that nothing at all is wrong. It is also incoherent to combine excuses that cannot both be true—for example, in simultaneously claiming not to have been told about some danger in advance and to have been unable to do anything about it. Such contradictory stances will tend to undermine the credibility of an officeholder or organization whatever the cultural context.

Similarly, when it comes to agency strategies for blame avoidance, it is logically incoherent both to renounce responsibility and to have some involvement (for instance, in a partnership arrangement). Such a combination can undermine the blame-avoidance efficacy of those top individuals who (as discussed in chapter 4) are attracted to a variable-geometry approach to agency strategies that involves a hands-off stance whenever blame is in the offing but a hands-on one when credit is to be taken. Likewise, for the policy and operational strategies of blame avoidance discussed in chapter 5, there is an obvious mismatch between simultaneously adopting herd and blame individualization approaches. But of course it is possible for different approaches to be followed at different levels in the same organization—for example, by frontline operators adopting herd approaches in response to blame individualization targeted from the higher corporate levels.

Moreover, blame avoidance can be incoherent in the cultural sense that was discussed in the previous section if it mixes approaches that are congruent with different worldviews or ways of life. Such incoherence may have its uses—after all, there is a school of thought that sees "clumsy" or culturally hybrid institutions and practices as more robust than cultural monotypes (see Verweij and Thompson 2006). But what seems to distinguish the practiced blame avoider from the more artless type of operator is both the ability to spot and prevent logical incompatibilities (in the set of approaches being used at any one point in time) and to produce a coherent mix of strategies that resonates with the cultural mood of a particular time and place.

Combining Blame-Avoidance Strategies over Time: Searching for that Perfect Teflon Coat

The previous section argued that there are some combinations of blame-avoidance strategies that would seem absurd or ineffective if they are pursued concurrently. But organizations and officeholders can and frequently do shift from one position to another over time. The example given in the previous section, of officeholders combining problem denial and responsibility denial, is a case in point, since organizations and officeholders do frequently shift from the first to the second position as a blame episode unfolds. Once we move from statics to dynamics and introduce the element of time into the analysis of the blame game, the focus goes onto the way the players make a succession of moves switching from one combination of blame-avoidance strategies to another as the blame they face continues, increases, or goes away. As with the statics of mixing and matching discussed earlier, many of those choices will no doubt be shaped by the individual personalities and life experience of particular officeholders, along with other imponderables.

Nevertheless, three broad propositions about the dynamics of mixing and matching blame-avoidance strategies can be offered here, most of which have been mentioned briefly in previous chapters. One is that agency and policy strategies are likely to be most effectively used in an anticipative way, while presentational strategies are likely to be the main preoccupation of organizations and officeholders when they are in the eye of the storm over some blame issue or in the immediate aftermath. A second, reflected in the epigraph to this chapter, is that if blame persists or increases after the adoption of an initial set of moves, beleaguered organizations or officeholders will tend to switch tactics, though such switching will usually not be costless. And a third proposition, reflecting a basic assumption about blame avoidance as a central motivating force in politics and institutional behavior, is that the moves made by those beleaguered individuals and organizations over time are likely to follow some sort of stages-of-response pattern. At the least we can expect them normally to adopt other stances in the course of a blame episode before they make any full admission of both agency and loss or harm.

Presentational Strategies Are Easier to Use in the Heat of Battle than Agency and Policy Strategies

The blame-avoidance strategies discussed earlier in the book do not seem to be equally deployable at any point in time during a blame event. Except in their softest form, where they are all but indistinguishable from presentational strategies (the areas marked d, e, and g in the Venn diagram presented in figure 1.2), agency and policy strategies are most likely to be useful *before* a blame crisis strikes. While disputation about the precise scope of an officeholder's formal responsibilities very commonly figures in blame games, at least the harder elements of policy and organizational structure cannot be changed after the event, except in the grosser types of history rewriting. Similarly, hastily changing the organogram or the policy procedures in the midst of a feeding frenzy is unlikely to stave off critical questioning about precisely who was responsible for whatever adverse events occurred under the old rules or organizational arrangements. It may even make that questioning worse, if it is seen as an admission that the old arrangements have failed. So to work most effectively, the blame-avoiding agency arrangements or policy procedures will normally need to be in place in advance of a blame event.

However, the mopping-up stages that occur in the aftermath of blame crises often include new applications of agency or policy strategies, at the point where dealing with the past meets anticipation of the future. A dramatic case in point is the eventual response to the bovine spongiform encephalopathy (BSE) crisis in Britain in the 1980s and 1990s. BSE is a severe and fatal brain disease in cattle, which seems to be capable of jumping species barriers and is linked to Creutzfeld-Jakob disease (CJD) in humans.[4] BSE killed over 175,000 of the UK's 12 million beef and dairy cattle in the 1980s and 1990s and led to a total EU ban on exports of UK cattle and cattle products, thereby ruining the country's cattle industry. By the later 1990s, scientists were concluding that an alarming new strain of CJD was probably linked to exposure to BSE-infected meat. BSE challenged every "roll-back-the-state" principle espoused by the Thatcherite

Conservative government, leading as it did to an avalanche of ever-increasing regulation of farms, abattoirs, and other industries (including cosmetics, drugs, fertilizers, and health care, as well as the food industry), prohibitions on everyday food and garden products, and massive state subsidization of farmers and rendering plants.

BSE created a blame crisis because of numerous errors in the government's efforts to handle the risks posed by the disease since it was first officially recognized in the mid-1980s. At first the government and its expert advisers wrongly believed the disease was not dangerous to humans and could not be passed from mother to calf, and the initial control measures adopted to control the incidence of the disease were ineffective. That in turn led to a loss of confidence in the capacity of the British government in this area by the EU and a loss of public confidence in the wider food safety regime. The government in general and its Ministry of Agriculture, Fisheries and Food in particular were seen to have been slow and foot-dragging in their response to what turned out to be the biggest twentieth-century crisis in UK farming. Their presentational strategies for blame avoidance backfired too. Numerous unqualified statements by agriculture ministers and the government's chief medical officer denying that there was a problem and asserting that beef was safe to eat (made, for example, in 1990 and 1993) came to be seen as evidence of complacency, as BSE cases continued to mount and a new variant of CJD began to claim human lives.

The government was also seen as administratively inept in its handling of the BSE crisis, since it took some ten years before all routes by which contaminated "ruminant material"[5] could enter the animal food chain were finally closed off by regulation, and even then there were widespread allegations that those regulations were not being effectively enforced. In addition, the government was seen as having created a major and damaging conflict with the EU as a result of its sluggish responses to the crisis, leading up to a "killer punch" in 1996 when the EU imposed a total ban on exports of cattle and cattle products from the UK, ruining the very industry the government had been trying to protect.

The mopping-up stage of this blame episode took place under the newly elected New Labour government under Tony Blair. In addition to setting up a heavy-duty inquiry into the mistakes and follies of its predecessor, the new regime adopted new agency and policy strategies over the handling of food safety risks. New agency strategy took the form of the creation of an autonomous Food Standards Agency, taking government ministers even further from the front line of formal responsibility for food risk issues than had been the case with the previous regime (under which food safety was handled by a ministerial department advised by expert committees).[6] New policy strategies took the form of procedures for assessing food safety that relied heavily on standard protocols, giving experts more standardized frameworks to work with.

While, as in that case, agency and policy strategies often get changed after a blame episode, presentational strategies are blame-avoidance measures that can be used equally readily before, during, and after such episodes. In fact, when a blame crisis strikes, presentational strategy is the main approach to blame avoidance that those in the firing line can use and change, while the agency and policy approaches are likely to be a constant in the short term. The emphasis on the use of presentational strategy in the heat of battle is reflected in the literature on crisis management and the handling of media feeding frenzies (see, for example, Linsky and Scott 1992). Such accounts bring out the way the news cycle tends to shape much of top officeholders' activity, and the huge investment of their scarce time that such individuals often devote to striking the right tone (for instance, over how contrite or unrepentant to sound) and finding the exact words to limit the blame damage, as in the Formula 1 racing case discussed at the outset of this chapter. When officeholders and organizations are in the eye of the storm of a blame crisis, they are therefore more likely to be preoccupied with what variants of presentational strategy to use than they are with crafting new agency or policy strategies.

Any Port in a Storm, but Changing Course Can Be Costly

Just as in any other tricky decision situation, those who are exposed to a blame crisis can be expected to hunt around, moving from one combination of strategies to another if the first does not succeed in making the problem go away, and seizing on the first that seems to be effective. As with the old adage quoted in the epigraph—"any port in a storm"—a strategy of hunting around is what people often follow when they are faced with complex choices with uncertain effects.

So the search for whatever blame-free haven might be available can be expected to start from where the beleaguered organizations and individuals happen to be when a blame crisis occurs. That search will be shaped by those individuals' history and experience and by existing institutional structures and routines. What has worked for the people concerned in the past is likely to be their first response, with a switch to something else only if those tried-and-tested recipes of the past do not produce the desired result.

But the central message of "path-dependency theory" in institutional analysis (see Peters, Pierre, and King 2005) is that switching from one strategy to another can be costly. So individuals and institutions often continue to follow a less than ideal course, because the various costs of switching to something better are so high. An example is the persistence of laws that prescribe driving on different sides of the road in different countries of the world, which remain through inertia, given the very high costs of switching, even though it would obviously be preferable to have a single global rule if every country was starting out afresh.[7]

In principle the same thing can be expected to apply when it comes to switching among blame-avoidance strategies, and the costs of switching come in at least three different forms. One is the time that it takes to move from one course to another. Irrespective of any other resource limits, time is needed for new scripts to be written, new job titles to be created, meetings to be arranged, formalities to be enacted. In a fast-moving blame episode, time costs can be central. And there are other kinds of costs that officeholders have to pay in making a switch from one blame-avoidance approach to another. Even with unlimited flunkeys at your command, switching from a familiar routine to something different often involves personal stress, whether in persuading and negotiating with other key actors or in making high-stakes speeches and statements. And a third kind of switching cost involves the organizational resources that need to be deployed—for instance, in arranging the legal or formal drafting needed for changes such as alterations in organizational responsibilities.

For presentational strategies, most of the switching costs involved are likely to be of the second type. It is often relatively costless in time and organizational resources to switch from this excuse to that or from one line of argument to another. It can be and often is done overnight. The main costs lie in the effort and political capital that has to be expended in persuading skeptical observers about the compatibility between yesterday's firmly held stance and today's apparently contradictory one, as when winning-the-argument strategies shift from the problem-denial variety to the problem-admission-but-responsibility-denial variety. Switching from one broader type of presentational strategy to another may incur similar sorts of costs—for instance, if a previously hyperactive blame-avoidance stance suddenly turns into a tactic of going to ground or vice versa. But there may also be different kinds of cost constraints in switching from one broader type of presentational strategy to another. For instance, it is likely to be harder to draw the line with a preemptive apology approach if officeholders or organizations have been previously following other approaches for an extended period.

When it comes to switching among and within agency and policy strategies, the second type of switching costs (expressed in terms of officeholders' personal effort and political capital) is likely to be important as well. But the first and third type of switching costs (that is, time and organizational resource costs) will ordinarily tend to figure rather larger than in the case of presentational strategies. Time costs will not necessarily be high if such strategies are so soft as to be almost indistinguishable from presentational strategies (that is, areas d and e in the overlapping circles depicted in in figure 1.2, as mentioned before). For instance, in cases where changes are made in distributions of organizational responsibilities that are not enshrined in formal law (as with the case of soft delegation, as discussed in chapter 4), there need be no gap between announcement and enactment. Nor will the time costs be heavy if top-level officeholders can mobilize the support necessary for extraordinary meetings or one-day legislative sessions for the necessary processes of formal authorization and enactment. But in such cases time costs are saved by paying a correspondingly heavier price in expenditure of personal political capital. And those kinds of changes also often need other tangible organizational resources as well, such as the scarce legal, financial, or negotiating expertise that could be put to other uses.

The example given in the previous section, of the remodeling of the UK's administrative architecture to distance ministers further from direct responsibility for handling food safety crises such as BSE, is a case in point. Whereas several media briefings can be given in a single day to change a presentational line, that reorganization of the government machine required heavy lifting that took years to carry out and involved complex negotiations with various players, such that the new Food Standards Agency (more distant from government ministers) only came into existence some three years after the Blair government came to power. Some switches in policy strategies can also take years to work out.

Those Under Fire in a Blame Crisis Will Ordinarily Respond in a Sequence

Finally, when it comes to those blame-avoidance crises in which office-holders have to rely on presentational strategies in the first instance (as discussed above), what sequence of responses can we expect? The idea that there will normally be a sequence of responses in such cases can be partly derived from the psychological literature on self-presentation and attribution of blame, but in part it also reflects the basic logic of blame avoidance as a political imperative. A decade or so ago, Astrid Schütz (1998: 121) drew on that literature to identify seven separate steps in responses by officeholders to political scandals. For Schütz, those steps are (loosely translated from the original German):

- denial (claim that nothing has happened)
- positive spin (claim that what has happened is positive rather than negative)
- denial of responsibility (claim that the officeholder was not responsible for what has happened)

- claims of procedural correctness or inevitability (claim that the issue had to be handled in the way that it was, or that the outcome was in some way unavoidable)
- claims of limited foresight or foreseeability (claim that the office-holder was not able to foresee at the time the negative consequences of his or her action)
- claims that the issue was a blip (not typical of the officeholder's general conduct)
- apology (expression of regret for what happened and assurance that it will not recur)

Schütz argues (in line with what has been said above) that these steps can be combined up to a point, but also suggests that they can form a set of stages of defensive self-presentation by officeholders in a blame crisis. That implies a logic of staged retreat in the use of presentational strategies, with more defensible positions abandoned only when they become untenable. And as was suggested in the first chapter, many readers will have dealt with organizations that do precisely that (in spite of PR portraying the organization as warm, friendly, and approachable) and from which the slightest admission of fault can only be dragged out after a tortuous process in which every other escape route has been blocked off by the aggrieved client producing criminal-standard evidence. Indeed, if organizations and officeholders were to respond to every problem by immediately accepting responsibility and making apologies, the notion of blame avoidance would have no value as a proposition about political and organizational behavior.

Of course, there are several reasons why Schütz's seven steps will not necessarily occur in the order given above. One is that in some circumstances, the safest defensive position—that there is no problem and therefore no possibility of blame—will simply never be tenable. If everyone can see that the roads are blocked or garbage is rotting uncollected in the streets or the country is submerged under floodwater, problem denial is hardly likely to be a viable option even for those officeholders with the greatest chutzpah.[8] The only issue in such cases will be who or what is to blame for what has happened. Second, as was noted in chapter 5, routinely following the advice to "never admit liability" (typically offered by insurers when we are involved in an auto accident) can sometimes be less effective in deflecting blame than a quick, preemptive admission of the problem and a (carefully worded) apology. Such preemption takes the wind out of critics' sails and allows the organization or officeholder to draw a line under the problem and move on before heavy-duty calling-to-account procedures have time to get started. Intelligent and light-footed blame avoidance might be expected sometimes to follow this pattern,

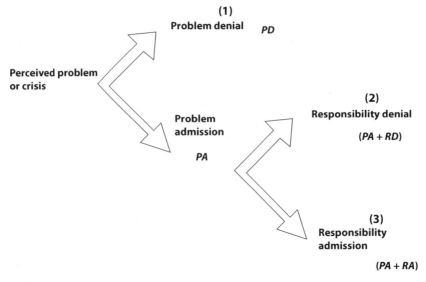

Figure 7.1. Presentational Strategies in a Blame Crisis: Stages of Retreat from Problem Denial. Source: Adapted from Hood et al. 2009: 697.

avoiding implausible first-stage defensive positions that may only make the individuals or organizations involved appear all the more culpable when they are eventually obliged to abandon those positions.

All the same, the logic of blame avoidance suggests that when it comes to presentational strategies, admission of the problem coupled with admission of personal culpability will ordinarily come after *either* problem denial (steps one and two of Schütz's analysis) or problem admission but responsibility denial (steps three and four of her analysis) *or* problem admission plus forms of responsibility admission that stops short of unambiguous admission of personal culpability (steps five through seven of her analysis).[9] Stated formally and as depicted in figure 7.1, the expectation is that $(PA + RA)$ will normally be adopted only after either PD or $(PA + RD)$, where PD = problem denial (in several possible variants, as we have seen earlier), RD = responsibility denial (several possible variants), PA = problem admission, and RA = responsibility admission (see Hood et al. 2009: 697–8).

Of course there are some variants of $(PA + RA)$ that do not necessarily involve an officeholder or organization admitting culpability for some adverse event. Perhaps the mildest form of $(PA + RA)$ merely consists of explaining what the problem is and how the issue (whatever it is) has been mishandled, as in the common use of the so-called past exonerative tense when officeholders or their spokespersons use the passive voice to admit that "mistakes have been made" without saying who precisely was responsible for those mistakes.[10] And once we start to look at the various ways that the different players in the blame game can blame each other for problems once acknowledged, there are many other possible variants of $(P + A)$—for example, when top bananas blame subordinate staff for adverse events or vice versa. After all, even if we leave aside the sort of abject confessions of guilt that were extracted from high-ranking officials during the show trial era of Stalin's rule in the former USSR, it often happens in modern liberal democracies that lower-level actors can be pressured by the top bananas into taking the rap for adverse actions at an early stage in a blaming sequence. But when it comes to uncoerced behavior, we can expect the version of $(PA + RA)$ that involves a personal admission of culpability to come after PD and/or $(PA + RD)$ and/or $(PA + RA)$ of some of the other varieties mentioned above.

Basic as that proposition might seem, to date we have relatively few systematic studies that test it carefully over time, though numerous scholars have explored the changing stance of officeholders under fire in one way or another (see, for instance, Linsky and Scott 1992; Bovens et al. 1999). The proposition was broadly held up in a study of ministerial behavior over fiascos in the handling of public university entrance exams in Scotland in 2000 and England in 2002, conducted by the author with three colleagues (Hood et al. 2009). In that study, the level of blame facing the responsible ministers over a period of approximately a hundred days after the exams were (mis)processed was measured by coding articles appearing in a selected set of newspapers on each of those days (to give an indication of the heat those officeholders faced on each day of the process). The actions taken by those ministers on each one of those hundred days were also coded in terms of various forms of PD, various forms of $(PA + RD)$, and various forms of $(PA + RA)$. Ministerial conduct in both of those cases followed the pattern predicted earlier.

These operational fiascos in the delivery of public services differ from the sort of high-stakes personal-conduct blame event faced by Bill Clinton in 1998 over allegations about his behavior with White House intern Monica Lewinsky, by Irish *Taoiseach* Bertie Ahern in 2007–8 over allegations about the conduct of his personal finances, or by François Mitterand toward the end of his term of office about his early political career in Vichy France. In cases such as those, the $(PA + RD)$ shot is not on the board and it comes down to a choice between PD and $(PA + RA)$. But the general point remains that if blame avoidance means anything, it will tend to mean that the sequencing approach will be commonly observable.

CONCLUSION

As was noted at the outset, mixing and matching blame-avoidance strategies is a process of human creativity and often takes place under fire (as it were). Much of the fascination in observing blame avoidance in institutional architecture, organizational operating routines, and presentational tactics is precisely the creativity that can be brought to the process.

But in this chapter (beginning with some fairly obvious propositions and proceeding to look at some of the complexities) we have argued that there are logical, practical, and cultural constraints that apply both to mixing and matching strategies at any one time and to switching among approaches over time.

As we have just seen, blame avoidance would mean nothing if individuals and organizations always responded to every adverse event by following an immediate $(PA + RA)$ line of presentational strategy. And the simile that was used earlier, likening blame-avoidance strategy to the problem of finding the numbers that open a combination lock or a perfect cookery recipe, is complicated both by the path-dependency issue and by the plasticity of culture. It is as if the numbers needed to open that lock depended on changes in micro-climate from moment to moment and also on what numbers had been used before.

But focusing on those practical or logical constraints that shape the way blame-avoidance strategies can be linked together or used in sequence by officeholders and organizations does not of itself tell us about the theme with which this book began, namely what might be positive or negative about blame avoidance and blame games. That is the issue to which we return in the next chapter.

CHAPTER EIGHT

Democracy, Good Governance, and Blame Avoidance

> Any frying pan in a fire.
>   —Austin 1956: 3

> Those who have attained the chief places are led to seek
> the character of "safe men,"—which is gained by avoiding
> entering into questions or giving reasons, that they may "not
> commit themselves;" by evading difficulties neatly; and by
> speciously turning away from troublesome duties, and letting
> evil principles work themselves out at the expense of the
> public, unless forced into notice by clamour,—applying the
> rule—"Never to act until you are obliged, and then do as
> little as you can," ...
>   —Chadwick 1854: 190

REPRISE: UNDERSTANDING BLAME-AVOIDANCE ENGINEERING AND ARCHITECTURE

This book began with puzzles about why organizational responsibilities for the problems we all face in our daily lives in dealing with government and public services are so rarely clear and joined up (despite all that earnest rhetoric of customer-focused, joined-up government); why the regulation of risk is so rarely flexible, well-judged, and proportionate (despite an apparently never-ending succession of "better regulation" initiatives); and why it is often so difficult to pin down responsibility and find out exactly who knew what when after some major adverse event has happened (despite so many loudly trumpeted governance reforms ostensibly intended to clarify lines of accountability and increase transparency so that muddles can never recur).

The earlier chapters of this book provide at least a partial answer to those puzzles. When blame avoidance (itself typically exacerbated by negativity bias embedded in various institutional mechanisms) dominates organizational design and functioning, and is the central motivation of all or many of the various blame game players discussed in chapter 2, the sort of experiences described at the outset of chapter 1 will be anything but accidental. They are wholly predictable results of blame-avoidance engineering and architecture.

Indeed, once we start looking at the structure and operations of government and public services through blame-avoidance spectacles, much that would otherwise be hard to make sense of starts to come into sharper focus. If policy and operational strategies for blame avoidance dominate organizational routines, flexibility, common sense, or nuanced human judgment will almost inevitably come to be squeezed out of the equation. If agency strategies for blame avoidance trump other considerations, it will hardly be surprising if problem cases turn out to fall between all those convenient cracks of organizational responsibility. And if everyone is ingeniously trying to spin their way out of blame through carefully crafted presentational strategies, unambiguous accounts of who knew what or even who did what when will be the last thing to emerge, whatever official bromides about transparency and accountability were pronounced by the architects of the last organizational restructuring or shuffling of portfolios. There is even a kind of beauty—albeit perhaps a chilling one—in blame-avoidance engineering and architecture, since it so starkly reflects a logic of design utterly different from the conventional clichés of good regulation, risk management, and organizational design.

Of course, blame avoidance is only one aspect of government and public services. To take blame avoidance as the master key to understanding all human behavior would be like the often noted tendency of those with hammers to treat everything as if it were a nail.[1] There are important competing motivations and counter-pressures at work, as we have already noted, and there are times when things get so bad for governments, organizations and officeholders that physical self-preservation becomes more important than warding off blame. But the earlier chapters of this book have tried to show that blame avoidance is important enough to be taken seriously. So in this chapter we step back from both the stamp collection and the analysis of combinations and dynamics to explore some broader questions about the significance of blame-avoidance behavior. Do the various blame-avoidance strategies actually work, or are they better understood as superstitious behavior? Whether or not those strategies work, is the pursuit of blame avoidance by organizations and officeholders something that is positive or negative? Can we identify good and bad forms of blame avoidance? And if so, what if any remedies are available for bad blame avoidance?

BLAME-AVOIDANCE STRATEGIES: EVER IMPROVING TEFLON TECHNOLOGY OR TRIUMPH OF HOPE OVER EXPERIENCE?

Oscar Wilde once famously described second marriages as a triumph of hope over experience. Can the same be said for the use of blame-avoidance strategies, or are we seeing something like the steady advancement of technology for non-stick cooking pots and utensils, unknown to our great-grandparents? Is the apparently increasing investment in some types of blame-avoidance measures, as discussed in chapter 6, matched with a corresponding decrease in the incidence of blame affecting the various institutional players discussed in chapter 2?

We do not have anything approaching a systematic test of the efficacy of blame-avoidance strategies. The necessary evidence is of its nature often buried or unavailable, and the social science technology for testing such efficacy is still in its infancy. But there does seem to be evidence that blame-avoidance strategies work sometimes, at least in the form of persuasive case examples and some broader studies.

For example, the political science literature on cutbacks in welfare state services discussed in chapter 5 suggests that some democratic governments have been able to find ways of packaging policy changes that disadvantage significant groups of the electorate without suffering severe punishment at the polls. And Christopher Anderson's (1995) comparative study, discussed in chapter 4, on the way institutional structures seemed to shape the extent to which voters blamed their governments for adverse economic circumstances, also suggests that some forms of delegation can shield politicians from blame they might otherwise incur. After all, when unemployment soared in East Germany in the early 1990s after unification with the west, reflecting a combination of the policy of valuing the former East German currency at par with the Deutschmark and of rapid privatization of East Germany's over 8000 state-owned enterprises, it was the head of the autonomous *Treuhandanstalt* (the privatization agency), not federal ministers, who was assassinated by the Red Army Faction.[2]

But equally it is clear from the scattered literature on the subject that efforts at blame avoidance are far from universally successful. For example, Raanan Sulitzeanu-Kenan (2006) found evidence of 'conditional credibility' (perhaps another version of negativity bias) in an experimental study of the effects of public inquiries on blame conducted in England in the mid-2000s, concluding that inquiries were more believable to his experimental subjects when the inquiry report condemned governmental authorities than when the inquiries exonerated such authorities from all blame. Similarly, in the study of levels of media blame leveled at British ministers after exam crises in Scotland and England in the early 2000s, as discussed in the previous chapter, impact intervention analysis showed that many ministerial presentational responses had no effects on the next day's level of blame and in some cases seemed to have had a reverse effect, unintendedly pouring gasoline on the very blame firestorm they were trying to douse (Hood. et al 2009).

From such studies and some of the examples given in earlier chapters, it is clear that the investment of time and money that officeholders and organizations put into their presentational, agency, and policy strategies by no means always protects them when the going gets rough. Sometimes that blame-avoidance activity does look like superstitious behavior—like wearing lucky shoes or carrying a rabbit's foot—and it frequently seems to be ineffective or even counterproductive. There are some ineluctable limits as well. As we have seen, policy strategies cannot be effective at the equilibrium point where all activity attracts equal blame. Agency strategies cannot be effective where the public credibility of any formal institutional arrangements is low. Presentational strategies, at least of the winning the argument kind, cannot be effective when public suspicion of all government statements or activity has become high enough. And none of those circumstances is exactly rare.

How can we make sense of such observations? One possible conclusion is that effective blame avoidance needs cultural congruence, as suggested in the previous chapter. That means that public mood and cultural bias among the potential blamers will be what determines whether any given blame-avoidance move will be effective or otherwise. The clearest example is the honeymoon period that new officeholders are often said to enjoy, when their blame-avoidance tactics are more likely to be effective because enough of the media and the electorate, like a new spouse, will for a time be disposed to be indulgent about giving second chances and the benefit of the doubt to the fresh faces at the top. A case in point is Barack Obama's disarming admission on TV news that he had "screwed up" ("I've got to own up to my mistake") over a key appointment early in his presidency in 2009.[3] But when that honeymoon is over and "the mood shifts, and every slip, every ill-advised step, indeed every sign of simple human fallibility, is eagerly pounced upon" (McCall Smith 2008: 223), such blame-avoidance moves will be launched into a far less forgiving or tractable environment. Another is the way that partisan ties shape who gets blamed for what, as revealed by numerous studies of which agencies and levels of government were blamed by whom for failures in the response to Hurricane Katrina which struck New Orleans in 2005 (see Maestas et al. 2008). And culture (or "conversational context," in the language of Clarke et al. 1997) more generally seems to be what explains why the same strategies can have different effects at different points in time as the mood changes in the media, among the public at large, or in the relevant institutional arena. It can be seen as a catalyst that determines the sign—positive or negative—that blame avoidance takes.

Of course, culture can be hard to measure, and explaining blame-avoidance efficacy by cultural context can easily turn into tautology—impossible to falsify because in effect true by definition. But still the effect of the cultural mood among potential blamers in shaping outcomes seems impossible to dismiss. As was suggested in the previous chapter, the sorts of blame-avoidance measures that will be effective are likely to differ according to the kind of worldviews that are held by the potential blamers in the game, meaning that what works in blame avoidance will not be the same in times when the dominant cultural mood is egalitarian as they are when hierarchism or individualism is dominant. An all-purpose approach to blame avoidance that will work whatever the cultural weather will therefore be elusive if not impossible.

As we have already seen, that point was learned the hard way by the much discussed and supposedly mighty spin doctors of Bill Clinton and Tony Blair in the 1990s and early 2000s, respectively. Those players discovered that their presumed ability to control the media to deflect blame away from themselves depended heavily on changing cultural moods that they could not readily control, except insofar as they themselves inadvertently generated the shift in public attitudes. In both of those cases, public attention started to turn away from policy substance to presentational technique, the spin doctors turned into the main story rather than the behind-the-scenes controllers of other stories, and once-Teflon politicians turned into blame magnets. What changed? It was not the selection of spin techniques that were used, but the social context, in the form of a growing climate of public distrust.

Figure 8.1 takes the example of delegation (one of the key agency strategies we discussed in chapter 4), traces some of the ways that cultural bias can shape the blame outcome, and also shows how agency strategies can link to policy strategies. It shows how attitudes and beliefs can shape whether the outcome of the delegation approach is *blame reversion* (blame makers see through the attempted delegation), *blame displacement* (blame makers find other things to blame the delegators for), *blame shifting* (delegators successfully transfer the blame to others), *blame sharing* or *blame reversion* (delegators cannot escape some or all of the blame because delegatees pass some or all of it it back), or *blame dissolution* (if delegatees cannot pass any of the blame back and are obliged to handle it by defensive policy strategies). And if defensive policy strategies by delegatees are the most likely outcome where blame-avoidance imperatives meet negativity bias, there are wider social implications that we shall discuss in the next two sections.

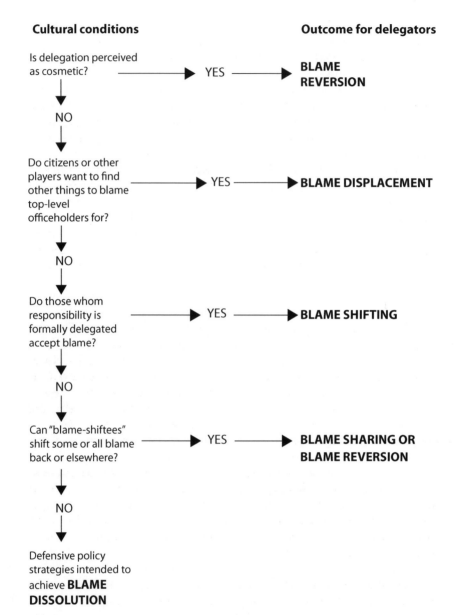

Cultural conditions

Is delegation perceived as cosmetic? → YES → **BLAME REVERSION**

NO ↓

Do citizens or other players want to find other things to blame top-level officeholders for? → YES → **BLAME DISPLACEMENT**

NO ↓

Do those whom responsibility is formally delegated accept blame? → YES → **BLAME SHIFTING**

NO ↓

Can "blame-shiftees" shift some or all blame back or elsewhere? → YES → **BLAME SHARING OR BLAME REVERSION**

NO ↓

Defensive policy strategies intended to achieve **BLAME DISSOLUTION**

Outcome for delegators

Figure 8.1. Delegation Agency Strategies and Policy Strategies: How Culture Can Shape the Outcomes of the Blame Game for Would-Be Delegators.

Whether or Not It Works, Can the Pursuit of Blame Avoidance Have Positive Effects?

Like social conflict (Coser 1956), blame avoidance gets a bad press. Perhaps itself showing negativity bias, this book began with the problems, showing how blame avoidance can skew institutional behavior. And indeed most commentators, going back at least to the nineteenth-century views of Sir Edwin Chadwick given in this chapter's second epigraph, see blame avoidance as an undesirable and unattractive feature of modern political and organizational behavior. They commonly portray it as a craven, defensive jobsworth world of endless weasel words, buck-passing, small print, and box-ticking, in contrast to an implicit golden age or at least imagined alternative world in which politicians and bureaucrats boldly take personal risks for the public good. Everyone loves to ridicule the latest instance of back-covering and evasive language by politicians and bureaucrats.

But should we get too worked up about such activity in modern government and corporate life? If blame-avoidance activity was mostly ineffective and merely a form of superstitious behavior (as it clearly is sometimes), shouldn't we conclude it is harmless even if misguided? After all, if blame avoidance-strategies generally did not work, erring officeholders and organizations would get their just deserts, irrespective of their wiles in spinmanship and the other blame-avoidance arts.

Even if blame avoidance activity is effective for at least some of the time, shouldn't we see it as having positive as well as negative effects, for example in keeping individuals and organizations on the straight and narrow, rather than just the negative effects with which this book began? After all, if a desire for blame avoidance makes those who lead us try to lead blameless lives, shouldn't that be applauded rather than derided? If it motivates public officeholders to take care with the policies they design, to avoid egregious risks to the lives, health, and financial security of the rest of us, and to vigorously defend what they do against challenge, whatever could be wrong with that?

If either of those propositions were true for a significant part of blame-avoidance behavior, we could not conclude that blame avoidance was all bad news. Maybe we could even consider the urge to avoid blame as one of those human drives (like the drive for sex or other kinds of gratification) that may seem less than noble when viewed dispassionately, but can unintentionally have positive consequences for the society as a whole and even be a recipe for better government through some sort of "invisible hand."

Such an argument, going radically against the sort of observations with this book began, would evoke the classic observation that positive results can result from inglorious motivations and from actions not intended by the perpetrators to be socially beneficial, such as Adam Smith's (1910 [1776]: 400) idea that the pursuit of individual selfishness could sometimes unintentionally lead to collective benefit, or Charles Lindblom's (1965) idea that the activity of vote-obsessed politicians living from one short-term political fix to the next could unintentionally lead to policies that were actually superior to the products of apparently far more cerebral and long-sighted central planners.[4] Can we say something similar about blame-avoidance behavior? And if so, might we even be able to conclude—contrary to the tone of all those barroom conversations and media derision of jobsworths and spin—that we need *more* blame avoidance in leadership and government rather than less?

Some readers will no doubt dismiss any such idea, in the same way that Voltaire (1965 [1759]) in his classic *Candide* ridiculed the idea of Gottfried Leibniz's eighteenth-century philosophy that positive harmony can always be discovered under apparent confusion if we only know where to look for it.[5] But the possibility that blame-avoidance activity might, albeit unintentionally, serve to enhance democracy and good governance in some conditions should give us pause. So let us briefly consider what might be positive effects of the application of the presentational, agency, and policy strategies we explored in Chapters Three to Five, before turning to the negatives.

Potentially Positive Effects of Presentational Strategies

Efforts by blame-avoiding officeholders and organizations to put their conduct and decisions in the most favorable possible light could well be positive in some circumstances. Even if the scheming spin doctors never consciously intend to improve public debate and accountability in their efforts to control the story and mainly aim to get the media off their case by fair means or foul, their activity could in principle have positive effects in at least two ways (though probably not simultaneously). One is by the reverse effect mentioned earlier, when excessive or inept use of presentational strategies unintentionally turns the spin doctoring itself into the story. In that way, the public at large ends up being better informed than the spin doctors might like about how officeholders and organizations work behind the scenes to shape what appears in the news media. By unintentionally turning itself into the main story, spin doctoring can sometimes serve to increase the very accountability it is often trying to avoid.

But winning-the-argument forms of presentational blame-avoidance activity can also in some circumstances improve public debate over the hot issues of the day by providing an effective and maybe even necessary counterweight to the negativity bias that would otherwise go unchallenged in public and media debate—for instance, if no government spokesperson is ever on hand to counter accusations of incompetence or corruption. There is a possible parallel here with the social case for advertising, as put forward by authors like John Hood (2005).[6] Their argument is that ads—even irritating and utterly banal telemarketing pitches, jingles, and junk mail—can give us useful information about products and services that are available to us but of which we might otherwise be unaware. The classic example is that of those catalogues that tell us about all the latest gadgets and gizmos we didn't know we needed because we hadn't heard of them. Hood's argument is that such processes make advertising a value-adding component of modern economic activity.

The parallel case for blame-avoiding presentational activity would be that well-framed excuses and justifications can better inform the potential blamers—voters, media, the commentariat—about the issues, the difficult trade-offs, and all the tricky judgment calls of the life political and bureaucratic. Such activity can thus in some conditions provide the basis for more sophisticated judgments about the blameworthiness of individuals or organizations. That will apply especially when the blame-avoiding spin activity serves to counterbalance the spin put on blame issues by non-elected media, NGOs, or unrepresentative well-funded pressure groups with particular and often concealed axes to grind. That is a modern version of Georg Hegel's 1820s argument (1896) for a bureaucracy that was not a captive to any one interest group in society, even though Hegel might not exactly have had today's spin doctors in mind when he framed that high-minded idea two centuries ago.

Potentially Positive Effects of Agency Strategies

The agency strategies for blame avoidance that were discussed in chapter 4 can also in some conditions serve to enhance the accountability of organizations and officeholders and indeed to improve the functioning of government and public services in other ways as well. The hidden hand of unintended benefit seems to function at least sometimes in blame-avoiding bureaucracies and political organizations as well as in profit-seeking markets.

For instance, as we saw in chapter 4, partnership arrangements for service delivery can serve as convenient ways for each of a group of individual or corporate actors to avoid being singled out for blame in the event of something going wrong, be it Olympic deficits, operational fiascos, convicted pedophiles who re-offend after having been injudiciously released into the community, or financial institutions that fail after errors of commission or omission by the authorities. But the outcome may nevertheless sometimes be the collection of intelligence that is superior to what any organization could ever conceivably muster on its own for the complex problem at hand. After all, more angles of vision may be brought to bear than would apply in a single-organizational structure, and more interests are likely to be considered as well.

Similarly, arrangements for delegating potentially blame-worthy operational tasks away from ministers or other elected government officials into the hands of more or less autonomous agencies might be heavily influenced by a less than noble desire by elected politicians or senior bureaucrats to avoid taking the bullet, however well-deserved, for operational failures that occur on their watch. But such arrangements could still unintentionally lead to better policy or service delivery. That positive outcome could come about if the by-product of institutional arrangements primarily intended to shield the delegator from blame was greater managerial or policy effectiveness on the part of those doing the job. And that could happen if such delegated arrangements gave professional managers and technical experts more decision space to do what they know best (tackling the details of technical advice, project management, and implementation). That is, after all, the conventional case for the better service outcomes that are claimed for managerial or technocratic styles of politics (Hood 2002).

So even if driven by blame-avoidance imperatives, such delegation arrangements can give the various players roles that provide them a comparative advantage. Elected politicians can be argued to have a comparative advantage in setting broad targets reflecting their perceptions of what the voters want, and in trading off conflicting values in some explicit political choice made by direct or representative democracy. But experts and managers might equally be considered to have a comparative advantage in weighing up abstruse technical evidence and looking after detailed delivery arrangements. Arrangements that provide for each of those parties to perform the tasks for which they are best fitted could be considered a formula for a marriage (if not of love, at least of convenience) between blame avoidance and good policy execution in a democratic framework.

Potentially Positive Effects of Policy and Operational Strategies

Policy strategies for blame avoidance might also in some conditions have strong potential advantages for society at large. After all, there is much to be said for an approach to public policy that puts the stress on avoiding harm rather than producing positive benefits, if avoiding harm is indeed the logic of blame avoidance in policy strategies. Two hundred years ago, the great utilitarian philosopher Jeremy Bentham (1962, 1: 301) thought it was entirely appropriate that public policy should be biased in that way. He declared that "the care of providing for his enjoyments ought to be left almost entirely to each individual; the principal function of government being to protect him from sufferings." Bentham probably meant that as an argument for government concentrating on relief of poverty rather than on (say) providing New Year's fireworks parties or putting on sporting extravaganzas. But at another level it could be read as an argument for avoiding the sort of egregious harm that brings blame, as in the case of the shifting policy stance on asbestos over a century (noted in chapter 5).

More recently, Kristin Shrader-Frechette (1991) used an argument based on Bentham's to defend a "precautionary" approach to public policy towards harm as superior to conventional "science-based" policies in justice and democratic effect. She argued that the difference between those policy stances concerns the relative weight to be given to Type I errors as against Type II errors. In conventional science and statistical theory, Type I errors involve rejection of a null hypothesis (for example, that there is no relationship between smoking and cancer) that turns out to be true. Type II errors involve acceptance of a null hypothesis that turns out to be false. If the null hypothesis is taken to be the assumption that a product or practice is not harmful, as it conventionally is in assessments of risk and hazard, debates about appropriate policy and management turn on whether we prefer to avoid Type I errors (the conventional bias of science and the 'innocent until proved guilty' presumption embedded in liberal systems of law) as against Type II errors (following the precautionary principle of being better safe than sorry). Shrader-Frechette argues that public policy based on the precautionary principle of avoiding Type II errors rather than Type I errors is more just and democratic than policy based on the opposite principle. Her claim is that the precautionary approach is more likely to serve a broader range of interests, while the bias toward avoiding Type I errors is more likely to serve less representative producer interests.

Such are some of the lines on which blame avoidance might be seen as a potentially positive force in democratic government and modern society more generally, even if many of its positive effects were unintended by the actors concerned. Moreover, the sort of blame games that start when the public becomes aware of adverse events—with the various parties engaging in processes of vigorous problem or responsibility denial—can, even if unedifying, function as an important social discovery process over blame, one that could not easily be achieved by some sort of synoptic rationality, given that formal allocation of responsibilities is often ambiguous, inappropriate, or out of line with practice.[7] And if blame avoidance can sometimes have positive social effects, however craven the motives from which it springs, there might indeed be some conditions in which more rather than less blame avoidance can result in better governance and improved welfare to society at large.

THE NEGATIVE SIDE OF BLAME AVOIDANCE

But it is hard to deny that there is also a negative side to blame avoidance. The first defense of blame-avoidance activity, noted in the previous section, was that it may be harmless if it is ineffective, as it clearly often is. The problem with that defense is that, even if they are unsuccessful, efforts at blame avoidance can still damage government and public services in other ways. Not all superstitions are harmless. At the least, such efforts can be a diversion from other, more worthy things that corporate or individual attention might otherwise be concentrated on. And they can do harm in other ways as well, as with the sharply raised health-care costs and harm to patients that can be caused by excessive testing or medication resulting from medical defensiveness, as discussed earlier.

The second defense of blame-avoidance activity, also noted in the previous section, was that even when it succeeds in deflecting or dissipating blame, such activity can at least sometimes have effects that are positive for accountability, public debate, and the effective functioning of government. But the problem with that argument is that for every example or assertion of positive effects of blame-avoidance activity we can find at least one negative example or assertion. Each of the three types of blame-avoidance strategies that have been analyzed in this book can clearly have negative effects as well.

Potentially Negative Effects of Presentational Strategies

When blame-avoiding presentational strategy is the dominant preoccupation in politics or organizational life, it can have at least three detrimental effects on the quality of governance. First, it can divert the limited time of top-level leaders away from other activities in which they might be engaged—such as actually running their organizations. And if, as was noted in chapter 3, those at the top of executive government spend much of their time on handling the media so as to avoid blame and claim credit, how can they find time for things that are so often said to increase organizational effectiveness—such as "management by walking around"? The presentational focus can turn into a recipe for focusing that scarce leadership attention on day-to-day media fire-fighting operations over today's soon-to-be-forgotten trivialities at the expense of any longer-term concerns (see Mulgan 2009: 21 and UK Public Administration Select Committee 2009: 20–1).

Second, it can mean that power at the top of politics and organizations passes from those who have substantive knowledge about law or the technicalities of policy to a new class of political functionary that has little or no technical expertise. If that happens, organizations can start to be controlled by journalists (or by those who have the skills of journalists) rather than those with more traditional bureaucratic engineering skills. The risk of that kind of dominance for organizational performance is that it can mean excessive concern with appearance rather than substance, and decision-making over life-or-death issues by those whose main skill is to make their masters look good in the media, craft eye-catching "announcables" and turn complex policy issues into superficial sound-bites. The risk of engineering and operational errors may be correspondingly increased if those who have the skill to minimize those errors are pushed down the pecking order so that what they have to say gets less attention.

Third and relatedly, if preoccupation with presentational strategy to the exclusion of all else means an iron grip over any information that could be potentially embarrassing and a tendency to hector and intimidate anyone whose actions or views could put the officeholder or organization concerned in a bad light, that too can undermine some familiar recipes for organizational effectiveness. It can mean a stultifying centralization that slows up decision-making and a blaming, bullying culture that flies in the face of conventional precepts for high-reliability organization (Sagan 1993). It may even encourage sabotage or damaging leaks by those who are disaffected by those sorts of controls and have no respect for the authority of those who impose them.

Finally, as noted in chapter 3, heavy emphasis on presentational strategy can ironically help to feed a culture in which no public statement is taken at face value, and public cynicism about politics and institutions controlled by spin doctors increases to the point that mendacity or at least half-truths start to be taken as the norm. Strategies intended to produce Teflon-coated organizations or officeholders can sometimes serve to exacerbate public cynicism and disaffection without contributing reasoned argument in defense of potentially blameworthy actions.

Potentially Negative Effects of Agency Strategies

Agency strategies of the kind described in chapter 4 can also have their negative side for the quality of governance in several ways. They can blunt the accountability that is so often said to be at the heart of effective governance. After all, if government organization is carefully structured in such a way that deniability is the be-all and end-all, how can office-holders be said to be accountable in any meaningful sense? What are citizens to make of a representative democracy whose elected rulers are so concerned to avoid political blame that they end up (apparently) hardly being in a position to decide or run anything when adverse events have occurred, or of institutional structures that are so finely tuned for blame avoidance that no one can readily be blamed for anything? (That is precisely what Bentham argued to be wrong with early nineteenth-century British government, as we saw in chapter 5.)

If government and policy delivery is organized primarily with a view to muddying the waters of blame when adverse events happen, it can make organization far more costly and cumbersome than it would otherwise be. It can be a recipe for duplication, for overly complex structures that expend their energies in managing their internal interactions over the ambiguities of who is responsible for what rather than concentrating on policy delivery, and for endless defensive reorganizations that confuse customers and absorb the limited time of managers at the expense of all else. Complex and ambiguous administrative structures may represent a triumph of functionality for short-term blame-avoidance engineering but still be dysfunctional for effective regulation or project management.

Agency blame-avoidance strategies can be negative for the quality of governance in those cases where, far from facing a "dream ticket" or a win-win of reaping cost, performance, and blame-avoidance advantages simultaneously, officeholders have to choose between blame avoidance and the functional goals of low cost or high efficacy. The same thing can happen if blame-avoidance considerations lead to a continuation of institutional arrangements that have plainly failed to achieve the functional getting-the-job-done goals that were originally used to justify those arrangements (such as cost reduction, business efficiency, the sharing or transfer of financial risks). And we do not have to look far to find cases in which delegated arrangements are retained to shield top bananas even when the organizations concerned have manifestly failed to deliver cheaper or more effective services. The UK provided a commonly claimed instance of that kind when provision of rail services by private companies continued after 1997 in spite of the failure of the privatized regime to provide rail services at lower cost to the taxpayer than the previous nationalized rail operator (indeed, subsidies rose about fivefold after the shift from public to private company provision (see Wolmar 2005)). A similar situation is the continuation of very costly private financing systems across the public services even after a long list of cases where the eventual risk has had to be borne by governments and taxpayers—as for instance, when the government of the state of Victoria in Australia had to buy back La Trobe hospital from the contractor concerned in 2000 when losses had reached a point unacceptable to the contractor (see Australian Senate Community Affairs Reference Committee 2000). Blame avoidance can be an important part of the reason why failing institutions (Meyer and Zucker 1989) survive.

Third and relatedly, the effects on those at the receiving end of organizational structures designed primarily to blunt all attempts to pin down responsibility for anything that goes wrong can be negative for political culture as well. If accountability leads to a dead end as a result of carefully crafted agency strategies, is it any wonder that public confidence and trust in politicians and big corporations seems to have declined in many of the advanced countries? Indeed, more delegation of policy or operational responsibilities to non-elected bodies may have the unintended effect of focusing public attention on sleaze or petty abuse of office by elected politicians and their families—a blame-displacement effect of the kind highlighted in figure 8.1. After all, if politicians cannot be blamed for policy or operational failures because, like T. S. Eliot's famous cat Macavity, they somehow contrive never to be there at the scene of the crime,[8] they can at least be blamed for their own personal indiscretions in financial or sexual conduct or other undelegatable activity. Politicians often criticize the media for an unseemly obsession with the details of their private lives—their amorous dalliances, personal financial transactions, behind-the-scenes dealings, and the like—rather than the substance of the policies they pursue. But if they have used agency strategies to deflect blame for all substantive policies, what else do voters and the media have to blame them for?

Potentially Negative Effects of Policy and Operational Strategies

Policy and operational strategies intended to avoid blame can also have negative effects in some conditions. Narrowly defensive observance of protocols—like the much discussed phenomenon of "management to audit" rather than management for positive value—can increase frustration and alienation by citizens or service users, as with those rigid failsafe systems that make ordinary services less reliable as a result of a propensity toward false positives. Protocolization designed to produce back-covering alibis can lead to a mechanical following of inappropriate procedures even when those actions are patently contrary to what common sense or intelligent professional judgment would suggest. For instance, White and colleagues (2009: 14) argue that the elaborate protocolization of child safety work in English local authorities over the past decade or so brought no demonstrable reduction in the incidence of serious harm and deaths and indeed suggest those changes may well have increased risks to children.

Further, protocolization can make service provision organizations harder for politicians to control, limiting the ability of elected representatives to reprogram some of the very back-covering procedures that make service delivery most frustrating to voters or users. As mentioned in chapter 5, it may inadvertently result in overall welfare loss or increase some social risks while trying to reduce others, as in the well-known phenomenon of "iatrogenic risks"—the risks created by ostensibly risk-reducing policies (Wiener 1998).

Similarly, avoidance or abstinence forms of policy strategy can result in the best becoming the enemy of the good—harming users by withdrawal of services that could potentially cause blame to service providers. For instance, the most vulnerable users may be hit by closure of advice services that could potentially lead to blame, and, as we saw earlier, avoidance behavior such as closure of rural rail lines because they do not generate enough revenue to pay for the latest top-specification, state-of-the-art safety engineering equipment may expose the travelers affected to greater risk of death on the roads.[9]

Blame individualization can also have negative effects of various kinds. While in principle it can be an incentive for frontline operators or service operators to take care and avoid the blunting of responsibility for such individuals, it can also result in transfer of blame from those who are best placed to take steps to reduce risks of harm onto those who are worst-placed to do so. For instance, if all the blame is laid on front-line troops (or service users) for making faulty judgment calls, attention is taken away from the ability of the top and middle-level players to develop operating systems less likely to be lead to errors (for instance, by siting rail signals so they are not likely to obscured by sunlight or by developing health-care equipment that does not allow operators to use it erroneously in ways that will produce harm to patients). Blaming the victim or the operator can mean putting the responsibility for error on those who are not in a position to develop systems that are less vulnerable to error, and it can thus be seen as a violation of the principle famously enunciated by the Judge Learned Hand, that responsibility for avoiding risk should be placed in the hands of those best placed to manage it (for example, adults rather than children).[10]

Similar problems can apply to herding behavior. For instance, apart from allowing individuals to shelter behind the actions of a group, thereby blunting clear accountability for adverse events, it can lead to the well-known phenomenon of groupthink (Janis 1972), which endangers effective decision-making as a result of shared blind spots about risks and hazards. Other kinds of dysfunctional conformity can also arise from herding behavior (see, for instance, Prat 2005), and the herding approach can slow down decision-making with complex schedules of endless committee meetings or case conferences, with no individual ever able to say yes or no to anything on the spot. It can produce "horses designed by committee," with layers of complexity or elaborate fudges to square all the various factions or individual preferences. Herding may serve to protect against attack but it will not always have the positive effects on quality of governance that were noted in the previous section.

An Overall Perspective

Such arguments and examples suggest that we cannot dismiss all worries about blame avoidance in modern government and organizations by some Panglossian claim that the structures and behavior it engenders always work out for the general welfare. And indeed, quite apart from the potentially negative effects we have noted for each of the three main types of blame-avoidance strategy, the interaction among those strategies can compound and amplify those effects. For example, as we have seen, when top-level players in the blame game try to deflect the heat away from themselves to other players by delegation (agency) strategies, the delegatees' logical counter-move is to pursue defensive policy strategies such as herding or protocolization, meaning that loss of accountability comes to be combined with loss of welfare for service users.

Indeed, the latter effect is all too predictable as part of the logic of blameworld and it can easily result in increased overall risk or danger. The phenomenon of organization tunnel vision is one of the institutional dysfunctions that have long been identified in the literature on bureaucracy. That effect is often compounded by the complex outsourcing and partnership arrangements that have been so popular in recent decades. And it will tend to intensify if complex delegation is undertaken in the context of a high-blame culture, with all the players trying to reduce their personal or institutional liability for policy failure or adverse outcomes.

So Where Does the Balance Lie? Good and Bad
  Blame Avoidance

The two previous sections suggest that we can find prima facie arguments both for and against blame avoidance as affecting the quality of governance and democracy, as so often happens with debates about governance or public management. So where does the balance lie? Is blame avoidance like so many other aspects of organization and governance (Simon 1946), in which contradictory assertions exist alongside each other, like proverbs that give diametrically opposite maxims for what to do in any situation?

Judging the positivity or otherwise of blame-avoidance tactics cannot, of course, be divorced from an assessment of the goals the blame avoiders are trying to pursue. If public officeholders or organizations are pursuing goals of which we disapprove (particularly if we think they are putting their own self-interest above that of others, or serving unrepresentative interests for personal gain), then we will also naturally come to negative judgements about their efforts to avoid blame for those efforts. Indeed, we are likely to see it as positive if the outcome of their blame-avoidance tactics is ineffective or counterproductive.

But is it equally obvious that blame-avoidance activity can be justified when the officeholders or organizations concerned are pursuing sincerely held goals that are at one level unexceptionable, believe they are doing good for society, and are just trying to stay out of trouble? Matters become more complicated at this point. Of course it can always be argued that there is no such thing as a bad instrument, only a bad purpose. The ax that a murderer can use to take an innocent life can equally be used by a firefighter to rescue other innocents trapped in a burning building. The ax itself is only as good or bad as the use to which it is put. Is blame avoidance like that? The discussion earlier would suggest not, because as we have shown there are plainly at least some approaches to blame avoidance that blunt accountability, debase political argument, or inflict avoidable harm on vulnerable individuals or groups. So can we distinguish between good and bad approaches to blame avoidance and if so, how?

Aristotle faced a similar problem several millennia ago in evaluating different types of rule. For Aristotle (1981, originally c. 330 BC), the basic types of rule (which he defined as rule by one person, rule by a few, or rule by many) were each capable of taking a positive form or a negative form. In a similar way, we can perhaps think of each of the three strategic approaches to avoidance considered in this book as containing potentially positive variants that can enhance the quality of governance and democratic accountability as well as negative variants that will tend to have the opposite effect.

Table 8.1 sketches out such an analysis. Simplifying the discussion in the previous two sections, it identifies three possible effects of blame-avoidance activity (namely, sharpening or blunting policy debate, pinpointing or diffusing accountability, and increasing or reducing transparency). And it shows how subtypes of the three main types of blame-avoidance strategy discussed in part 2 of the book can be negative or positive on those three criteria.

Thus a key test of the positivity or otherwise of presentational blame-avoidance strategy is how far it serves to engage the citizenry in serious argument about the merits of policy or operational choices to be made by officeholders and organizations, and clarifies where fault lies after allega-

TABLE 8.1
Positive and Negative Blame-Avoidance?

Blame Avoidance Strategies and Selected Variants		Selected Governance Criteria		
Strategy	Variant(s)	Sharpening or blunting debate	Pinpointing or diffusing accountability	Increasing or decreasing transparency
Presentational strategies	Winning the argument	**POSITIVE** (sharpening)		
	Changing the subject or non-engagement	**NEGATIVE** (blunting)		
Agency strategies	(Hard) delegation		**POSITIVE** (pinpointing)	
	Soft delegation or defensive reorganization		**NEGATIVE** (diffusing)	
Policy strategies	Abstinence or protocolization			**POSITIVE** (increasing)
	Herding			**NEGATIVE** (decreasing)

tions of avoidable losses have been made. The forms of presentational strategies that are most likely to have such an effect are those that serve to engage in rather than to evade policy arguments. So on that criterion we can argue that winning-the-argument approaches are broadly positive, but changing-the-subject and low-profile approaches (such as diversionary tactics, nonengagement, or backdoor pressures on media) are negative.

Similarly, if the key test of the positivity or otherwise of agency blame-avoidance strategy is how far it sharpens or diffuses accountability for failure, the forms of agency strategy that seem most likely to have the sharpening effect are the hard forms of delegation strategy rather than the more plastic or complex forms of delegation or partnership that were discussed in chapter 4. On that criterion we would score harder types of delegation as positive, but soft variable-geometry forms of delegation, together with opaque partnership arrangements and defensive forms of rotation and reorganization, as negative.

When it comes to policy and operational strategies, arguably the most important test of negative or positive effect would be the risk of physical harm to users or the public at large. That is hard to assess for policy strategies in the round, though it can be explored for particular sectors, as in the case of the net health effects of assurance and avoidance tactics in defensive medicine, and plainly (as was shown in the previous section) there are fairly clear-cut cases in other fields in which a narrow defensiveness puts the blame-avoiding interests of providers and producers ahead of the welfare of those they ostensibly serve. But if we stay with broad governance principles, as table 8.1 does, and take a key test of the positivity or otherwise of policy types of blame-avoidance strategy to be how far it tends to increase or decrease the transparency of organizational or institutional operation, the forms of policy strategy that are most likely to have a transparency-increasing effect are abstinence or protocolization approaches rather than herding strategies, in which the positions and influence of individual actors or organizations in the decision or implementation process are almost impossible to figure out.

That analysis picks up only a fraction of the wider discussion of potentially positive and negative features of blame-avoidance strategies in the previous two sections. But it nevertheless shows how we might distinguish between forms of blame avoidance that can have positive effects on policy, argument, accountability, and transparency from those that have negative effects on such qualities. We could of course add many other evaluative criteria and subdivide the variants further. But the main point that table 8.1 aims to make is that not all forms of blame avoidance are necessarily to be seen as negative phenomena.

REMEDIES FOR THE WRONG SORT OF BLAME AVOIDANCE?

If the analysis offered in the previous section is correct, the practical problem that then arises is how to avoid the wrong sort of blame avoidance while fostering or at least not discouraging the more positive forms. What, if any, remedies are available? Do we have to count blame avoidance as a "condition"—one of those facts of life that we just have to live with, like the common cold? Or is it something that can be shaped and engineered in some way?

At first sight, the scope for changing such behavior by official rules and formal institutional tweaks seems decidedly limited. After all, many of the negative blame-avoidance behaviors and institutional developments that are summarized in table 8.1 differ from the more visible kinds of malfeasance for which there are conventional hard legal remedies. They are not the sort of things that can be readily addressed by legal or constitutional provisions. They seem like the sort of elements whose elimination might feature in a wish-list for some ideal democracy as considered by political scientists (see Dahl 1989), but which are often considered to be less attainable than more basic machinery for electoral choice and party contestation, such as elected officials, inclusive suffrage, the right to run for office, alternative sources of information, and relative freedom of expression and association.

That is not to say that hard law remedies—black-letter law of one kind or another—could not be applied to some of the negative kinds of blame avoidance discussed in the previous section. For instance, when it comes to presentational strategies, we suggested that the more negative varieties are those that evade argument by resort to diversions or by backdoor pressures on media rather than open argument (including perhaps the punitive use of strict libel and privacy laws to suppress any public criticism of officeholders or organizations). If so, legal restraints on monopolies in the media could make it less possible for officeholders (or the political class generally) to hobble or corral the media by backdoor deals or arm-twisting to keep themselves out of trouble.

Similarly, if the most potentially damaging forms of agency strategy are those soft, plastic, and revocable forms of delegation that can be trimmed at will to fit the political conditions of the moment (and related arrangements that allow blame to slip between the cracks of jurisdictional ambiguity), the most appropriate hard law remedy would be greater legal and constitutional entrenchment of institutional forms, to put more procedural obstacles in the way of casual or opportunistic delegation or obfuscatory partnership arrangements.

When it comes to policy and operational strategies, it was suggested that these strategies take their most potentially damaging forms when a narrow defensiveness puts the blame-avoiding interests of providers and producers ahead of the welfare of those they ostensibly serve. Such behavior is obviously hard to check by hard law remedies, though there may be something to be gained from tough transparency laws, legal requirements for decision processes to include representation of user or client interests, or measures to mandate the existence of certain positions (such as safety or environmental officers) at given points within organizational structures. Those kinds of provisions can cut across officeholders' and organizations' ability to engineer systems that allow them to claim they had no knowledge of certain facts. Such an approach to the legal control of corporate behavior is advocated by authors such as Christopher Stone (1991), and it requires legislators and regulators to be able and willing to reach deep into organizational decision processes.

Still, hard law remedies have obvious limits for many of the kinds of negative blame-avoidance behavior discussed in the previous section. Legal measures such as transparency laws can be double-edged in their effects on blame avoidance, resulting in heightened defensiveness in forms such as tighter central management (Roberts 2006b), more disclaimers, increased protocolization of operations, and one-way communications of the kind Onora O'Neill (2006) sees as inimical to real transparency. Further, some conceivable hard legal remedies—such as extensions of no-delegation rules and restriction of partnership arrangements—could kill off important kinds of organizational dynamism at the same time that they limit certain avenues to blame avoidance.[11] And even if that was not the case, government and corporate lobbying power are likely to strongly resist any such measures, both because they would undercut much of the logic of private-sector governance and (less loftily) because public bureaucrats and private interests alike can often benefit from ambiguous delegation arrangements and other negative blame-avoidance approaches.

Such limitations of hard law remedies, particularly but not only for policy and operational strategies, mean that remedies must often be found in rules and institutions of the soft law variety. By soft law—a term whose usefulness is, needless to say, disputed—is meant quasi-legal instruments whose binding force rests heavily on convention and compliance rather than more heavy-duty forms of rules (see Chinkin 1989). Forms of soft law that could limit some of the more negative forms of blame avoidance discussed earlier include codes of conduct, good practice guidelines, and the regulatory impact assessment activity that has been adopted in many of the developed countries in an attempt to counterbalance the proliferation of back-covering regulations, typically allied with mechanisms of risk management to check whether procedures adopted are proportionate to the real risks involved.

But soft law itself depends on a culture in which institutional and individual behavior can be changed by shaming or administrative sanctions, and such cultures are hardly universal. Moreover, the subtlety and limited 'justiciability' of much of the more negative kinds of blame-avoidance activity—such as the changing-the-subject kind of diversionary activity or permanent revolutionary forms of reorganization—inevitably limit the effectiveness of both hard and soft law remedies, and mean that even soft law remedies will often be destined to make only small differences at the margin (as is typically said to apply to efforts at busting red tape in government).

Accordingly, the most effective remedies for the more negative kinds of blame-avoidance activity seem more likely to be found in political behavior than legal rules, in the form of spontaneous or programmed social or political action that raises awareness and mobilizes opinion. Such remedies consist of activity of the 'educate, agitate, organize'[12] type—driven by social awareness and political campaigning within and outside organizations, as social understanding of blame avoidance spreads. In the first chapter we referred to the "naming, blaming, claiming" analysis (Felstiner et al. 1980) of the development of legal claims, and similar processes may provide important checks on the negative kinds of blame-avoidance activity, as awareness of such activity spreads.

Such "people power" processes can be messy and fragile. They are liable to frequent reverses in the face of corporate, professional, and union power, and they will not even get off the starting-blocks in a whole society devoted to blame avoidance, as was often said to apply to the former Soviet Union (see Politskovaya 2003: 27). And given that blame avoidance approaches keep mutating as they come into public awareness, the frontier will always be moving. But if the more negative forms of blame-avoidance are to be checked, it seems that such a form of politics is what is most likely to produce a result. And even though pressure of this kind obviously goes against the institutional grain, there are forces that can play in its favor as well—such as an apparently growing public awareness of and interest in the way blame games are played and a tendency away from party tribalism to looser patterns of affiliation in politics driven by changing social structures.

Moreover, while keeping media independent from political incumbents is hard to achieve in a world of giant news corporations that control large swaths of broadcast and print media, the relative decline of mass-circulation newspapers and general broadcasting in the developed countries and more communication through less centrally controllable internet forms can work against at least some of the grosser forms of diversionary tactics, and function in the same way as the *samizdat* forms of informal publication that supplemented and even partly supplanted the official and state-controlled media of the former Soviet Union.

This sort of politics matters, because although the negative kinds of blame avoidance discussed in this book might at first sight seem to go well beyond the 'thin' conditions for democracy in conventional political science (which, as noted earlier, tend to relate to the openness of the voting system), they cut to some basic issues in democratic and responsive government. If democracy means the ability of the ruled to change their rulers, a media structure that is readily manipulable by blame-avoiding political incumbents strikes at the heart of that condition. If democracy means the ability of the ruled to hold the rulers to account, governance arrangements that are unstable and impenetrable to all but the cognoscenti (sometimes not even that) fatally undermine that condition (see O'Donnell 1999). So these issues are not so far from the thin conditions for democratic government after all.

CHAPTER NINE

The Last Word

> To err is human. To blame someone else is politics.
> —Attributed to Hubert Humphrey (1911–78),
> U.S. Vice President 1965–69[1]

This book has tried to show that blame avoidance is an important and central feature of political and institutional life. Of course blame avoidance is not everything. Sometimes the imperatives of credit-claiming will trump it, and sometimes, as we saw in chapter 5, defensiveness gets to a point where it moves away from blame avoidance altogether and turns into efforts to ensure the physical safety of officeholders and their families, irrespective of the blame they may attract from everyone else. But it is nevertheless a powerful force in shaping the architecture of organizations. It often dominates their standard operating routines. And it goes far to explain why political and organizational leaders often seem to spend as much if not more of their time on presentational issues and elaborate restructuring schemes as they do in actually managing the organizations they head.

This book has shown how the imperatives of blame avoidance can lead to forms of organizational architecture and behavior that seem to run entirely counter to commonly advanced precepts of good public service management, like joining up, customer focus, and clear accountability. It has shown how arrangements that are typically presented as purely functional means for better service provision—like complex partnership structures, preoccupation with presentation and publicity, delegation, privatization, and outsourcing of critical tasks,—can be understood at least equally well from a blame-avoidance perspective. And it has shown that blame avoidance behavior does not just apply to political leaders and high officeholders, who are understandably the focus of most commentary on the subject. The same sort of behavior can reach down deep into organizational life in the front line and the middle ranks, and indeed into society more generally.

The book has also traced out some of the different routes through which blame avoidance can be pursued. It began by defining blame as a product of something that someone sees as an avoidable loss or harm and that is perceived to result from some act of commission or omission. Then it looked at three main ways of trying to avoid blame in that sense—by presentational, agency, and policy strategies. As we have seen, there are many interesting specimens of blame-avoidance behavior at the point where these strategies overlap (the overlapping circles that we drew in chapter 1)—as when policy strategies meet presentational strategies in the realm of information management, or when agency strategies meet policy and presentational strategies in the often labyrinthine processes of setting up inquiries after failures and foul-ups when blame and credit are at stake.

When these strategies come into play and are pursued with all the energy and ingenuity that human beings can summon up, they can combine to produce a hall-of-mirrors world in which the extent and avoidability of every loss is ambiguous or contested and in which it is just as hard to get to the bottom of who or what is responsible for anything untoward. As we have seen, big organizations, public and private, often carefully build defensive tactics into their operating routines, in everything from the way their websites work to screen out direct human contact with any identifiable name to their complaints procedures and the presentational strategies pursued by their high commands.

Blame avoidance has probably always been with us in some form, and claims that it is a peculiarly modern preoccupation need to be treated with caution. As we saw in chapter 6, tracing change over time in presentational effort, in the range of delegation, and in the extent of defensive policy routines is far from straightforward and does not always lead to simple conclusions. The key changes, such as those found in the workings of organizations at their middle or lower levels, are often qualitative and not easily captured in standard statistical runs of numbers. But it seems clear that the absolute number of spin doctors has grown at the top of some government systems over the last three or four decades, that creative new forms of responsibility-fudging agency strategies have come into existence over that period as well, and that the defensive tag first applied to the practice of medicine in the late 1960s is now coming to apply to other forms of professional and public service as well, as reflected in social work and education.

Blame-avoidance activity will be found wherever motive combines with opportunity. Motive will be strong when potential blame takers have high stakes in preserving their future careers and when potential blame makers can reap benefits from blame-attribution activity. The professionalization of politics as an occupation, the rise of general management rather than specialist expertise as a key skill in public services, and the marked growth in the "blaming professions" over recent decades—such as the worlds of lawyers, journalists, academics, official and unofficial watchdogs, and indeed salaried politicians and their political class hangers-on more generally—provide precisely those conditions today.

Likewise, opportunity for blame avoidance will be strong when scope presents itself for altering the loss perception and agency perception elements that make up blame. Moves away from older tribal or primordial forms of politics to political parties and institutions more shallowly rooted in civil society may increase such opportunity, inasmuch as they produce an electorate that does not make up its mind about politics on the basis of bred-in-the-bone loyalties alone. More opportunity for blame avoidance is also provided by the proliferation of governance and service delivery institutions at every level over recent decades, from supranational to neighborhood bodies, often comprising a dizzying complex of public, private, and third-sector organizations. That institutional world, reflected in the rise of the term "governance" rather than "government" to describe today's public policy and public service environment (Rhodes 1996; Osborne 2010), is particularly rich in the scope it provides for blame games and strategies focused on the agency element of blame. On top of that, the "devil-in-the-details" management that modern organization lends itself to—such as the ability to constrain choice and avoid direct human contact through software systems, the provision of websites that reflect continually rewritten history, and the opportunity of continuous micro-management through e-mail—also potentially increases those opportunities.

If such motive and opportunity elements are what shape the extent of blame-avoidance behavior, most of them seem to be here to stay. If that is the case, we can expect such behavior to continue to figure large in public discontents about dealings with corporations and public officeholders. Rulers will continue to use elaborate propaganda machines to spin blame away. Organizational structures will go on being crafted in baroque complexity to ensure that no one turns out to be responsible for anything when bad things happen. Individuals dealing with organizations whose self-presentation is suffused to the saturation point with a self-congratulatory language of service and care will continue to be brought up short against policies and procedures apparently designed to protect those organizations and their staff when anything troublesome happens (and to place the maximum obstacles in the way of anyone who wants to identify and speak to the people actually making the decisions). That is hardly a formula for high popular trust in governance and organizations. Indeed, it is likely to provide a context in which populist politicians who choose to run against the bureaucracy will be able to tap into deep popular frustrations—but will also risk raising public expectations on which they cannot deliver.

If the long-term social underpinnings of blameworld are unlikely to go away by a normal process of self-correction, there are some perplexing what-to-do issues to be faced. How should blame-avoidance activity be evaluated? What if anything can be done to shape or change it?

As we have seen, blame avoidance gets a bad press. The superheroes of popular culture typically do not concern themselves with blame avoidance. Blame avoidance is often portrayed as craven and cowardly behavior on the part of politicians, bureaucrats, and so many functionaries in modern organizations. Start a conversation about the subject in a bar or at some social occasion, and that is the tone it will usually take. Search the internet for jokes about blame, and you will find the emphasis is overwhelmingly on the negative aspects of blame and blame avoidance. Listen to politicians or public managers talking about the subject, and you will often find they take it as axiomatic that we need to get away from "blame culture" into a more adventurous, less blame-avoiding world.

It is true that there are many things to worry about when blame avoidance leads officeholders and organizations to make sure that accountability trails always run cold, that no one ever gets a straight answer to a simple question, and no one seems to be responsible for anything. We have already pointed out some of the obvious dysfunctions that such preoccupations can lead to. For example, at the extreme, blame avoidance can help to drive negative selection processes in organizations in which individuals are recruited not for their potential talents or brilliance but for their lack of ability or propensity to challenge their bosses and their potential to serve as "blame fodder" when something goes wrong, as is said to have happened in the former Soviet Union at every level from the Politburo downwards.

But it also needs to be said that not all blame is bad, not all blame games are to be deplored, and blame avoidance more broadly can have positive as well as negative effects, as was suggested in the previous chapter. Blame and the fear of blame are not all bad, if we are led to think twice about bending or disobeying important rules, what we say to whom, how we conduct our personal lives. A world without social or legal blame would be one in which the only pressure to stay on the straight and narrow would have to come from individuals' own moral compasses —notoriously cranky instruments. It would be a world in which there were no penalties for shamelessness. Unattractive as blameworld may often seem, a no-blame world would be far from problem free either. Imagine what it would be like to drive your car in a society where no blame attached to driving errors or accidents. Imagine how those who govern us might behave if they never had to fear any blame.

Blame games are not all bad either. We cannot just leave evaluation of policy or operational failures to professionals or technocrats, because such evaluations often run up against the limits of knowledge and inherently contested values. And where complex organizational or institutional arrangements are concerned, agency will almost always be ambiguous too. Short of some imagined nirvana in which those difficulties could be made to disappear by a technical fix or a general outbreak of social altruism, how are societies to decide what exactly constitutes an avoidable loss and who or what is responsible for such a loss? The sort of blame game with which we began this book, in which different actors and organizations try to pin responsibility onto others, often in the glare of media attention, can serve as an important process of social "discovery" that would often be in practice impossible to achieve by technocratic means or by elaborately writing all the rules or contractual terms in advance.

Nor is blame avoidance in a wider sense all bad. As we have seen, both anticipative and reactive forms of blame avoidance can sometimes (even if unintentionally) produce positive outcomes in policy and governance. They can lead rulers or leaders to show self-restraint which would otherwise be absent. They can lead to productive forms of delegation to technical or managerial experts. They can even sometimes lead to more balanced argument about the conduct of policy or operations than would otherwise occur, when the authorities are under pressure to put their case or defend their actions as persuasively as they can in the face of potential media or public blame.

Nevertheless, some variants of the three blame-avoidance strategies discussed in this book have far from benign effects on the quality of institutional life. That applies particularly if institutions and officeholders under pressure choose forms of presentational strategy other than the winning-the-argument type, choose agency strategies other than those of hard delegation, and choose policy strategies that either make individual responsibility impossible to pin down or end up putting the onus of responsibility on those least fitted to reduce the risks of adverse events.

In fact, as we saw in the last chapter, the difficulty is how to tell good from bad blame avoidance and how to encourage the good kinds and discourage the bad forms that undermine the quality of governance. But remedies for the negative effects of individual and corporate blame avoidance are elusive and demanding, as we have seen. And while a few bits of bad blame avoidance might be swept away by constitutional provisions, Acts of Parliament, or international agreements, most of the problematic forms cannot readily be dealt with that way. The changes needed reach deep down into corporate behavior. So it is mostly to politics—the social process of naming, shaming, and claiming—that we need to look for controlling this phenomenon. That, after all, is what democracy is for.

Notes

1. On BBC Radio 4 *Today* program, December 19, 2005.

2. As happened in London in the summer of 2009. See *Metro* (London) July 3, 2009: 1.

3. Something that has apparently happened in several European countries. See Hood, Rothstein, and Baldwin 2001: 27.

4. Some say we live in a "risk society" (Beck 1992). In many ways, of course, life is far less risky for most people in the rich countries of today than it was for their grandparents or great-grandparents, when millions of lives were at risk from catastrophic wars and the incidence of infant deaths, deaths in childbirth, and deaths from contagious disease was vastly higher than it is now. (Maternal death rates were 50 per 10,000 births in West European countries in the early twentieth century, compared to 1 or so per 10,000 births today, infant deaths per 1000 live births were 70 or so in the USA in the 1920s as against 10 or so today [see Loudon 1991].) Go back only two or three generations in even the most advanced societies of today, and you will find that people risked their lives making voyages in engine-less sailing ships, lived in towns and villages with open sewers, and gave birth at home with at best the aid of midwives but none of the high-tech hospital facilities available today. That was hardly a risk-free lifestyle, even if the people of those days did not have to contend with uniquely modern hazards such as computer viruses or cyber-crime. Nevertheless, the use of the term "risk" in the titles of academic books and articles has demonstrably increased over the last decade or so, as indicated by web searches for titles including the word "risk" over the five years from 2003 to 2008.

5. Of course the global financial collapse of 2008 dramatically undermined the credibility of government regulators' ability to act in a way that the original advocates of risk-based regulation (Ayres and Braithwaite 1991) argued for.

6. Power (2004) has ironically termed the phenomenon "the risk management of everything," and writers such as Dryzek (1996) and Furedi (2005) have commented on the growth of the "risk industry" (Dryzek 1996). Or perhaps we should say "risk industries," because today's world of risk is increasingly compartmentalized in different categories, with financial risk divided from health risk, occupational risks divided from transport risks and lifestyle risks, organizational risks divided up into reputational risks, operational risks, financial risks, and so on and on.

7. That is the essence of dictionary definitions of the term.

8. See Sulitzeanu-Kenan and Hood 2005: 2-3.

9. The term came to be used widely by journalists, cartoonists, and popular writers, has been used as the title of at least two media shows, and has even been taken up by an American punk band that adopted the phrase as its name in 1999.

10. See Bloom and Price 1975; Kernell 1977; Weaver 1986; 1988; Baumeister et al 2001; Rozin and Royzman 2001; Soroka 2006. Slovic's (1993) observation that favorable traits require more confirmation than unfavorable traits (what he calls "trust asymmetry") is a related observation, and Kahneman and Tversky (1979) and others have also observed human tendencies to incur greater risks when faced with a choice among potential losses than occurs when faced with a choice among equivalent potential gains.

11. As reflected in maxims such as "Failures are written in stone, successes in sand," or Mark Antony's speech making the same point in Shakespeare's *Julius Caesar* Act 3, Scene 2.

12. Referring to an episode in which the then UK Foreign Secretary, the late Robin Cook, abruptly parted from his wife in 1997 after an extramarital affair with his secretary came to light a few months after he had been appointed.

13. The argument, originally developed by a group at Clark University in the 1980s, is that the signals about hazards that shape individuals' perceptions of risk are filtered through "social amplification stations" (including politicians, bureaucracies, scientists, mass media, and activist groups) that amplify or attenuate risks in ways that are predictable from the social circumstances of those stations.

14. See Eiser and White 2005.

15. Indeed, it was once reported that Cherie Booth, wife of former British Prime Minister Tony Blair, had bought precisely such a pendant. See Suzy Austin: "Give Me Strength." *Metro*, May 4, 2006).

16. For the term "fear entrepreneurs" see Furedi 2009; for Furedi's underlying argument about the promotion of fear see also Furedi 1997: 20–42 and Furedi 2005: 126–32 and 138–9. Furedi does not explicitly link fear and fear entrepreneurship to blame, though he tellingly notes a comment to the effect that governments who do not 'do' the politics of fear are likely to have the politics of fear done to them (Furedi 2005: 125).

17. See, for instance, Pierson (1994, 1996 and 2001); Ross (1997); Bonoli (2001), and Lindbom (2001).

18. Definitively satirized in Laurence Sterne's great eighteenth-century, novel *Tristram Shandy*, which mock-seriously identifies the *Argumentum Fistulatorium* (argument by whistling) as a new specimen and declares that it is to "rank hereafter with the *Argumentum Baculinum* and the *Argumentum ad Crumenam*, and for ever hereafter be treated of in the same chapter." (Sterne 1984: 56–7).

19. Christopher Pollitt (1984: ix) comments on the "generous slice" of their time that British Prime Ministers and their top official advisers devoted to "machinery of government" changes from 1960 to 1983, and asks, "Why did oppressively busy and usually very able persons spend time on such ... matters?"

20. A phrase that refers to the Fifth Amendment to the US Constitution, part of the Bill of Rights that became part of the Constitution in 1791. The Fifth Amendment states that no one shall be compelled to be a witness against himself in any criminal case. By analogy, one possible strategy for blame avoidance is simply to stay silent and hope the blame crisis will pass.

21. A distinction popularized by the American management gurus David Osborne and Ted Gaebler (1993) fifteen years or so ago.

NOTES TO CHAPTER TWO

1. For example, Marista Leishman (2006: 183), daughter of John Reith, the founder of the BBC, recalls that her father and his deputy adopted a private naval language to talk about life at the top of the corporation in the 1930s, as if they were on the bridge of a warship, using terms like "shipping it green" when they encountered political resistance to or criticism of their operations.

2. Gelbert, a well-known satirist, wrote the play for BBC radio in 2006 and it is set during an imaginary congressional hearing investigating the abrogation of human rights under the Bush regime. See http://www.fictionfactory.co.uk/Abrogate details.htm (accessed October 2007).

3. Something that Gennaro's seven predecessors had all failed to do, in spite of having apparently sweeping powers. See Pomeroy 2008.

4. A position often lamented by celebrities and top leaders but seen as just by others, including a character in Emily Barr's (2002: 272) novel *Baggage* who declares, "It's a fair price to pay for all the benefits. I abhor the idea of a society where celebrity comes free, when people can use the press to promote themselves, without the danger of a comeback."

5. Normality in these matters is a conservative assumption for the purposes. There have been some well-documented instances of top-level leaders who seem to have a proclivity for controversial sexual relations, and the pressures of celebrity lifestyles may themselves tend to produce needs for release in the form of drink, drugs, or sexual adventures. But the major difference seems to be that whatever weaknesses exist will be more consequential for these individuals than for those at the bottom of the heap. John Thompson's (2000: 125) work on accounts of scandals in public life suggests that, 'sexual political scandals may serve as credibility tests for actual or aspiring political leaders...."

6. As chronicled by his personal physician, Li Zhisui (1994: ix, 144, 365 and *passim*).

7. See also Cristina Forsne's (1997) account of her life with Mitterand during his presidency and William Styron's (1998) contrast of the erotic atmosphere of Mitterand's inaugural in 1981 with American puritanism during the Clinton presidency.

8. Mitterand had not fully revealed his World War II record, which remained moot until it was finally exposed by the journalist Pierre Péan (1994) in his book *Une Jeunesse Française* in the last year of Mitterand's presidency.

9. For example, the well-known 2001 Kennedy report on the deaths of over thirty children who underwent heart surgery at the Bristol Royal Infirmary in England between 1991 and 1995 inveighed against a "blame and shame" approach in dealing with medical failures (see *Learning from Bristol: the Report of the Public Inquiry into Children's Heart Surgery at the Bristol Royal Infirmary 1984–1995*. CM 5207, London, HMSO 2001). A key academic exposition of the idea of blaming systems rather than individuals for adverse events in health care is Braithwaite, Healy, and Dwan 2005: 18.

10. A graphic account of such a culture is given by the Fitzgerald Commission of Inquiry into police misconduct in the Australian state of Queensland in the 1980s.

See *Report of a Commission of Inquiry Pursuant to Orders in Council 1987–9*: 200ff.

11. To quote a case given by the columnist Howard Jacobson (2008) in describing his frustrations in trying to cancel a standing order at his bank.

12. The most high-profile example of a British government minister coming to grief when damaging e-mails came to light is that of former Home Secretary David Blunkett, who resigned in December 2004 after an inquiry found an e-mail from his private secretary to the director general of the Home Office Immigration and Nationality Department asking for an "update on the settlement (domestic worker) case I faxed through to you the other day." See "Blunkett Resigns over Visa Accusations." BBC News December 15, 2004 http://news.bbc.co.uk/onthisday/hi/dates/stories/december/15/newsid_4361000/4361728.stm (accessed November 2009). Of course it is possible for top-level people to ban or limit e-mail access to themselves, or not to use it at all, but such a safety-first strategy comes at a high cost in terms of communication ability.

13. See "Boy Drowned as Police Support Officers 'Stood By.'" *Guardian*, September 21, 2007 http://www.guardian.co.uk/uk/2007/sep/21/1 (accessed September 2008).

14. Page and Jenkins do not portray this "invited authority" behavior as blame avoidance, but it can be understood in that light.

15. A term that has come into academic papers and policy reports—for example, Whitehead 2007 and the 2007 British Foresight Report on Obesity (Butland et al. 2007).

16. For instance, some years ago Tony Abbott, then Australia's federal health minister, was reported to have said that obesity "was a self-inflicted illness" See "Abbott "Blames Fat People for Obesity,'" *Sydney Morning Herald* October 19, 2006. www.smh.com.au/news/National/Abbott-blames-fat-people-for-obesity/2006/10 (accessed April 2009).

17. "…Wäre es da/Nicht doch einfacher/Die Regierung/Löste das Volk auf und Wählte ein anderes?" ("Would it not be simpler if the government dismissed the people and chose another one?"). (Berthold Brecht, "Die Lösung." In Brecht, 1967: 1009.

NOTES TO CHAPTER THREE

1. See Danto 2005: 58n16.

2. According to Moloney (2000: 124), spin and presentation in modern politics "… are no longer the salt and pepper; they are the meal."

3. The term is said by Bernard Ingham (2003: 121) to have been first used by Saul Bellow in his Jefferson lectures in 1977, and to have been taken up by *The New York Times* in 1984 in an article about the aftermath of a televised debate between Ronald Reagan and Walter Mondale.

4. Reported under Chatham House rules at a Better Government Initiative conference at Ditchley Park, Oxfordshire, October 19–20, 2007.

5. In his *Bride of Lammermuir* ([1819] 1991: 15).

6. Something similar can apply to the world of public management. For example, in 2008 British Home Secretary Jacqui Smith claimed that there had been a fall in the number of people in England caught carrying knives and that those found guilty of possessing knives were receiving longer sentences (a claim that spectacularly backfired after it was promptly dismissed by the official statistics regulator as relying on "premature, irregular, and selective" statistics). See Richard Ford: 'Statistics Watchdog Chief Accuses Home Office of Abusing Crime Statistics" *The Times*, December 12, 2008. http://www.timesonline.co.uk/tol/news/politics/article5332170.ece?token=null&offset=12&page=2 (accessed April 2009).

7. Aristotle (1984: 2155) famously described rhetoric as "the facility of observing in any given case the available means of persuasion."

8. The epigram was coined by Paul Flynn (1999), a seasoned MP, in his account of the maneuverings within the Welsh Labour Party when it governed Wales in the early years of Tony Blair's UK government.

9. See letter to the editor from Jenny Jordan: "Back to the Future." *Metro* (London edition), October 6, 2008: 18.

10. "The best ink for Vanity Fair use would be one that faded utterly in a couple of days …" (Thackeray ([1853] 2003): 213–4).

11. Nominated by Neville Friedlander for inclusion in a short list of "great lies." See his letter to the editor of the *Sydney Morning Herald* on May 20, 1988.

12. This famous phrase originated from a statement by Terry Worrall, British Rail's Director of Operations. On February 11, 1991, he said that "we are having particular problems with this type of snow," (an unusually soft and powdery snow that was not deep enough to be cleared by snowplows and snow-blowers and that penetrated train electrical systems with devastating effect). Many electric services had to be replaced by diesel locomotives, causing long delays (see *Motive Power Monthly*, May 1991). Worrall's earnest explanation backfired, because journalists mockingly coined the phrase "the wrong kind of snow" to portray his statement as yet another feeble excuse for poor train service, and indeed to denote implausible official excuses as a group.

13. For example, a cartoon lampooning the then British Home Secretary John Reid in the satirical magazine *Private Eye* in 2007 was captioned, "No one told me I was Home Secretary." (*Private Eye* 1176, January 19–February 1, 2007, 19).

14. The statement was made on BBC Five Live weekend news on April 22, 2006 (http//newsvote.bbc.co.uk/mpapps/pagetools/print/news.bbc.co.uk/1/hi/health 49358.stm, accessed May 2007; see also Sam Jones "Disbelief as Hewitt Claims Best Year Ever for NHS." *The Guardian*, April, 24, 2006. http://politics.guardian .co.uk/publicservices/story/0..1759887.00.html (accessed May 2007)

15. In the Christian reform church tradition, the stool of repentance was a seat in front of the congregation in which penitent sinners, and especially adulterers, were obliged to sit. See Hood 2006: 7n6.

16. The statement was made in *New Nation*, a newspaper aimed at Britain's black community, in November 2006, as the government was deciding what it should do to mark the bicentenary of the abolition of the transatlantic slave trade. The statement did not satisfy those (such as the Pan African Reparation Coalition) who were calling for a full apology to be followed by financial compensation.

Tony Blair's culture minister at that time, David Lammy, defended the approach by saying that the bicentenary should be used positively, to celebrate those who abolished the slave trade and commemorate those who died, but that he "did not want to get into a blame fest." See BBC news November 24, 2006, November 27, 2006. http://news.bbc.co.uk/1/hi/uk_politics/6185176.stm (accessed September 2007).

17. The minister was making a speech in Dublin to mark the arrival of a replica of a Viking ship from Roskilde in August 2007. His speech, expressing some regret at the damage done to the Irish people by the Viking raiders, was reported by Irish and British newspapers as an official apology for the destruction and havoc of a millennium before, but Mr. Mikkelson was careful to deny that it had any such official force. See Eric Larsen, "Dane Guilt," *Guardian Unlimited News Blog* August 16, 2007. http://blogs.guardian.co.uk/news/archives/2007/08/16_guilt.html (accessed September 2007).

18. The notorious memo, written at 2:55 pm British time on September 11, when millions of people around the world were preoccupied by the terrible television images of the terrorist attack, said: "It is now a very good day to get out anything we want to bury. Councillors' expenses?" See Andrew Sparrow, "Sept. 11: 'A Good Day to Bury Bad News.'" *Daily Telegraph* October 9, 2001. http://www.telegraph.co.uk/news/main.jhtml?xml=/2001/10/10/nmoor10xml (accessed September 2007).

19. A quotation attributed to many people, including George Eliot and Mark Twain, but probably originating in the Hebrew Bible (Proverbs 17: 28).

20. "Sarkozy Walks Out of TV interview." BBC news October 29, 2007. http://news.bbc.co.uk/1/hi/world/europe/7067167.stm (accessed November 2008).

21. For example, when Harriet Harman, then a minister in Tony Blair's Labour government, decided to send her son to a selective school rather than the non-selective comprehensive schools that have been the preferred instrument of school education for the Labour party since the 1960s, Alastair Campbell chose to "brief Indy and the Mirror" on the subject in the hope of more friendly coverage (Campbell 2007: 100).

22. A case in point is a 2009 legal "super-injunction" to prevent media reporting of proceedings in the UK Westminster parliament about alleged dumping of toxic waste in Ivory Coast by the oil-trading company Trafigura. See David Leigh, "Trafigura drops bid to gag Guardian over MP's Question," *Guardian* October 13, 2009, http://www.guardian.co.uk/media/2009/oct/13/trafigura-drops-gag-guardian-oil (accessed August 2010).

23. See "The Simple Sword of Truth." *Guardian* April 11, 1995. www.guardian.co.uk/politics/1995/apr/11/uk1 (accessed November 2008).

24. See "Diary of Disgrace for ex-Minister," *Guardian* March 5, 1999. www.guardian.co.uk/politics/1999/mar/05/uk3 (accessed November 1999).

NOTES TO CHAPTER FOUR

1. See Ellis 1994 for an account of the elaborate effort and energy that goes into trying to achieve this outcome in US executive government. Likewise, Christopher Pollitt (1984: ix) opened a detailed study of British machinery-of-government changes from the 1960s to the early 1980s by observing that such activity "absorbed a generous slice of the energies of several recent prime ministers and their most senior official advisers" and asking, "Why did oppressively busy … persons spend time on such apparently unglamorous … matters?' Efforts to avoid blame, however, did not feature in Pollitt's answer to that question.

2. "Sir-Multi-agency Approach: Definition, No One Will Ever Be Responsible for the Outcome." Letter to the *Daily Telegraph* from Bill Underwood, April 10, 2010: 19.

3. See "Politicians Flock to Flood Zone," DW-World DE, Deutsche Welle. http://dwelle.de/southasia/germany/1.151994.1html (accessed November 2008).

4. See "Country Profile: Libya," BBC News March 11, 2009. http://news.bbc.co.uk/1/hi/world/middle_east/country_profiles/819291.stm (accessed June 2009).

5. See, for instance, Ellis 1994.

6. See, for instance, Fiorina 1982 and 1986.

7. See "Dome Woes Haunt Blair." BBC News February 15, 2001. http://news.bbc.co.uk/1/hi/uk_politics/1172367.stm (accessed November 2008).

8. See "Legacy Loses Exclusive Dome Bidding Rights," *The Guardian* February 15, 2001. http://www.guardian.co.uk/uk/2001/feb/15/dome (accessed November 2008).

9. Such a role was assumed several times by Tony Blair during his premiership, including taking "personal charge" of the National Health Service during a winter flu crisis in January 2000, but his assumption of personal charge for tackling an epidemic of foot-and-mouth disease in March 2001 in the period leading up to the 2001 general election is perhaps the most dramatic instance. See Lindord 2004.

10. Murray Horn (1995: 19) uses the term "agency costs" to refer to this type of risk.

11 The logical opposite of the merry-go-round strategy of constant reorganization is the strategy of "freezing," also commonly adopted as a defensive strategy in the animal kingdom. Freezing seems to map more closely onto the lying doggo approach to presentation discussed in the previous chapter than onto agency strategies, so is not discussed here.

12. The English Audit Commission (2008) reviewed these arrangements after some years of operation and found little evidence that they had improved outcomes for children and young people or delivered better value for money than ad hoc voluntary cooperation arrangements. The death of another child ("Baby Peter") in 2007, in the same local authority area (Haringey) where the Victoria Climbié death had occurred seven years earlier, produced fresh ministerial pledges to improve cooperation, and there were numerous leaked allegations of warnings, concern, and information having been ignored or overridden in the way the case had been handled by social services. See "Child Protection Plans Revealed," BBC News

November 18, 2008. http://news.bbc.co.uk/1/hi/uk/7734576.stm (accessed November 2008).

13. A characteristically irreverent interpretation by the columnist Simon Carr (2006), put on British Prime Minister Tony Blair's plans for improving standards in problem schools by bringing in external partners such as universities, business firms, or better schools. By contrast, the academic public management literature on joint working among agencies (such as Bardach 1998; Pfeffer and Salancik 2003; Ruiter 2005) tends to focus on factors such as resource dependency and transaction costs rather than blame avoidance.

NOTES TO CHAPTER FIVE

1. A saying that can be traced back nearly a thousand years, according to the *Oxford Dictionary of Proverbs*, running from the mid-eleventh-century Latin form *Si non caste tamen caute* to an early twentieth-century song of that title.

2. "The fully developed bureaucratic mechanism compares with other organizations exactly as does the machine with the non-mechanical modes of production" (Weber 1948: 214).

3. See Simon Carr, "If It's Not Outlawed Yet, It Soon Will Be." *The Independent*, November 19, 2007. http://www.independent.co.uk/opinion/commentators/simon-carr/simon-car-if-its-not-outlawed-yet-it-soon-will-be-400940.html (accessed April 2009).

4. This issue was sharply highlighted in late 2008 in the aftermath of a report on the death of a seventeen-month-old boy, Peter Connolly, after months of torture in the London borough of Haringey when just the previous year the borough's social services department had been warmly praised by central government inspectors after a desk-based inspection of its paperwork rather than an inspection of its activities in the field. See Ross (2008).

5. Rose later (1990) pointed to the prevalence of inertia bias in policy-making more generally.

6. See Jonathan Margolis, "A Mission to State a Load of Old Guff," *Evening Standard* January 15, 1997: 24.

7. The singer-songwriter-impresario Noel Coward records in a 1957 diary entry a robust statement to that effect from the then British Governor of Bermuda. See Payn and Morley 1982: 365.

8. In 1936 tithe-owners in England and Wales were compensated with special bonds guaranteed by the government and funded by redemption annuities which were payable by the owners of the land previously charged with tithe rentcharge.

9. See David Fickling, "Dusty Death: How Asbestos Hit Australia," *The Observer* August 22, 2004. http://www.guardian.co.uk/world/2004/aug/22/australia/davidfickling (accessed June 2009).

10. It is a variant of the well-known Pareto principle of optimality in policy (defined as the point at which no one can be made better off without making someone worse off).

11. Leading exponents of this approach included George Stigler (1971) and Sam Peltzman (1980). For a fuller account, see Hood 1994: 22–26.

12. Some or even much of the time, the data and calculations that would in principle be required for the computer-program assumptions about policy making that were sketched out earlier may not be feasible even for the most intelligent and well-resourced officeholders.

13. See also Bernzweig 1973; Garg et al. 1978.

14. See "Bank Refuses Armless Man an Account." http://news.uk.msn.com/ odd-news/article.aspx?cp-documentid=149503282 (accessed November 2009).

15. Though it is sometimes also used to refer to driving behavior designed to keep the police at bay—for example, by employing radar detection devices, using license plates from places with slow or bad motor vehicle information systems, frequently repainting vehicles, etc. See, for instance, SBF Glossary. http://www .plexoft.com/SBF/D02.html (accessed October 2007).

NOTES TO CHAPTER SIX

1. www.columbia.edu/cu/augustine/arch/solzhenitsyn/harvard1978.html. (accessed August 2008).

2. The New Zealand–born scientist Ernest Rutherford (1871–1937) directed the Cavendish laboratory at Cambridge that first "split the atom" in 1932. For the quotation, see Birks 1962: 108.

3. See McFarland 1991: 257.

4. As an alternative to shutting down the internet entirely, as the Myanmar government did in 2007, or to censorship of hostile websites, as the Chinese government does. See Rhoads et al. 2009.

5. See Wolff 2009.

6. On the growth of the White House media staff, see Hess 1998: 749, 751 and Nelson 1998: 373. For data on the growth of the staff of the White House Office, see Ragsdale 1996: 257–61.

7. See House of Lords Communications Committee (2009), "Government Communications." Chapter 5, p.2, table 2: 34.

8. For example, in 2004 the Liberal Democrat Party made much of an increase in the costs of running the Downing Street Press Office and claimed that those costs had risen by some 130 percent in the seven years since Tony Blair's government had come to power. (BBC March 24, 2004. www.bbc.co.uk/1/hi/politics/ 3565305.stm [accessed July 2008]).

9. For example, Civil Service Statistics 1973, table 4, p.14, notes the number of "information group" staff in British central departments at 1310 in 1972; 36 years later the figure for total communications staff given to the House of Lords Communication Committee (2009: chapter 5, table 2) by the Cabinet Office for 2008 was 1376.

10. For instance, Tony Blair's chief press secretary, Alastair Campbell, appears to have routinely attended cabinet meetings, attracted more press mentions than

half the cabinet, and personally bawled out ministers who created embarrassments (Ingham 2003: 227 and 237).

11. For example, commenting in his diary in the mid-1960s on a bill to create a new development authority in Scotland, Reith remarked, "… it is … merely a body which the … [relevant minister] can blame if things go wrong, himself taking the credit when they go right … the politician and civil servant can interfere in any way they like when they want to, but … [can] blame the board, disown and criticise, whenever they want to, particularly of course when the mess has been made as a result of … [their own] interference.…" (diary entry for March 1, 1965 [consulted in BBC archives, Reading, UK], commenting on a bill that introduced what later became the Highlands and Islands Development Board).

12. The invention of the term is described in Barker 1982: 10–14. It derived from the term "quasi-nongovernmental organization," originally coined in the late 1960s by Alan Pifer (1967), President of the Carnegie Corporation of New York, to mean bodies that were formally independent of government but in practice served as instruments of government. That term was shortened to "quango" by Anthony Barker in the early 1970s, but soon came to be used by politicians and journalists to refer to quasi-government bodies and official boards of various kinds.

13. Indeed, commenting some fifteen years ago on recurring British debates about 'quango explosions," Brian Hogwood (1995: 223) judiciously observed that: "government categorizations are not based on systematic distinctions and are at least in part motivated by a desire to keep the body count down. Much of the journalistic and independent coverage, by contrast, seems to be concerned to establish that the number of bodies is high and increasing and that there has been an increase in patronage. The only shared value seems to be that quangos are rather shameful.…" The same point could be made with equal force today.

14. The British government's official count shows numbers of non-departmental public bodies (NDPBs) falling by nearly 40 percent between the early 1980s and the 2000s—from nearly 2000 in 1982 to only just over half that twenty-four years later. But alternative sources indicate a diametrically opposite conclusion about the direction of travel. In particular, the campaigning NGO Democratic Audit, created in the early 1990s, produced two hard-hitting publications during that decade that put the number of quangos in Britain at about ten times the official NDPB count and painted a picture of dramatic growth in numbers, spending, and patronage associated with "extra-governmental bodies" from the late 1970s to the late 1990s (see Weir and Hall 1994; Hall and Weir 1996). While the official NDPB numbers are clearly incomplete, the dramatic claims about the growth of quasi-government bodies made by the Democratic Audit rest heavily on decisions about categorization that can be contested, in particular the exclusion of public corporations (which have been substantially reduced, particularly in terms of employment, with successive bursts of privatization), as Hogwood (1995) has shown.

15. From a Dutch perspective, Van Thiel (2001: 25-6) comments on the huge disparity among the various estimates of the numbers of quangos in Britain.

16. See Laegreid et al. 2003.

17. After all, churches receive tax funds in many European countries (see Madeley 2008), often provide welfare services (such as night shelters for vagrants in cities), run schools and universities, keep official registers of births, marriages, and deaths in some countries, and together with other religious institutions often feature in government dealings with "community leaders"—for instance over youth crime.

18. Congressional Budget Office 2004 table S–2. Budget Summary by Category http://www.whitehouse.gov/omb/budget/fy2004/tables.html (accessed June 2009).

19. The ratio of avoidance to assurance types of defensive behavior in medicine could be expected to depend on the legal regime. Where malpractice law imposes the heaviest liabilities for failure to treat patients, doctors will have an incentive to put the stress on assurance behavior (which may produce significant amounts of "iatrogenic"—doctor-induced—injury, for instance, through the side effects of unnecessary testing and scanning). Where such law imposes the heaviest liability for negative side effects, doctors will have an incentive to put the stress on avoidance behavior by not treating high-risk patients or by not practicing high-risk procedures (Wiener 1998: 50).

20. See, for instance, U.S. Congress, Office of Technology Assessment 1994.

21. For instance, a report into police paperwork in England was commissioned in 2002 after an investigation discovered that the average police officer spent only 17 percent of the day on the street, compared to 43 percent of the day at the police station, two fifths of which was devoted to paperwork, since arresting someone, even for a minor offense, took up an average of three-and-a-half hours on paperwork and associated procedures. See Philip Johnston, "Paper Chase Keeps Officers Off the Beat," *Daily Telegraph*, March 21, 2002. http://www.telegraph.co.uk/news/uknews/1388353/Paper-chase-keeps-officers-off-the-beat.html (accessed May 2009).

22 "For the mind does not require filling like a bottle, but rather, like wood, only requires kindling to create in it an impulse to think independently" (Plutarch 1927: 258–9).

23. See *The Macmillan Dictionary of Contemporary Slang*, London: Macmillan 1995.

NOTES TO CHAPTER SEVEN

1. In that case, the response seemed to depend on leadership by a single powerful agency—the police—who were able to coordinate working jointly in a way that other organizations would probably not have been able to do.

2. In the mid-1990s, Jane Broadbent and colleagues (1994) documented different ways that English schools responded to inspections, ranging from closing ranks against the enemy to settling scores with one another and using other tactics of "buffering."

3. The expert testimony view reflected the (hierarchist) view that juries were incapable of judging what could reasonably be expected of physicians and was succeeded by the equally controversial doctrine of *res ipsa loquitur* (broadly, the

egalitarian notion that facts speak for themselves). See *Duke Law Journal* 1971: 940–41n4; Broder 1969; Knisely 1964.

4. The official inquiry set up in 1997 by the incoming Labour government into the way BSE was handled by its Conservative predecessor, which was led by Lord Phillips and reported in 2000, contains an exhaustive history of the progression of the BSE crisis and the way it was handled. See http://www.bseinquiry.gov.uk/index.htm (accessed February 2009).

5. That is, parts of sheep and cattle infected by spongiform brain disease and used as protein in cattle feed, conventionally thought to be the cause of BSE infection.

6. Something similar happened after a major blame crisis in 2006 over failures to deport foreign prisoners after release, leading to the resignation of the then Home Secretary. After that, responsibility for this issue was passed out to a newly created executive agency, the Border Control Agency.

7. One frequently cited example of this phenomenon is the QWERTY English-language keyboard, which was originally devised to minimize type-bar clashes on the manual typewriters that emerged in the nineteenth century (David 1986). The QWERTY keyboard continues in use long after the problem of clashing mechanical type bars has disappeared (as a result of computerization), even though anyone starting to develop a new arrangement of letters on a keyboard from scratch today would adopt a different convention.

8. Though official denial of the existence of problems that would otherwise appear obvious to the meanest intelligence (as in Hans Anderson's story of the emperor's new clothes) is often a feature of authoritarian and totalitarian regimes, and their corporate equivalents.

9. Indeed, to the various responses listed by Schütz in her steps five through seven might be added the commonly observed phenomenon of top bananas blaming the institutions they lead (rather than themselves) and taking steps to discipline errant middle or front-line players or to offer compensation to the victims of whatever went wrong, while more or less subtly portraying themselves as part of the solution rather than part of the problem.

10. See Broder 2007. William Safire (2008: 431) traces this classic phrase back at least as far as 1876, when it was used by President Ulysses S. Grant, and it has been a regular stand-by of Washington politicians over the last thirty years.

NOTES TO CHAPTER EIGHT

1. An aphorism used by various writers, including Bernard Baruch and Ernst Nagel. Arthur Wirth includes it in his foreword to Abraham Maslow's *The Psychology of Science*, observing that "if the only tool you have is a hammer, it is tempting to treat everything as if it was a nail" (Maslow 1966: x).

2. It should be pointed out that this assassination represented a return to action by the German Red Army Faction, and Detlev Karsten Rohwedder was arguably an "extension" of the Red Army Faction's targets from the 1980s.

3. The admission, on NBC news, concerned the nomination of Senator Tom Daschle for the key role of Secretary of Health and Human Services, which was withdrawn in February 2009 when it came to light that Mr. Daschle and another major appointee had failed to pay all their taxes. The admission came only twenty-four hours after Obama had declared his firm commitment to Daschle's nomination. See "Obama: 'I screwed up,'" Washington Times, February 4, 2009. http://www.washingtontimes.com/news/2009/feb/04/obama-i-screwed/ (accessed June 2009).

4. Lindblom's argument was that (unlike technocratic central planning systems) a pluralist democratic process could ordinarily be trusted to produce outcomes that did not violate common sense or important values, and in that sense would produce more intelligent policy than any non-democratic alternative. The policy would be more "intelligent," Lindblom claimed, because almost any value that a group of citizens wanted to be reflected in policy would come to be weighted "at some value significantly above zero."

5. In Voltaire's biting satire on this idea, the character of Dr. Pangloss ludicrously holds that all is for the best in the best of all possible worlds as one undeserved disaster after another overtakes him and the other characters in the story.

6. No relation, as far as I know!

7. The parallel is with Hayek's (1948) famous argument that markets work as social discovery processes.

8. The analogy with the fictional cat who was never around at the scene of the crime was controversially used by former British Cabinet Secretary Lord Turnbull to describe the political style of the then Chancellor Gordon Brown in March 2007, in an interview with the *Financial Times* newspaper which Turnbull later said he had understood to be a background chat on which he would not be quoted verbatim. See Philippe Naughton, "Brown hit by 'Stalinist' attack on Budget eve," *Times Online* March 20, 2007. http://timesonline.co.uk/tol/news/politics/article 1542111.ece (accessed June 2009).

9. This case is an example of what in earlier work (Hood 1976: 17) I have termed "multi-organizational sub-optimization," in which segmenting responsibility for interlinked safety issues among a set of autonomous or various quasi-autonomous actors (in this case separating road and rail safety responsibility into separate organizations) leads to those actors making decisions that lead to outcomes that are negative at the level of the system as a whole.

10. See Posner 1986: 147–51. Judge Learned Hand's argument (much criticized for its ambiguity in practice) implies that legal liability for negligence in the causing of injury should lie with those who face the lowest costs in preventing it, as with the case of loss from the sort of automobile collision that driver A could only have prevented by driving a tank but driver B could have prevented by driving more slowly.

11. A similar issue applies to changes in civil service law in the Westminster-model democracies to clarify the relationship between politicians and appointed officials and make it clearer who is to be held responsible for what. While such measures could serve to check some applications of variable-geometry agency strat-

egy, opponents argue that such a change can damage the "marriage-type" relationship between politicians and civil servants that they see as necessary for the effective operation of executive government (see Hood and Lodge 2006, 2007).

12. A phrase widely associated with Dr. Bhimrao Ramji Ambedkar (1891–1956), the campaigner for political rights and social freedom for India's untouchables (see Jaffrelot 2005), but long used as a maxim on the left by organizations such as the British Fabian Society.

NOTE TO CHAPTER NINE

1. See for example http://www.imdb.com/name/nm0401921/bio (accessed December 2009).

References

Ames, Glenn J. 2008. *The Globe Encompassed: The Age of European Discovery, 1500–1700*. Upper Saddle River, New Jersey: Prentice Hall.

Anderson, Christopher. 1995. *Blaming the Government: Citizens and the Economy in Five European Democracies*. London: M.E. Sharpe.

Aristotle. [c. 330 BC] 1981. *The Politics*, trans. Thomas A. Sinclair and Trevor Saunders. Harmondsworth, Middlesex: Penguin.

Aristotle 1984. *The Complete Works of Aristotle*. Princeton, NJ: Princeton University Press.

Armor, David A. and Shelley E. Taylor. 2002. "When Predictions Fail: The Dilemma of Unrealistic Optimism." In *Heuristics and Biases: The Psychology of Intuitive Judgement*, ed. Thomas Gilovich, Dale Griffin, and Daniel Kahneman, 334–47. New York: Cambridge University Press.

Audit Commission. 2008. *Are We There Yet? Improving Governance and Resource Management in Children's Trusts*, London: Audit Commission.

Austin, John. 1956. "A Plea for Excuses." *Proceedings of the Aristotelian Society* LVII: 1–30.

Australian Senate Community Affairs References Committee. 2000 *Healing Our Hospitals*. Canberra: Commonwealth of Australia.

Bardach, Eugene. 1998. *Getting Agencies to Work Together: The Practice and Theory of Managerial Craftsmanship*. Washington, DC: Brookings Institution Press.

Barker, Anthony, ed. 1982. *Quangos in Britain: Government and the Networks of Public Policy-Making*. London: Macmillan.

Barr, Emily. 2002. *Baggage*. London: Review.

Baumeister, Roy, Ellen Bratslavsky, Catrin Finkenauer, and Kathleen Vohs, 2001. "Bad Is Stronger than Good." *Review of General Psychology* 5 (4): 323–70.

Beck, Ulrich. 1992. *Risk Society*. London: Sage.

Bentham, Jeremy. 1962. *The Works of Jeremy Bentham*. Bowring edition. Vol. 2. New York: Russell and Russell.

——— 1983. *Constitutional Code*. Oxford: Clarendon.

Bernzweig, Eli P. 1973. "'Defensive Medicine' Appendix: Report of the Secretary's Commission on Medical Malpractice." U.S. Department of Health, Education, and Welfare. DHEW Pub No 73-89, Washington, D.C.: U.S. Government Printing Office.

Birks, J. B. 1962. *Rutherford at Manchester*. London: Heywood.

Black, Julia. 2005. The Emergence of Risk Based Regulation and the New Public Management in the UK. *Public Law*: 512–49.

Bloom, Howard S, and H. Douglas Prince. 1975. "Vote Response to Short-Run Economic Conditions: The Asymmetric Effect of Prosperity and Recession." *American Political Science Review* 69 (December): 1240–54.

Boeker, Warren. 1992. "Power and Managerial Dismissal: Scapegoating at the Top." *Administrative Science Quarterly* 37: 400–21.

Bogdanor, Vernon, ed., 2005. *Joined-up Government*. Oxford: British Academy/ Oxford University Press.

Bonoli, Giuliano. 2001. Political Institutions, Veto Points and the Process of Welfare State Adaptation." In *The New Politics of the Welfare State*, ed. P. Pierson. Oxford: Oxford University Press.

Borraz, Olivier. 2007. "Les Politiques du Risque" Mémoire pour l'habilitation à diriger des researches en Science Politique soutenue le 31 janvier 2007, Paris: Sciences-Po.

Bovens, Mark, Paul t'Hart, Sander Dekker, and Gerdien Verheul. 1999. "The Politics of Blame Avoidance: Defensive Tactics in a Dutch Crime Fighting Fiasco." In *When Things Go Wrong: Organizational Failures and Breakdowns*, ed. Helmet K. Anheir, 123–47. Thousand Oaks: Sage.

Boyne, George A, Oliver James, Peter John, and Nikolai Petrovsky. 2008a. "Executive Succession in Local Government." *Public Money and Management* 28(5): 267–274.

———. 2008b. "Does Public Service Performance Affect Top Management Turnover?" Discussion Paper 0802. Oxford, ESRC Public Services Programme.

———. 2010. "Does Public Service Performance Affect Top Management Turnover?" *Journal of Public Administration Research and Theory* 20(3): i261–i279.

Braithwaite, John, Judith Healy, and Kathryn Dwan. 2005. *The Governance of Health Safety and Quality*. Canberra: Commonwealth of Australia.

Brecht, Berthold. 1967. "De Lösung." In *Gesammelte Werke*, ed. Elisabeth Hauptmann, 1009. Frankfurt-am-Main: Suhrkamp.

Broadbent, Jane, Richard Laughlin, David Shearn, and Heidrun Willig-Atherton. 1994. "Absorbing LMS: The Coping Mechanism of a Small Group." *Accounting, Auditing and Accountability Journal* 7 (1): 152–67.

Broder, Aaron J. 1969. "Res Ipsa Loquitur in Medical Malpractice Cases." *De Paul Law Review* 18: 421.

Broder, John M. 2007. "Familiar Fallback for Officials: 'Mistakes Were Made.'" *New York Times*, March 14, 2007. http://www.nytimes.com/2007/03/14/washington/14mistakes.html (accessed October 2009).

Broszat, Martin. 1981. *The Hitler State: The Foundations and Development of the Internal Structure of the Third Reich*, trans. J.W. Hiden. London: Longman.

Bryson, John M. and Barbara C Crosby. 1992. *Leadership for the Common Good: Tackling Public Problems in a Shared-Power World*. San Francisco: Jossey-Bass.

Buchanan, James M., Robert D. Tollison, and Gordon Tullock, eds. 1980. *Toward a Theory of the Rent-Seeking Society*. College Station: Texas A&M University.

Butland, Bryon, Susan Jebb, Peter Kopelman, Kim McPherson, Sandy Thomas, Jane Mardell, and Vivienne Parry. 2007. *Foresight: Tackling Obesities: Future Choices—Project Report*. London: Department of Innovation, Universities and Skills.

Butler, David, Andrew Adonis, and Tony Travers. 1994. *Failure in British Government: The Politics of the Poll Tax*. Oxford: Oxford University Press.

Campbell, Alistair, and Richard Stott. 2007. *The Blair Years: Extracts from the Alastair Campbell Diaries*. London: Hutchison.

Carr, Simon. 2006. "The Sketch: A Lot of Double-Speak and Plain Rubbish. To Be Fair." *The Independent* March 16, 2006.

———. 2008. "Sometimes You Need a Man in Tights." *The Independent* December 4, 2008: 6.

———. 2009. "The Sketch: Vengeful Tories May Laugh Last at Bercow." *The Independent* May 22, 2009.

Chadwick, Edwin. 1854. Written Submission August 1, 1854. In HMSO (1855) *Papers Relating to the Re-organisation of the Civil Service*. London: HMSO: 135–228.

Chinkin, Christine M. 1989. "The Challenge of Soft Law: Development and Change in International Law." *International and Comparative Law Quarterly* 38 (4): 850–66.

Clarke, Harold, Nitish Dutt, and Jonathan Rapkin. 1997. "Conversations in Context: The (Mis)Measurement of Value Change in Advanced Industrial Societies." *Political Behavior* 19 (1): 19–39.

Clemens, Michael, and Todd Moss. 2005. "Dateline Zimbabwe: Who's to Blame?" *The Globalist*, Center for Global Development, August 24, 2005 http://www.cgdev.org/content/opinion/detail/3612/ (accessed December 2007).

Coleman, Marie. 2005. "A Terrible Danger to the Morals of the Country: The Irish Hospitals Sweepstake in Great Britain, 1930–87" *Proceedings of the Royal Irish Academy* 105C (5): 197–220.

Coser, Lewis. 1956. *The Functions of Social Conflict*. London: Routledge and Kegan Paul.

Craig, David. and Richard Brooks. 2006. *Plundering the Public Sector: How New Labour are Letting Consultants Run Off with £70 Billion of Our Money*. London: Constable.

Crawford, Craig. 2005. *Attack the Messenger: How Politicians Turn You Against the Media*. Lanham, MD: Rowman and Littlefield.

Dahl, Robert A. 1989. *Democracy and its Critics*. London: Yale University Press.

Danto, Arthur C. 2005. *Nietzsche as Philosopher* (expanded edition). New York: Columbia University Press.

Davenport, Thomas, and James Short. 1990. "The New Industrial Engineering: Information Technology and Business Process Redesign." *Sloan Management Review* Summer 1990: 11–27.

David, Paul A. 1986. "Understanding the Economics of QWERTY: The Necessity of History." In *Economic History and the Modern Economist*, ed. W. N. Parker. Oxford: Basil Blackwell.

de Tocqueville, Alexis. 1946. *Democracy in America*. Oxford: Oxford University Press

Dehousse, Renaud. 2007. "Delegation of Powers in the European Union: The Need for a Multi-Principals Model." Paper presented to Connex Thematic Conference on Accountability, EUI, Florence, June 29–30, 2007.

Department of Health. 2006. *National media coverage of public health issues and the NHS*. http://www.dh.gov.uk/enFreedomOfInformationpublicationscheme feedback/Classesofinformation/Communicationsresearch/DH_4130120.

Dickens, Charles. 1850. *The Personal History Of David Copperfield*. London: Bradbury & Evans.

Douglas, Mary. 1970. *Natural Symbols: Explorations in Cosmology*. London: Barrie and Rockliff.

———. 1982. "Cultural Bias" In *In the Active Voice*, ed. M. Douglas. London: Routledge and Kegan Paul.

———. 1990. "Risk as a Forensic Resource." *Daedalus (Proceedings of the American Academy of Arts and Sciences)* 119 (4): 1–16.

Dryzek, John. 1996. Review of A. Wildavsky, *But is it True? A Citizen's Guide to Environmental Health and Safety Issues* (Harvard University Press 1995). *Journal of Public Policy* 15 (2): 299–304.

Duke Law Journal. 1971. "The Medical Malpractice Threat: A Study of Defensive Medicine." *Duke Law Journal* 5 (December): 939–93.

Dunsire, Andrew. 1978. *Control in a Bureaucracy: The Execution Process*. Vol. 2. Oxford: Martin Robertson and Company Ltd.

Edwards-Jones, Imogen, and Anonymous. 2006. *Air Babylon*. London: Corgi.

Elliott, Carl. 1992. "Diagnosing Blame: Responsibility and the Psychopath." *Journal of Medicine and Philosophy* 17(2): 199–214.

Elgie, Robert. 2006. "Why Do Governments Delegate Authority to Quasi-Autonomous Agencies? The Case of Independent Administrative Authorities in France." *Governance* 19(2): 207–27.

Ellis, Richard. 1994. *Presidential Lightning Rods: The Politics of Blame Avoidance*. Kansas: University Press of Kansas.

Evans, Tony and John Harris. 2004. "Street-Level Bureaucracy, Social Work and the (Exaggerated) Death of Discretion." *British Journal of Social Work* 34: 871–95.

Felstiner, William L.F., Richard L. Abel, and Austin Sarat. 1980. "The Emergence and Transformation of Disputes: Naming, Blaming, Claiming." *Law and Society Review* 15(3–4): 631–654.

Fenno, Richard. 1978. *Home Style*. Boston: Little, Brown.

Fielding, Helen. 2006. "Bridget Jones's Diary." *The Independent* (extra section), April 27, 2006: 7.

Fildes, Christopher. 2005. "Hedonomics: It's the Dismal Science with its Own Happy Ending." *Daily Telegraph*, August 30, 2005: 32.

Fiorina, Morris. 1982. "Legislative Choice of Regulatory Forms: Legal Process or Administrative Process?" *Public Choice* 39 (1): 33–66.

Fiorina, Morris. 1986. "Legislator Uncertainty, Legislator Control and the Delegation of Legislative Power." *Journal of Law, Economics and Organization* 2 (1): 133–51.

Finer, Samuel E. 1970. *Comparative Government*. London: Penguin Press.

Flanagan, Ronnie. 2008. *The Review of Policing: Final Report*, Home Office. http://police.homeoffice.gov.uk/publications/police-reform/Review_of_policing_final_report/flanagan-final-report?view=Binary (accessed May 2009).

Flinders, Matthew. 2004. "MPs and Icebergs: Parliament and Delegated Governance." *Parliamentary Affairs* 57 (4): 767–84.

Flynn, Paul. 1999. *Dragons Led by Poodles: The Inside Story of a New Labour Stitch-Up*. London: Politico's.

Forder, James. 2001. "Some Methodological Issues in the Statutory Characterisation of Central Banks." *West European Politics* 24 (1): 202–16. (Also see Robert Elgie's reply in the same issue: 217–21.)

Forsne, Christina. 1997. *François*. Paris: Le Seuil.

Franchino, Fabio. 2007. *The Powers of the Union: Delegation in the EU*. Cambridge: Cambridge University Press.

Frederickson, H. George. 2003. "Easy Innovation and the Iron Cage: Best Practice, Benchmarking, Ranking and the Management of Organizational Creativity." Kettering Foundation Occasional Paper, Dayton: Kettering Foundation.

Freedland, Jonathan. 2007. "Next up on Newsnight, an Empty Chair." *The Guardian*, April 12, 2007. www.guardian.co.uk/media/2007/apr/12/politicsand themedia.comment (accessed November 2008).

Fuess, Claude M. 2007. *Calvin Coolidge—The Man from Vermont*. Alcester: Read Books.

Furedi, Frank. 2009. "What Swine Flu Reveals About the Culture of Fear: A Guide to Today's Various Species of Scaremonger." *Spiked* May 5, 2009. http://www.spiked-online.com/index.php?/site/article/6633 (accessed June 2009).

Furedi, Frank. 2005. *The Politics of Fear*. London: Continuum.

Furedi, Frank. 1997. *Culture of Fear: Risk Taking and Morality of Low Expectations*. London: Cassell.

Garg, Mohan L. Werner A. Gliebe, and Mounir B. Elkhatib. 1978. "The Extent of Defensive Medicine: Some Empirical Evidence." *Legal Aspects of Medical Practice* February 1978: 25–9.

Garland, David. 2001. *The Culture of Control: Crime and Social Order in Contemporary Society*. Oxford: Oxford University Press.

Giddens, Anthony. and Simon Griffiths. 2006. *Sociology*, 5th ed. Cambridge: Polity.

Gilardi, Fabrizio. 2002. "Policy Credibility and Delegation to Independent Regulatory Agencies: A Comparative Empirical Analysis." *Journal of European Public Policy* 9(6): 873–93.

Gill, Tom. 2005. "Whose Problem? Japan's Homeless People as an Issue of Local and Central Governance." In *Contested Governance in Japan: Sites and Issues*, ed. Glenn D. Hook. London: Routledge Curzon.

Gill, Tim. 2007. *No Fear: Growing up in a Risk Averse Society*. London: Calouste Gulbenkian Foundation.

Godoy, Julio. 2003. "Politics—France: Dollars Stuffed into Monsieur Africa's Salad." IPS News June 9, 2003. http://ipsnews.net/interna.asp?idnews=18662 (accessed November 2008).

Goffman, Erving. 1986. *Frame Analysis: An Essay on the Organization of Experience*. Boston: Northeastern University Press.

Gore, Al. 1993. *From Red Tape to Results: Report of the National Performance Review*. Washington, DC: U.S. Government Printing Office.

Graham, John D. and Jonathan B. Wiener. 1995. "Confronting Risk Tradeoffs." In *Risk versus Risk: Tradeoffs in Protecting Health and the Environment*, ed. J. D. Graham and J. B. Weiner. London: Harvard University Press.

Hague, Douglas C., William J. M. Mackenzie, and Anthony Barker. 1975. *Public Policy and Private Interests: The Institutions of Compromise*. London: Macmillan.

Hall, Wendy and Stuart Weir. 1996. "The Untouchables: Power and Accountability in the Quango State." Democratic Audit of the UK. London: Charter 88 Trust.

Hammer, Michael. 1990. "Reengineering Work: Don't Automate, Obliterate." *Harvard Business Review,* Jul/Aug 1990: 104–12.

Hanusch, Horst, ed. 1980. *Anatomy of Government Deficiencies*. Berlin, Springer-Verlag.

Hart, Albert B. and Herbert R. Ferleger, ed. [1941] 1989. *Theodore Roosevelt Cyclopedia*. Rev. 2nd ed. New York: Theodore Roosevelt Association and Meckler.

Hayek, Friedrich A. 1948. *Individualism and Economic Order*. Chicago: Chicago University Press.

Heald, David A. and George Georgiou. 2008. "The Regulation and Substance of Accounting for Public-Private Partnerships," Paper presented to the Financial Reporting and Communication Unit's Tenth Annual Conference, Cardiff Business School, July 3–4, 2008.

Heath, Chip, Richard Larrick and George Wu. 1999. "Goals as Reference Points." *Cognitive Psychology* 38 (1): 79–109.

Hegel, Georg W. F. 1896. *Philosophy of Right*. Trans. S.W. Dyde. London: Bell.

Heinrich, Carolyn J. 2002. "Outcomes-Based Performance Management in the Public Sector: Implications for Government Accountability and Effectiveness." *Public Administration Review* 62 (6): 712–25.

Herring, Pendleton. 1940. *Presidential Leadership*. New York: Farrar and Rinehart.

Hess, Stephen. 1998. "The Once to Future Worlds of Presidents Communicating." *Presidential Studies Quarterly* 28 (4): 748–53.

Hirschman, David. 1981. "Development or Underdevelopment Administration? A Further Deadlock." *Development and Change* 12(3): 459–79.

Hiwatari, Nobuhiro. 2000. "The Reorganization of Japan's Financial Bureaucracy: The Politics of Bureaucratic Structure and Blame Avoidance." In *Crisis and Change in the Japanese Financial System*, ed. Takeo Hoshi and Hugh T. Patrick. London, Kluwer Academic: 159–200.

Hogwood, Brian W. 1995. "The 'Growth' of Quangos: Evidence and Explanations." *Parliamentary Affairs* 48: 207–25.

Holt, Tim. 2008. "Official Statistics, Public Policy and Public Trust." *Journal of the Royal Statistical Society* A 171 Part 2: 1–20.

Hood, Christopher. 1976. *The Limits of Administration*. London: Wiley.

———. 1978. "Keeping the Centre Small: Explanations of Agency Type." *Political Studies* 26 (1): 30–46.

———. 1994. *Explaining Economic Policy Reversals*. Buckingham: Open University Press.

———. 1998. *The Art of the State: Culture, Rhetoric and Public Management*. Oxford: Clarendon.

———. 2002. "The Risk Game and the Blame Game." *Government and Opposition* 37 (1): 15–37.

———. 2006. "Transparency in Historical Perspective." In *Transparency: The Key to Better Governance*, ed. Christopher Hood and David Heald. Oxford: Oxford University Press.

Hood, Christopher, and Michael W. Jackson. 1991. *Administrative Argument*. Aldershot: Dartmouth.

Hood, Christopher, Will Jennings, Ruth Dixon, Brian W. Hogwood, and Craig Beeston. 2009. "Testing Times: Exploring Staged Responses and the Impact of Blame Management Strategies in Two Exam Fiasco Cases." *European Journal of Political Research* 48 (6): 695–722.

Hood, Christopher, and Martin Lodge. 2006. *The Politics of Public Service Bargains: Reward, Competency, Loyalty—and Blame*. Oxford: Oxford University Press.

———. "'Putting It in Writing' Is Not the Best Way to Make Peace with Sir Humphrey." *Parliamentary Brief* 11(6) August 2007: 17–18.

Hood, Christopher, and Helen Margetts. 2007. *The Tools of Government in the Digital Age*. London: Palgrave Macmillan.

Hood, Christopher, and B. Guy Peters, eds. 1994. *Rewards at the Top: A Comparative Study of High Public Office*. London: Sage.

Hood, Christopher, B. Guy Peters, and Grace O. M. Lee, eds. 2003. *Reward for High Public Office: Asian and Pacific Rim States*. London: Routledge.

Hood, Christopher, Henry Rothstein, and Robert Baldwin. 2001. *The Government of Risk: Understanding Risk Regulation Regimes*. Oxford: Oxford University Press.

Hood, Christopher, and Gunnar F. Schuppert. 1988. *Delivering Public Services in Western Europe: Sharing Western European Experience of Para-Government Organization*. London: Sage.

Hood, Christopher, Colin Scott, Oliver James, George W. Jones, and Tony Travers. 1999. *Regulation Inside Government: Waste-Watchers, Quality Police and Sleaze-Busters*. Oxford: Oxford University Press.

Hood, John. 2005. *Selling the Dream: Why Advertising is Good Business*. New York: Praeger.

Horn, Murray J. 1995. *The Political Economy of Public Administration: Institutional Choice in the Public Sector*. Cambridge: Cambridge University Press.

House of Lords Communications Committee. 2009. "Government Communications." *First Report of Session 2008–9*, HL Paper 7. London: The Stationery Office Limited.

Huntingdon, Samuel. 1971. "The Change to Change: Modernization, Development and Politics." *Comparative Politics* 3 (3): 283–322.

Hupe, Peter, and Michael Hill. 2007. "Street-Level Bureaucracy And Public Accountability." *Public Administration* 85 (2): 279–99.

Ingham, Bernard. 2003. *The Wages of Spin*. London: John Murray.

Jacobson, Howard. 2008. "No Wonder the Public is Deranged When the People Paid to Serve Us Do Such a Bad Job." *The Independent*, May 1, 2008: 40.

Jaffrelot, Christophe. 2005. *Dr. Ambedkar and Untouchability: Fighting the Indian Caste System*. New York: Columbia University Press.

James, Oliver and Peter John. 2007. "Public Management Performance Information and Electoral Support for Incumbent English Local Governments." *Journal of Public Administration Research and Theory* 17 (4): 567–80.

Janis, Irving. 1972. *Victims of Groupthink*. Boston: Houghton Mifflin.

Javeline, Debra. 2003. "The Role of Blame in Collective Action: Evidence from Russia." *American Political Science Review* 97 (1): 107–21.

Jennings, Will J. 2009. "The Public Thermostat, Political Responsiveness and Error-Correction: Border Control and Asylum in Britain, 1994–2007," *British Journal of Political Science* 39(4): 847–70.

———. 2004. "Public Policy, Implementation and Public Opinion: The Case of Public Celebrations (Canada 1967, USA 1976, Australia 1988 and the UK 2000)." Oxford: DPhil thesis.

Jones, Bill. 1993. "The Pitiless Probing Eye: Politicians and the Broadcast Political Interview." *Parliamentary Affairs* 46 (1): 66–93.

Jones, Nicholas. 1996. *Soundbites and Spin Doctors: How Politicians Manipulate the Media—and Vice Versa*. London: Indigo.

———. 1999. *Sultans of Spin*. London: Gollancz.

Jordana, Jacint, and David Levi-Faur. 2006. "Towards a Latin American Regulatory State? The Diffusion of Autonomous Regulatory Agencies across Countries and Sectors," *International Journal of Public Administration* 29(4–6): 335–366.

Kahneman, Daniel, and Amos Tversky. 1979. "Prospect Theory: An Analysis of Decisions under Risk." *Econometrica* 47: 263–91.

Kasperson, Roger. 1992. "The Social Amplification of Risk: Progress in Developing an Integrative Framework." *Social Theories of Risk*, ed. Sheldon Krimsky and Dominic Golding Westport, Conn.: Paeger.

Kaye, Robert. 2002. "'Regulating Westminster: The House of Commons Select Committees on Members' Interests and Standards and Privileges," Oxford: DPhil thesis.

Kelemen, R. Daniel. 2006. "Suing for Europe: Adversarial Legalism and European Governance," *Comparative Political Studies* 39(1): 101–27.

Kernell, Samuel. 1977. "Presidential Popularity and Negative Voting." *American Political Science Review* 71: 44–66.

Knisely, Anne M. 1964. "Modern Medico-Legal Trends." *Ohio State Law Journal* 25: 360.

Koren, Gideon, and Naomi Klein. 1991. "Bias against Negative Studies in Newspaper Reports of Medical Research." *Journal of the American Medical Association* 266: 1824–26.

Kurtz, Howard. 1998. *Spin Cycle: Inside the Clinton Propaganda Machine.* New York: Free Press.

Laegreid, Per, Vidar W. Rolland, Paul G. Roness, and John-Erik Aagotnes. 2003. "The Structural Anatomy of the Norwegian State, 1947–2003." Paper presented to the COBRA network conference, Bergen, 2003.

Larsen, Egon. 1980. *Wit as a Weapon: The Political Joke in History.* London: Frederick Muller.

Laski, Harold. 1940. *The American Presidency.* New York: Harper.

Lau, Richard R. 1982. "Negativity in political perception." *Political Behavior* 4: 353–378.

———. 1985. "Two Explanations for Negativity Effects in Political Behavior." *American Journal of Political Science* 29: 119–38.

Lawrence, Gary M. 1994. *Due Diligence in Business Transactions.* New York: Law Journal Press.

Lee, Ronald, and Matthew H. Barton. 2003. "Clinton's Rhetoric of Contrition." In *Images, Scandal and Communication Strategies of the Clinton Presidency.* ed. Robert E. Denton Jr. and Rachel L. Holloway, 219–46. Westport, Conn., Praeger.

Legendre, Pierre. 1968. *Histoire de l'Administration de 1750 à nos jours.* Vendôme: Presses Universitaires de France.

Leishman, Marista. 2006. *My Father: Reith of the BBC.* Edinburgh: St. Andrew's Press.

Lessig, Lawrence. 2000. *Code and Other Laws of Cyberspace.* New York: Basic Books.

Levi-Faur, David. 2005. "The Global Diffusion of Regulatory Capitalism." *Annals of the American Academy of Political and Social Science.* 598 (1): 12–32.

Levin, Bernard. 1971. *The Pendulum Years: Britain in the Sixties.* London: Jonathan Cape.

Lindblom, Charles. 1965. *The Intelligence of Democracy.* New York: Free Press.

———. 1982. "Another State of Mind." *American Political Science Review* 76: 9–21.

Lindbom, Anders. 2001. "Dismantling the Swedish Welfare Model: Has the Swedish Welfare State Lost its Defining Characteristics?" *Scandinavian Political Studies* 24 (3): 171–193.

———. 2007. "Obfuscating Retrenchment: Swedish Welfare Policy in the 1990s." *Journal of Public Policy* 27 (2): 129–50.

Linford, Paul. 2004. "Blair Taking on All the Summits." *The Journal.* 10.4.2004, http://icteesside.icnetwork.co.uk/thejournal/paullinford/tm_objectid=14135266 &method=full&siteid=50081&headline=blair-taking-on-all-the-summits -name_page.html (accessed August 2008).

Linsky, Marty, and Esther Scott. 1992. "Managing a Press 'Feeding Frenzy': Gregory Coler and the Florida Department of Health and Rehabilitative Services," Case 1135.0, Kennedy School of Government, Harvard University. http://www.ksgcase.harvard.edu/caseTitle.asp?caseNo=1135.0 (accessed February 2009).

Lipsky, Michael. 1980. *Street-Level Bureaucracy: Dilemmas of the Individual in Public Services.* New York: Russell Sage Foundation.

Loudon, Irvine. 1991. "On Maternal and Infant Mortality 1900–1960." *The Society for the Social History of Medicine* 4 (1): 29–73.

McCubbins, Matthew D. and Thomas Schwartz. 1984. "Congressional Oversight Overlooked: Police Patrols Versus Fire Alarms." *American Journal of Political Science* 28: 165–79.

McFarland, Andrew S. 1991. "Interest Groups and Political Time: Cycles in America." *British Journal of Political Science* 21: 257–84.

McGivern, Gerry, and Ewan Ferlie. 2007. "Playing Tick-Box Games: Interrelating Defences in Professional Appraisal." *Human Relations* 60 (9) 1361–1385.

McGraw, Kathleen M. 1990. "Avoiding Blame: An Experimental Investigation of Political Excuses and Justifications." *British Journal of Political Science* 20 (1): 119–42.

McLean, Iain, and Martin Johnes. 2000. "'Regulation Run Mad': The Board of Trade and the Loss of the Titanic." *Public Administration* 78 (4): 729–49.

Machiavelli, Niccolò. 1961. *The Prince.* Harmondsworth: Penguin.

Maestas, Cherie D., Lonna Rae Atkeson, Thomas Croom, and Lisa A. Bryant. 2008. "Shifting the Blame: Federalism, Media and Public Assignment of Blame

Following Hurrican Katrina." *Publius: The Journal of Federalism* 38(4): 609–32.

Mackenzie, William J. M. 2002. *The Secret History of SOE: The Special Operations Executive*, 1940–1945. London: St. Emin's Press.

Margetts, Helen. 2010. "Modernization Dreams and Public Policy Reform." In *Paradoxes of Modernization: Unintended Consequences of Public Policy Reform*, ed. Helen Margetts and Christopher Hood. Oxford: Oxford University Press.

Marks, Gary, and Liesbet Hooghe. 2004. "Contrasting Visions of Multi-Level Governance." In *Multi-Level Governance*, ed. Jan Bache and Matthew Flinders, 15–30. Oxford: Oxford University Press.

Maslow, Abraham H. 1966. *The Psychology of Science: A Reconnaissance*. Foreword by Arthur G. Wirth. New York: Harper and Row.

Menzies, Isabel E. P. 1960. "A Case Study in the Functioning of Social Systems as a Defence Against Anxiety." *Human Relations* 13(2): 95–121.

Meyer, Marshall W. and Lynne G. Zucker. 1989. *Permanently Failing Organizations*. Newbury Park: Sage.

Minogue, Kenneth. 1986. "Loquocentric Society and its Critics." *Government and Opposition* 21 (3): 338–61.

Mitchell, Neil. 2004. *Agents of Atrocity: Leaders, Followers, and the Violation of Human Rights in Civil Wars*. Basingstoke: Palgrave Macmillan.

Moloney, Kevin. 2000. "The Rise and Fall of Spin: Changes of Fashion in the Presentation of UK Politics." *Journal of Public Affairs*. 1(2): 124–135.

Moorehead, Alan. 1963. *Cooper's Creek*. London: Hamish Hamilton.

Monnet, Jean. 1978. *Memoirs*. Trans. Richard Mayne. London: Collins.

Morrow, Lance. 1996. "Naysayer to the Nattering Nabobs." *Time* Magazine, September 30, 1996. www.time/com/time/magazine/article//0.9171.985217.00 .html (accessed November 2009).

Mudge, Stephanie. 2006. "'Two Chess Games at Once': Blame Avoidance and the Future of Social Rights in Europe's Multilevel Politics." Paper presented at the annual meeting of the American Sociological Association, Montreal Convention Center. Montreal, Quebec, Canada, August 11, 2006. http://www.allacademic .com/meta/p105060_index.html (accessed July 2008).

Mulgan, Geoff. 2009. *The Art of Public Strategy: Mobilizing Power and Knowledge for the Common Good*. Oxford: Oxford University Press.

Nelson, Michael, (ed.) 1998. *The Presidency A to Z*, 2nd ed. Chicago: Fitzroy Dearborn Publishers.

Neustadt, Richard. 1960. *Presidential Power: The Politics of Leadership*. New York: Wiley.

Norris, Pippa, John Curtice, David Sanders, and Maggie Scammell. 1999. *On Message: Communicating the Campaign*. London: Sage.

Nye, Joe S. Jr., Philip D. Zelizhov, and David C. King. 1997. *Why People Don't Trust Government*. Cambridge, MA: Harvard University Press.

O'Donnell, Guillermo. 1999. "Horizontal Accountability in New Democracies." In *The Self-Restraining State: Power and Accountability in New Democracies*, ed. Andreas Schedler, Larry Diamond, and Marc F. Plattner, 29–52. Boulder, CO: Lynne Reinner.

O'Neill, Onora. 2002. *A Question of Trust*. The BBC Reith Lectures 2002. Cambridge: Cambridge University Press.

———. "Transparency and the Ethics of Communication." In *Transparency: The Key to Better Governance*, Christopher Hood and David A. Heald, 75–90. Oxford: Oxford University Press.

Oborne, Peter. 1999. *Alastair Campbell: New Labour and the Rise of the Media Class*. London: Aurum.

Ogilvy, David. 1964. *Confessions of an Advertising Man*. London: Longmans.

Ogilvy-Webb, Marjorie. 1965. *The Government Explains: A Study of the Information Services*. London: Allen and Unwin.

Osborne, David, and Ted Gaebler. 1993. *Reinventing Government: How the Entrepreneurial Spirit Is Transforming the Public Sector from Schoolhouse to Statehouse, City Hall to the Pentagon*. Reading, MA: Addison-Wesley.

Osborne, Stephen, ed. 2010. *The New Public Governance: Emerging Perspectives on the Theory and Practice of Public Governance*. London: Routledge.

Page, Edward C. and William Jenkins. 2005. *Policy Bureaucracy: Government with a Cast of Thousands*. Oxford: Oxford University Press.

Parker, Laura. 2004. "Medical Malpractice Battle Gets Personal." *USA Today* June 13, 2004. http://www.usatoday.com/news/nation/2004-06-13-med-mal practice_x.htm (accessed January 2009).

Payn, Graham, and Sheridan Morley eds. 1982. *The Noel Coward Diaries*. London: Macmillan.

Péan, Pierre. 1994. *Une Jeunesse Française: François Mitterand 1934–47*. Paris: Fayard.

Pepperday, Michael E. 2009. Way of Life Theory: The Underlying Structure of Worldviews, Social Relations and Lifestyles. PhD thesis, Canberra: Australian National University.

Peltzman, Sam. 1981. "Current Developments in the Economics of Regulation." In *Studies of Public Regulation*, ed. G. Fromm Cambridge, MA: MIT Press.

Penn, Robert, and Antony Woodward. 2007. *The Wrong Kind of Snow: The Complete Daily Companion to the British Weather*. London: Hodder and Stoughton.

Perrow, Charles. 1972. *Complex Organizations: A Critical Essay*. Glenview, IL: Scott Foresman.

———. *Normal Accidents*. New York: Basic Books.

Peters, B. Guy, Jon Pierre, and Desmond King. 2005. "The Politics of Path Dependency: Political Conflict in Historical Institutionalism." *The Journal of Politics*. 67 (4): 1275–1300.

Pfeffer, Jeffrey and Gerald R. Salancik. 2003. *The External Control of Organizations: A Resource Dependence Perspective.* Stanford, CA: Stanford Business Books.

Pierson, Paul. 1994. *Dismantling the Welfare State?* Cambridge: Cambridge University Press.

———. 1996. "The New Politics of the Welfare State." *World Politics* 48 (2): 143–179.

———, ed. 2001. *The New Politics of the Welfare State.* Oxford: Oxford University Press.

Pifer, Alan. 1967. *The Quasi Nongovernmental Organization.* Reprinted from the 1967 Annual Report of the Carnegie Corporation of New York. New York: Carnegie Corporation.

Plutarch. 1927. *De Auditu.* In Vol. 1 of *Moralia.* 201–59. Loeb Classical Library. Cambridge Mass.: Harvard University Press.

Politkovskaya, Anna. 2003. *A Small Corner of Hell: Dispatches from Chechnya.* Trans. Burry Alexander and Tatiana Tulchinsky, with an introduction by G. Derluguian. Chicago: University of Chicago Press.

Pollitt, Christopher. 1984. *Manipulating the Machine: Changing the Pattern of Ministerial Departments 1960–83.* London: Allen and Unwin.

Pollitt, Christopher, and Colin Talbot, eds. 2004. *Unbundled Government: A Critical Analysis of the Global Trend to Agencies, Quasi-Autonomous Bodies and Contractualization.* London: Taylor and Francis.

Pomeroy, Robin. 2008. "Italy's PM Orders 'Trash Tsar' to End Crisis." Reuter's UK Jan 8, 2008 http://uk/reuters.com/articleidUKPAR8618692008108 (accessed November 2009).

Posner, Richard A. 1986. *Economic Analysis of Law.* 3rd ed. Boston: Little, Brown.

Power, Michael K. 1997. *The Audit Society: Rituals of Verification.* Oxford: Oxford University Press.

———. 2004. *The Risk Management of Everything.* London: Demos.

———. 2007. *Organized Uncertainty: Designing a World of Risk Management.* Oxford: Oxford University Press.

Prat, Andrea. 2005. "The Wrong Kind of Transparency." *American Economic Review* 95 (3): 862–77.

Quah, Jon. 2003. "Paying for the Best and Brightest: Rewards for High Public Office in Singapore." In *Reward for High Public Office: Asian and Pacific Rim States*, ed. Christopher Hood, B. Guy Peters and Grace O. M. Lee, 144–62. London: Routledge.

Radcliff, Benjamin. 1994. "Reward Without Punishment: Economic Conditions and the Vote." *Political Research Quarterly* 47 (3): 721–31.

Ragsdale, Lyn. 1996. *Vital Statistics on the Presidency: Washington to Clinton.* Washington, DC: Congressional Quarterly, Inc.

Reder, Peter, and Sylvia Duncan. 2004. "Making the Most of the Victoria Climbié Report." *Child Abuse Review* 13 (2): 95–114.

Report of a Commission of Inquiry Pursuant to Orders in Council. May 26, 1987, June 24, 1987, August 25, 1988, June 29, 1989. *Commission of Inquiry into Possible Illegal Activities and Associated Police Misconduct* (the Fitzgerald Inquiry). Brisbane, Commission of Inquiry.

Rhoads, Christopher, Geoffrey A Fowler, and Chip Cummins. 2009. "Iran Cracks Down on Internet Use, Foreign Media." *Wall Street Journal*, June 17, 2009, http://online.wsj.com/article/SB124519888117821213.html (accessed November 2009).

Rhodes, Rod A. W. 1996. "The New Governance: Governing without Government." *Political Studies* 44(4): 652–67.

Roberts, Alasdair. 2006a. *Blacked Out: Government Secrecy in the Information Age.* Cambridge: Cambridge University Press.

———. 2006b. "Dashed Expectations: Governmental Adaptation to Transparency Rules." In *Transparency: The Key to Better Governance?*, ed. C. Hood and D.A. Heald, 107–26. Oxford: Oxford University Press.

Robson, William A. 1937. "The Public Service Board: General Conclusions." In *Public Enterprise: Developments in Social Enterprise and Control in Great Britain*, ed W. A. Robson New Fabian Research Bureau. London: Allen and Unwin.

Rose, Richard. 1990. "Inheritance Before Choice in Public Policy." *Journal of Theoretical Politics* 2 (3): 263–91.

Rose, Richard, and Terence Karran. 1987. *Taxation by Political Inertia.* London: Allen and Unwin.

Rosin, Paul, and Edward B. Royzman. 2001. "Negativity Bias, Negativity Dominance and Contagion." *Personality and Social Psychology Review* 5 (4): 296–320.

Ross, Fiona. 1997. "Cutting Public Expenditures in Advanced Industrial Democracies: The Importance of Avoiding Blame." *Governance* 10: 175–200.

Ross, Tim. 2008. "Ofsted Knew of Baby P Tragedy When it Gave Council Glowing Report." *Evening Standard*, November 14, 2008. http://www.thisislondon.co.uk/standard/article-23587003-details/Haringey+given+a+clean+bill+of+health+only+weeks+after+the+death+of+Baby+P/article.co (accessed December 2008).

Ruiter, Dick. 2005. "Is Transaction Cost Economics Applicable to Public Governance?" *European Journal of Law and Economics* 20(3): 287–303.

Safire, William. 2008. *Safire's Political Dictionary.* New York: Oxford University Press.

Sagan, Scott. 1993. *The Limits of Safety.* Princeton: Princeton University Press.

Savas, Emanuel S. 1982. *Privatizing the Public Sector: How to Shrink Government.* Chatham, NJ: Chatham House.

Savoie, Donald. 1995. *Thatcher, Reagan, Mulroney: In Search of a New Bureaucracy.* Pittsburgh, PA.: University of Pittsburgh Press.

Schlenker, Barry. 1980. *Impression management: The Self-Concept, Social Identity, and Interpersonal Relations*. Monterey: Brooks Cole.

Schütz, Astrid. 1996. "Selbstdarstellung in der Defensive—Reaktionen in politischen Skandalen." In *"Wir, Die Wir Gut Sind": Die Selbstdarstellung von Politikern zwischen Glorifizierung und Glaubwürdigkeit*. Lothar Laux and Astrid Schütz. München: Deutscher Taschenbuch Verlag.

Scott, Walter. [1819] 1991. The *Bride of Lammermuir*. Oxford: Oxford University Press.

Self, Peter. 1993. *Government by the Market?* London: Palgrave Macmillan.

Sharkansky, Ira. 1979. *Wither the State?* Chatham, NJ: Chatham House.

Shrader-Frechette, Kristin. 1991. *Risk and Rationality*. Berkeley: University of California Press.

Sieber, Sam. 1981. *Fatal Remedies*. New York: Plehum.

Simon, Herbert A. 1946. "The Proverbs of Administration." *Public Administration Review* 6 (1): 53–67.

Slovic, Paul. 1993. "Perceived Risk, Trust, and Democracy," *Risk Analysis*. 13: 675–682.

Smith, Adam. [1776] 1910. *The Wealth of Nations* Everyman's Library edition. London: J. M. Dent.

Smith, A. McCall. 2008. *The Unbearable Lightness of Scones*. Edinburgh, Polygon.

Smith, Craig A. 2003. "Bill Clinton in Rhetorical Crisis: The Six Stages of Scandal and Impeachment." In *Images, Scandal, and Communication Strategies of the Clinton Presidency*, ed. Robert E. Denton and Rachel L. Holloway, 173–94. Santa Barbara: Greenwood Publishing Group.

Smith, Vicki. 1994. "Manufacturing Management Ideology: Corporate Culture and Control in Financial Services." In *Critical Studies in Organization and Bureaucracy*. Rev. and exp. ed. Ed. Frank Fischer and Carmen Sirianni, 233–57. Philadelphia: Temple University Press.

Soroka, Stuart N. 2006. "Good News and Bad News: Asymmetric Responses to Economic Information." *Journal of Politics* 68(2): 372–85.

Standing, Sarah. 2009. "Standing Room." *The Spectator* July 4, 2009: 19.

Sterne, Laurence. [1759–67] 1984. *The Life and Opinions of Tristram Shandy, Gentleman*. Ed. Ian C. Ross. Oxford: Oxford University Press.

Stigler, George J. 1971. "The Theory of Economic Regulation." *Bell Journal of Economics and Management Science* 2 (1): 1–21.

Stone, Christopher D. 1991. *Where the Law Ends: The Social Control of Corporate Behavior*. Illinois: Waveland.

Styron, William. 1998. "Has Starr Humiliated Us All?" *New Yorker*, October 12, 1998.

Sulitzeanu-Kenan, Raanan. 2006. "If They Get it Right: An Experimental Test of the Effects of UK Public Inquiries' Appointment and Reports," *Public Administration*, 84 (3): 623–53.

———. 2007. "Scything the Grass: Agenda-Setting Consequences of Appointing Public Inquiries in the UK. A longitudinal Analysis." *Policy and Politics* 35 (4): 629–50.

Sulitzeanu-Kenan, Raanan, and Christopher Hood. 2005. "Blame Avoidance with Adjectives? Motivation, Opportunity, Activity and Outcome." Paper presented at the ECPR Joint Sessions, Granada, April 2005.

Sun Tzu [500 BC] 1983. *The Art of War*. Ed. J. Clavell. New York: Delta Books.

Taylor, Shelley and Jonathon Brown. 1994. "Positive Illusions and Well-Being Revisited: Seperating Fact from Fiction." *Psychological Bulletin* 116 (1): 21–7.

Thackeray, William M. [1853] 2003. *Vanity Fair: A Novel Without a Hero*. Harmondsworth: Penguin.

Thatcher, Mark. 2002. "Delegation to Independent Regulatory Agencies: Pressures, Functions and Contextual Mediation." *West European Politics* 25 (1): 125–47.

Therborn, Gøran. 2000. "Modernization Discourses, Their Limitations and Their Alternatives." In *Paradigms of Social Change: Modernization, Development, Transformation, Evolution*, ed. Waltraud Schelke, Wolf-Hagen Krauth, Martin Kohli, and George Elwert. Campus Verlag: St. Martins Press.

Thompson, Dennis. 1980. "Moral Responsibility of Public Officials: The Problem of Many Hands." *The American Political Science Review* 74 (4): 905–916.

———. 1987. "Legislative Ethics." In *Political Ethics and Public Office*. Cambridge, MA: Harvard University Press.

Thompson, John B. 2000. *Political Scandal: Power And Visibility In The Media Age*. Cambridge : Polity.

Thompson, Victor A. 1975. *Without Sympathy or Enthusiasm: The Problem of Administrative Compassion*. Alabama: University of Alabama Press.

Tiersky, Ronald. 2003. *François Mitterand: A Very French President*. Lanham, MD: Rowman and Littlefield.

Twight, Charlotte, 1991 "From Claiming Credit to Avoiding Blame: The Evolution of Congressional Strategy for Asbestos Management." *Journal of Public Policy* 11 (2): 153–86.

Twinch, Carol. 2001. *Tithe War 1918–1939: The Countryside in Revolt*. Norwich: Media Associates.

Tversky, Amos and Daniel Kahneman. 1981. "The Framing of Decisions and the Psychology of Choice." *Science* 211(4481): 453–58.

UK Public Administration Select Committee. 2009. *Good Government*, 8th Report of Session 2008–9, HC97-1. London: HMSO.

U.S. Congress, Office of Technology Assessment. 1994. *Defensive Medicine and Medical Malpractice*. OTA-H-602. Washington, DC: US Government Printing Office.

van Thiel, Sandra. 2001. *Quangos: Trends, Causes and Consequences*. Aldershot: Ashgate.

van Thijn, Ed A. 1998. *De Sorry-democratie: Recente politieke affaires en de ministeriële verantwoordelijkheid.* Amsterdam: Van Gennep.

Verweij, Marco, and Michael Thompson. 2006. *Clumsy Solutions for a Complex World.* Basingstoke: Palgrave.

Vibert, Frank. 2007. *The Rise of the Unelected: Democracy and the New Separation of Powers.* Cambridge: Cambridge University Press.

Voltaire. [1759] 1965. *Candide.* Oxford: Blackwell.

von Clausewitz, Claus. 1968. *On War.* Harmondsworth: Penguin.

von Neumann, John. 1928. "Zur Theorie der Gesellschaftsspiele." *Mathematische Annalen* 100: 295–300.

von Neumann, John, and Oskar Morgenstern. 1944. *Theory of Games and Economic Behavior.* Princeton: Princeton University Press.

Waddington, Peter A. J. 1999. "Police (Canteen) Sub-Culture: An Appreciation." *British Journal of Criminology* 39 (2): 287–309.

Walsh, Bryan. 2004. "Singapore Shapes Up: The Lion City's Aggressive Government Programs Show the Benefits of a Concerted, Nationwide War on Fat." *TimeAsia Magazine*, November 1, 2004.

Weaver, R. Kent. 1986. "The Politics of Blame Avoidance." *Journal of Public Policy* 6 (4): 371–98.

———. 1988. *Automatic Government: The Politics of Indexation.* Washington, DC: Brookings.

Weber, Max. 1948. *From Max Weber: Essays in Sociology.* Trans. and ed. H. H. Gerth and C. W. Mills. London: Routledge and Kegan Paul.

Weir, Stuart, and Wendy Hall, eds. 1994. "Ego Trip: Extra-governmental Organisations in the United Kingdom and Their Accountability," *Democratic Audit Paper No 2.* Human Rights Centre, University of Essex. London: Charter 88 Trust.

White, Matthew P., and J. Richard Eiser. 2005. "Information Specificity and Hazard Risk Potential as Moderators of Trust Asymmetry," *Risk Analysis* 25(5): 1187–98.

White, Sue, David Wastell, Sue Peckover, Chris Hall, and Karen Broadhurst. 2009. "Managing Risk in a High-Blame Environment: Tales from the 'Front Door' in Contemporary Children's Social Care." In *Risk and Public Services.* ESRC Public Services Programme and LSE Centre for the Analysis of Risk and Regulation. London: CARR.

Whitehead, Tanya D. 2007. "Combating The Obesogenic Environment: Helping Children Hold Onto Health," *Online Journal of Health and Allied Sciences* 6 (4):1–8.

Wiener, Jonathan B. 1998. "Managing the Iatrogenic Risks of Risk Management." *Risk: Health, Safety and Environment* 9 (1): 39–82.

Williams, Bernard. 2002. *Truth and truthfulness: An Essay in Genealogy.* Princeton: Princeton University Press.

Wilson, James Q. 1980. "The Politics of Regulation." In *The Politics of Regulation*, ed. J. Q. Wilson. New York: Basic Books: 357–94.

Wintour, Patrick. 2003. "Pen Pushing Police Urged to Get Back on the Beat." *The Guardian* October 15, 2003. http://www.guardian.co.uk/uk/2003/oct/15/uk crime.immigrationpolicy (accessed May 2009).

Wolfe, Tom. 1970. *Radical Chic and Mau-Mauing the Flak-Catchers*. New York: Farrar, Straus and Giroux.

Wolff, Michael. 2009. "The Power and the Story." *Vanity Fair*, July 2009. http://www.vanityfair.com/politics/features/2009/07/wolff200907, (accessed April 2010).

Wolmar, Christian. 2005. *On the Wrong Line: How Ideology and Incompetence Wrecked Britain's Railways*. London: Aurum Press.

Wouk, Herman. 1951. *The Caine Mutiny*. London: Jonathan Cape.

Yeung, Karen and Mary Dixon-Woods. 2010. "Design-based Regulation and Patient Safety: A Regulatory Studies Prespective." *Social Science and Medicine* 71: 502–9.

Zhisui, Li. 1994. *The Private Life of Chairman Mao*. Trans. Tai Hung-chao. London: Chatto and Windus.

Index

Abbott, Tony, 190n16
Abrogate, 27
abstinence, 93, 102–5, 137, 145, 172, 176
advertising, 165
Africa, 76
after-the-fact apologies, 55
Agnew, Spiro, 10
Ahern, Bertie, 155
air transport, 103
airbags, 96
airport security, 85, 97
Aitken, Jonathan, 62
ambulances, 109
Ambedkar, Dr Bhimrao Ramji, 200n12
Anderson, Christopher, 86, 87–8, 159
Anderson Committee on the Machinery of
    Government, 118
architecture: of organisations, 43, 72, 83,
    85–6, 95, 122, 137, 157–8; in UK, 152
Aristotle, 174, 191n7
army, 104; British, 102
arrow theories, 112–3, 118–9
asbestos, 167; in Australia, 103, 194n9; in
    US, 106
assurance behavior, 126, 129, 141, 176,
    197n19
audit-trail, 94, 128, 184
Audit Commission (England), 10, 193n12
Austin, John, 51
Australia, 103, 189n10, 190n16
Austrian Freedom Party, 110
automatic formulae, 20
avoidance behavior, 125–6, 129, 176,
    197n19

Baggage, 189n4
banks, 109, 190n11; central, 77, 85; in
    Japan, 80
Barker, Anthony, 196n12
Barton, Matthew, 54
BBC, 118, 189n1
Bellow, Saul, 190n3
benchmarking, 97–8, 129
Bentham, Jeremy, 15, 97, 117, 167, 170

Better Government Initiative, 190n4
Black, Julia, 16
black ops, 76
Blair, Tony, 26, 37, 48, 54, 55, 57, 60, 64,
    73–4, 116, 149–50, 161, 191n8, 193n9,
    194n13, 195n8
blame aversion, 13
blame avoidance, 14–23, 33, 81, 83, 95,
    105–8
blame avoidance engineering, 157–8
blame avoidance frontier, 104–5, 109
blame cultures, 8
blame deflectors, 21, 24, 27
blame displacement, 161–2, 171
blame dissolution, 161–2
blame games, 7, 167, 179
blame heat, 138–42
blame magnets, 21, 24, 27, 73, 87, 108, 161
blame prevention re-engineering, 91, 94, 137
blame reversion, 161–2
blame risk, 5–6, 8–9, 20, 33, 104
blame sharing, 161–2
blame shift fatigue, 56
blame shifting, 37, 67, 161–2
blind-trust arrangements, 89
blood transfusion, 96
Blunkett, David, 190n12
Board of Trade (UK), 57–8
boards, 97, 117
Boeker, Warren, 86
Booth, Cherie, 188n15
Border Control Agency (UK), 198n6
Borraz, Olivier, 10, 128–9
Bovens, Mark, 63
bovine spongiform encephalopathy. *See* BSE
box-ticking, 128–9, 163
Boyne, George, 86
Brecht, Berthold, 41
Bristol Royal Infirmary, 189n9
British Gazette, 116
Broadbent, Jane, 197n2
Brown, Gordon, 199n8
BSE, 148–9, 152, 198n4
budget allocations, 20; formula for 125

Made in the USA
Monee, IL
16 December 2022

21986410R00141